State of the Nation's Children
Ireland 2006

Office of the Minister for Children

FOREWORD

As Minister for Children, it is my great pleasure to publish the first *State of the Nation's Children* report. This report fulfils a commitment in the National Children's Strategy to the publication of a regularly updated statement of key indicators of children's well-being. As the first such report on children in Ireland, it provides us with a benchmark for the future and gives us a clear picture of the progress we have made and the challenges that lie ahead.

The report is an important resource for all those who seek to understand the experience of childhood in Ireland. It covers many different aspects of children's lives, including their health, behavioural and educational outcomes, their relationships with their parents and their friends, and the services available to and accessed by them.

The report brings together information from administrative, survey and census data, which is already in the public domain. Indeed, it is clear that we have a substantial amount of statistical information about children's lives, but this report also shows the gaps that exist. A commitment to improving data about children has been given in the recent Social Partnership Agreement, *Towards 2016: Ten-Year Framework Social Partnership Agreement 2006-2015*, and I will be ensuring that progress is made in that regard.

I am grateful to the Central Statistics Office, the Statistics Division of the Department of Health and Children, and the Health Promotion Unit at the National University of Ireland, Galway, who assisted the Research division at the Office of the Minister for Children in compiling this report.

This report is a good foundation on which to build our understanding of our children's lives. As such, it will help us in our task of making Ireland a better place for children.

Brian Lenihan, TD
Minister for Children
December 2006

Contents

Foreword   v

Authors and Acknowledgements   ix

Acronyms   x

Summary of main findings   xiii

Introduction   1
Overview of report   3
Some considerations   3
Conclusion   5

PART 1: SOCIO-DEMOGRAPHICS   7
Child population   11
Child mortality   15
Non-Irish national children   19
Family structure   23
Parental education level   27
Separated children seeking asylum   32
Traveller children   35

PART 2: RELATIONSHIPS   41
Relationship with parents   43
Relationships with peers   61

PART 3: CHILDREN'S OUTCOMES   73

EDUCATION   75
Early childhood care and education   76
School attendance   80
Achievement in Reading Literacy, Mathematics and Science   86

HEALTH   97
Birth weight   98
Breastfeeding practice   105
Chronic health conditions and hospitalisation   110
Disability   119
Abuse and neglect   130

SOCIAL, EMOTIONAL AND BEHAVIOURAL OUTCOMES 139
Participation in decision-making 140
Reading as a leisure activity 146
Use of tobacco, alcohol and drugs 150
Binge drinking 160
Illicit drug use 166
Sexual health and behaviour 173
Self-esteem 178
Self-reported happiness 183
Youth suicide 187
Physical activity 190
Eating habits 200
Homeless children 206

PART 4: FORMAL AND INFORMAL SUPPORTS 213
Public expenditure on education for children and young people 214
Economic security 221
Availability of housing for families with children 227
Community characteristics 232
Environment and places 238
Referrals to Garda Juvenile Diversion Programme 243
Antenatal care 247
Childhood immunisation 252
Screening for growth and development 262
Accessibility of basic health services for children and young people 268
Children and young people in care 273
Mental health referrals 278

Main data sources 285

Index 289

AUTHORS

The main authors of this *State of the Nation's Children* report are:

- Sinéad Hanafin, Head of Research, Office of the Minister for Children
- Anne-Marie Brooks, Research Officer, Office of the Minister for Children
- Hugh McGee, Senior Statistician, Department of Health and Children
- Gerry Brady, Senior Statistician, Central Statistics Office
- Gillian Roche, Statistician, Central Statistics Office
- Reamonn McKeever, Statistician, Central Statistics Office
- Saoirse Nic Gabhainn, Senior Deputy Director, Health Promotion Research Centre, National University of Ireland, Galway
- Michal Molcho, Lecturer, Health Promotion Research Centre, National University of Ireland, Galway

ACKNOWLEDGEMENTS

We would also like to thank all the people and organisations who provided data, especially Eileen Connolly, Department of Health and Children (Childcare Interim Dataset); Trevor Moylan and Greg Conlon, Health Promotion Research Centre, National University of Ireland, Galway; Mark Morgan, St. Patrick's College, Drumcondra (ESPAD); Eemer Eivers, Education Research Centre (PISA); Sheelagh Bonham, Economic and Social Research Institute (National Perinatal Reporting System); Steven Barron and Caraisoa Kelly, Health Research Board (National Intellectual Disability Database); Arthur O'Reilly, Health Research Board (National Psychiatric In-Patient Reporting System); Anne Doyle and Mary Ann O'Donovan, Health Research Board (National Physical and Sensory Disability Database); Anna Lloyd, Liz Shannon and Jason Sibley, National Treatment Purchase Fund (Patient Treatment Register); Suzanne Cotter, Health Protection Surveillance Centre (Immunisation Uptake Statistics); Finbarr Murphy, An Garda Síochána (crime statistics); Elaine O'Mahony, National Education Welfare Board (Education Welfare Board Database); Tom Healy, Department of Education and Science (statistics on education expenditure and school attendance); and Niamh Gallagher, Maire O'Mahoney and Lisa Clifford, Department of the Environment, Heritage and Local Government (Triennial Assessment of Housing Needs).

We are also very grateful to all the people who provided feedback on individual indicators.

ACRONYMS

ADHD	Attention Deficit Hyperactivity Disorder
ALSPAC	Avon Longitudinal Study of Parents and Children
CASE	Child and Adolescent Self-Harm in Europe Study
CDC	Centre for Disease Control and Prevention
CECDE	Centre for Early Childhood Development and Education
CPA	Combat Poverty Agency
CPI	Consumer Price Index
CSER	Centre for Social and Educational Research
CSO	Central Statistics Office
DEIS	Delivering equality of opportunity in schools
ENFO	A public information service on the environment, to encourage children and young people to be environmentally responsible
EPPE	Effective Provision of Pre-School Education Project
ERO	Education Review Office
ESPAD	European School Survey Project on Alcohol and Other Drugs
ESRI	Economic and Social Research Institute
EU25 average	Average result for the 25 EU Member States
EU SILC	EU Survey on Income and Living Conditions
GCSE	General Certificate of Secondary Education
GDP	Gross Domestic Product
GNP	Gross National Product
GRO	General Register's Office
HBSC	Health Behaviour in School-aged Children Survey
HEA	Higher Education Authority
HIPE	Hospital In-patient Enquiry System
HPSC	Health Protection Surveillance Centre
HRB	Health Research Board
HSE	Health Service Executive (formally Health Boards)
ICD-9 CM	Clinical modification of the 9th Revision of the International Classification of Diseases
ICD-10	World Health Organization's International Classification of Diseases category
ICD-10-AM	Australian modification of ICD-10
IYJS	Irish Youth Justice Service
LAAHN	Local Authority Assessment of Housing Need
LSP	Local Sports Partnerships
MABS	Money Advice and Budgeting Service
MHADIE	Measuring Health and Disability in Europe

X

MMR	Measles, Mumps and Rubella Vaccine
MSRB	Medico-Social Research Board
MVPA	Moderate-to-Vigorous Physical Activity
NAPS	National Anti-Poverty Strategy
NCCA	National Council for Curriculum and Assessment
NCCRI	National Consultative Committee on Racism and Interculturalism
NDA	National Disability Authority
NESC	National Economic and Social Council
NESF	National Economic and Social Forum
NEWB	National Educational Welfare Board
NHS	National Health Service
NICHD	National Institute of Child Health and Human Development
NIDD	National Intellectual Disability Database
NPIRS	National Psychiatric In-Patient Reporting System
NPRS	National Perinatal Reporting System
NPSDD	National Physical and Sensory Disability Database
NTPF	National Treatment Purchase Fund
OECD	Organisation for Economic Cooperation and Development
OMC	Office of the Minister for Children
PHN	Public Health Nurse
PISA	Programme for International Student Assessment Survey
PTR	Patient Treatment Register
QNHS	Quarterly National Household Survey
RTA	Road Traffic Accidents
SAHAP	Social and Affordable Housing Action Plans
SEU	Social Exclusion Unit
SPHE	Social, Personal and Health Education
SSI	Social Services Inspectorate
UNCRC	United Nations Convention on the Rights of the Child
UNICEF	United Nations Children's Fund
US DHHS	United States Department of Health and Human Services
WHO	World Health Organization
WLI	Waiting List Initiative
YPFSF	Young People's Facilities and Services Fund

SUMMARY OF MAIN FINDINGS

Notes:

- Percentage differences are presented for descriptive purposes only and may not reflect a statistically significant finding.
- Prior to 2005, for the purposes of the health services the country was geographically divided into health board areas and one regional health authority. The Health Service Executive (HSE) now has overarching responsibility and there are now four regional health authorities.

SOCIO-DEMOGRAPHICS

Indicator	Measure	Description	Comparisons	Data Source	Year
Child population	The number of children under 18, expressed as a proportion of the total population.	1,027,880 children	Ireland has a higher percentage of children under 18 than any other EU Member State. 25.0% of the population in Ireland are under 18 years. This compares with an EU average of 19.8%.	Census of the Population; Population Estimates	2005
Child mortality	The number of deaths among children under 18, expressed as a proportion of all children. This may be subdivided by principal cause of death.	The child mortality rate in 2004 was 4.6 deaths per 10,000 children. This represents a decline since 2000, when the child mortality rate was 5.5 deaths per 10,000 children. The infant mortality rate in Ireland in 2000 was 63 per 10,000. This had decreased to 49 per 10,000 in 2004.	Child mortality rates in 2004 for boys (5.3 per 10,000) are higher than those for girls (3.8 per 10,000).	Vital Statistics; Eurostat	2004
Non-Irish national children	The number of non-Irish national children in the population, expressed as a proportion of all children.	There were 39,838 non-Irish national children in Ireland according to the 2002 Census. 23.2% of these children were living in Dublin.	A little more than half (51%) hold British or Northern Irish nationality.	Census of the Population	2002
Family structure	The number of children under 18 who live in family household units with only one parent or primary caregiver resident, expressed as a proportion of all children.	According to the 2002 Census, 86.0% of children live with both parents/guardians and 14.0% live with a lone parent or guardian.	One in 3 lone-parent families with children (33.4%) are resident in Dublin.	Census of the Population	2002
Parental education level	The number of children under 18 whose parents have attained (a) primary; (b) lower secondary; (c) upper secondary; and (d) third-level education, expressed as a proportion of all children.	13.1% of children live in families where the head of the household has either no formal education or primary education only. 25.6% of children live in families where the head of the household has a third-level degree or higher educational qualification.	Younger children are more likely to live with a head of household with a higher educational qualification.	Census of the Population	2002
Children seeking asylum	The number of children seeking asylum, alone or as part of a family, expressed as a proportion of all children.	In 2004, there were 679 children seeking asylum. Over 90% of children seeking asylum were found in the former Eastern Regional Health Authority area.	There has been a decline in the number of children seeking asylum since 2002, when the numbers were 779. In 2004, 66.0% of children seeking asylum were re-united with their families.	Childcare Interim Dataset	2004
Traveller children	The number of Traveller children, expressed as a proportion of all children.	There were 11,725 Traveller children in Ireland, accounting for 1.2% of the total child population and 49.5% of the total Traveller population.		Census of the Population	2002

RELATIONSHIPS

Indicator	Measure	Description	Comparisons	Data Source	Year
Parental relationships					
Relationship with mothers	The proportion of children aged 10-17 who report that they find it easy or very easy to talk with their mother when something is really bothering them.	77.6% of children report that they find it easy to talk with their mothers when something is really bothering them.	Using the ages of 11, 13, and 15 only to draw international comparisons, Ireland ranked 27th among 35 WHO countries participating in the HBSC Survey. The average was 82.7%.	Health Behaviour in School-aged Children (HBSC) Survey	2002
Relationship with fathers	The proportion of children aged 10-17 who report that they find it easy or very easy to talk with their father when something is really bothering them.	56.2% of children report that they find it easy to talk with their fathers when something is really bothering them.	Using the ages of 11, 13, and 15 only to draw international comparisons, Ireland ranked 24th among 35 WHO countries participating in the HBSC Survey. The average was 64.2%.	Health Behaviour in School-aged Children (HBSC) Survey	2002
Talking to parents	The proportion of children aged 15 who report that their parents spend time just talking with them more than once a week.	61.6% of children report that their parents spend time just talking with them several times a week.	Ireland ranked 11th among 27 OECD countries participating in the PISA Survey. The average was 59.6%.	Programme for International Student Assessment (PISA) Survey	2000
Parental involvement in schooling	The proportion of children aged 15 who report that their parents discuss with them how well they are doing at school more than once a week.	47.9% of children report that their parents discuss with them how well they are doing at school several times a week.	Ireland ranked 14th among 27 OECD countries participating in the PISA Survey. The average was 52.3%.	Programme for International Student Assessment (PISA) Survey	2000
Eating a main meal together	The proportion of children aged 15 who report that their parents eat a main meal with them around a table more than once a week.	77.1% of children report that their parents eat dinner with them around a table several times a week.	Ireland ranked 16th among 27 OECD countries participating in the PISA Survey. The average was 78.9%.	Programme for International Student Assessment (PISA) Survey	2000
Peer relationships					
Friendships	The proportion of children aged 10-17 who report to have 3 or more friends of the same gender.	85.3% of children reported to have 3 or more friends of the same gender.	Using the ages of 11, 13, and 15 only to draw international comparisons, Ireland ranked 1st among 35 WHO countries participating in the HBSC Survey. The average was 78.8%.	Health Behaviour in School-aged Children (HBSC) Survey	2002
Bullying	The proportion of children aged 10-17 who report to have been bullied at school.	23.3% of children reported to have been bullied at school in the last couple of months. A higher proportion of boys (26.4%) reported being bullied than girls (21.0%).	Using the ages of 11, 13, and 15 only to draw international comparisons, Ireland ranked 27th among 35 WHO countries participating in the HBSC Survey. The average was 33.5%.	Health Behaviour in School-aged Children (HBSC) Survey	2002

CHILDREN'S OUTCOMES: EDUCATION

Indicator	Measure	Description	Comparisons	Data Source	Year
Enrolment in early childhood care and education	The number of children under 13 in various early childhood care and education arrangements, expressed as a proportion of all children in the same group. This can be subdivided into (a) pre-school; (b) compulsory school; (c) centre-based care outside school hours; (d) crèche or day-care; (e) professional childminder; and (f) family relative.	In 2005, the main type of childcare arrangement was by parent/guardian for pre-school children (59.7%) and primary school children (78.5%).	There was a small decrease from 62.1% to 59.7% from 2002 to 2005 in the percentage of parents/guardians as the main carer for pre-school children.	Quarterly National Household Survey (QHNS)	2005
Attendance at school	The number of children who are absent from school for 20 days or more in the school year, expressed as a proportion of all children.	In the 2004-2005 school year, 10% of primary school children were absent from school for 20 days or more.	14.9% of the primary school children in urban schools were absent from school for 20 days or more, compared with 7.8% of the primary school children in rural schools.	National Educational Welfare Board (NEWB) statistics	2005
Transfer to second-level education	The percentage of children leaving national school by destination.	Over the period 2001-2005, 96.3% of children leaving national schools were known to have progressed to another form of schooling, either at first or second level.		Department of Education and Science statistics	2005
Reading literacy	The mean scores for 15-year-old children based on the international reading literacy scales, set by the PISA Survey.	Children in Ireland achieved a mean average score of 515.5 on the reading literacy scale. This was higher than the OECD country mean of 494. Girls achieved a higher mean average score (530.1) than boys (501.1).	Irish children ranked 6th out of 29 OECD countries who took part in the PISA Survey. Children in higher social classes achieved higher mean average scores than children in lower social classes.	Programme for International Student Assessment (PISA) Survey	2003
Mathematics	The mean scores for 15-year-old children based on the international mathematics literacy scales, set by the PISA Survey.	Children in Ireland achieved a mean average score of 502.8 on the mathematics literacy scale. This was about the same as the OECD country mean of 500. Boys achieved a higher mean average score (510.2) than girls (495.4).	Irish children ranked 17th out of 29 OECD countries who took part in the PISA Survey. Children in higher social classes achieved higher mean average scores than children in lower social classes.	Programme for International Student Assessment (PISA) Survey	2003
Science	The mean scores for 15-year-old children based on the international scientific literacy scales, set by the PISA Survey.	Children in Ireland achieved a mean average score of 505.4 on the scientific literacy scale. This was marginally higher than the OECD country mean of 500.	Irish children ranked 13th out of 29 OECD countries who took part in the PISA Survey. Children in higher social classes achieved higher mean average scores than children in lower social classes.	Programme for International Student Assessment (PISA) Survey	2003

xvi

CHILDREN'S OUTCOMES: HEALTH

Indicator	Measure	Description	Comparisons	Data Source	Year
Low birth weight	The number of babies born weighing less than 2,500 grams, expressed as a proportion of all registered live and stillbirths.	In 2003, 5.4% of babies were born at low birth weight (weighing less than 2,500 grams). This measure was based on all live and stillbirths.	On average, 6.4% of babies in the EU are born at low birth weight. This figure takes account of live births only. Using live births only, in 2003, 5.1% of Irish babies were born at low birth weight.	National Perinatal Reporting System (NPRS)	2003
Breastfeeding practice	The number of newborn babies who are (a) exclusively breastfed and (b) partially breastfed throughout the first 48 hours of life, expressed as a proportion of all newborn babies.	The breastfeeding rate on discharge from hospital was 44.5% in 2003. 41% were exclusively breastfed, while 3.5% were partially breastfed. Mothers in higher socio-economic classes are more likely to breastfeed their babies.	Although Ireland still compares unfavourably with other EU Member States, there has been an increase in the breastfeeding rate since 1999, when it was 36.7%.	National Perinatal Reporting System (NPRS)	2003
Chronic health and hospitalisation	The 10 most frequent conditions resulting in hospitalisation among children.	In 2004, there were 140,528 hospital discharges of children (aged 0-17 years). 20.8% of discharges were among children aged <1; 28.8% among children aged 1-4; 20.5% among children aged 5-9; 16.6% among children aged 10-14; and 13.3% among children aged 15-17. Road traffic accidents accounted for 1,822 episodes in 2004.	The number of hospitalisations for children aged 0-17 has increased by 8,486 since 2000, when the number was 132,042.	Hospital In-patient Enquiry (HIPE) System	2004

Disability

Indicator	Measure	Description	Comparisons	Data Source	Year
Intellectual disability	The number of children under 18 registered as having an intellectual disability, expressed as a proportion of all children. This can be subdivided by grade of disability: (a) mild; (b) moderate; (c) severe; and (d) profound.	The number registered as having an intellectual disability was 7,385 in 2005. 41% of children registered as having an intellectual disability were identified as having a mild disability; 28% as having a moderate disability; 11% as having a severe disability; and 2% as having a profound disability.	This number has decreased from 7,960 in 2001.	National Intellectual Disability Database (NIDD)	2005
Physical and sensory disability	The number of children under 18 registered as having a physical or sensory disability, expressed as a proportion of all children.	In 2005, 7,039 children were registered as having a physical or sensory disability.	This number has increased from 6,412 in 2004.	National Physical and Sensory Disability Database (NPSDD) (approx. 68% national coverage)	2005

continued

SUMMARY OF MAIN FINDINGS

xvii

CHILDREN'S OUTCOMES: HEALTH (continued)

Indicator	Measure	Description	Comparisons	Data Source	Year
Abuse and maltreatment					
Assessments for child welfare and protection concerns	The number of children assessed through the Child Protection Notification System, expressed as a proportion of all children.	In 2004, 6,188 children were assessed by the former health board areas for child welfare concerns. This represents a rate of 61 children per 10,000 under 18 years. In 2004, 34% of these children were assessed for neglect; 20% for physical abuse; 28% for sexual abuse; and 18% for emotional abuse.	Since 2000, there has been an inconsistent decrease in the number of assessments for child welfare and protection concerns. This number was 8,269 in 2000 and 6,188 in 2004.	Childcare Interim Dataset	2004
Confirmed cases of child abuse and neglect	The number of children subject to substantiated notification, expressed as a proportion of all children.	In 2004, there were 1,425 substantiated notifications to the Child Protection Notification System. This represents a rate of 14 children per 10,000 under 18 years. In 2004, of all substantiated notifications to the Child Protection Notification System, 15% suffered sexual abuse; 19% suffered physical abuse; 24% suffered emotional abuse; and 42% suffered neglect.	Since 2000, there has been an inconsistent decrease in the number of substantiated notifications. This number was 3,085 in 2000 and 1,425 in 2004.	Childcare Interim Dataset	2004

CHILDREN'S OUTCOMES: SOCIAL, EMOTIONAL AND BEHAVIOURAL

Indicator	Measure	Description	Comparisons	Data Source	Year
Participation in making the school rules	The proportion of children aged 10-17 who report that students at their school participate in making the school rules.	In 2002, 23.5% of children reported that students in their school participate in making the school rules.	Using the ages of 11, 13, and 15 only to draw international comparisons, Ireland ranked 13th among 14 WHO countries participating in the HBSC Survey. The average was 36.1%.	Health Behaviour in School-aged Children (HBSC) Survey	2002
Reading as a leisure activity	The proportion of children aged 15 who report that reading is one of their favourite hobbies.	35.7% of children aged 15 agreed that reading was one of their favourite hobbies. This was higher for girls (48.2%) than for boys (22.9%).	Ireland ranked 9th among 27 OECD countries who took part in the PISA Survey.	Programme for International Student Assessment (PISA) Survey	2000
Daily smoking	The proportion of children aged 10-17 who report smoking cigarettes every day.	In 2002, 10.0% of children reported smoking cigarettes every day. This was higher among older children (19.7% of 15-17 year-olds).	Using the ages of 11, 13, and 15 only to draw international comparisons, Ireland ranked 24th among 35 WHO countries participating in the HBSC Survey.	Health Behaviour in School-aged Children (HBSC) Survey	2002
Weekly smoking	The proportion of children aged 10-17 who report smoking cigarettes every week.	In 2002, 13.4% of children reported smoking cigarettes every week. This was higher among older children (24.6% of 15-17 year-olds).	Using the ages of 11, 13, and 15 only to draw international comparisons, Ireland ranked 26th among 35 WHO countries participating in the HBSC Survey.	Health Behaviour in School-aged Children (HBSC) Survey	2002
Binge drinking	The proportion of children aged 15 who report to have had 5 or more alcoholic drinks in a row at least once in the last 30 days.	In 2003, 57.0% of children aged 15 reported to have had 5 or more alcoholic drinks in a row in the past 30 days. There were no differences between boys and girls.	Ireland ranked 3rd among 33 countries participating in the ESPAD Survey.	European School Survey Project on Alcohol and Other Drugs (ESPAD)	2003
Any illicit drug use	The proportion of children aged 15 who report having used any illicit drugs in their lifetime.	In 2003, 40% of children aged 15 reported to have used an illicit drug in their lifetime. There were no differences between boys and girls.	Ireland ranked 3rd among 36 countries participating in the ESPAD Survey. Irish girls ranked 1st and Irish boys ranked 6th among the 36 countries surveyed.	European School Survey Project on Alcohol and Other Drugs (ESPAD)	2003
Illicit drug use other than marijuana	The proportion of children aged 15 who report to have used any illicit drugs other than marijuana in their lifetime.	In 2003, 9% of children aged 15 reported to have used an illicit drug other than marijuana in their lifetime. There were no differences between boys and girls.	Ireland ranked 3rd among 36 countries participating in the ESPAD Survey.	European School Survey Project on Alcohol and Other Drugs (ESPAD)	2003

continued

CHILDREN'S OUTCOMES: SOCIAL, EMOTIONAL AND BEHAVIOURAL (continued)

Indicator	Measure	Description	Comparisons	Data Source	Year
Sexual health and behaviour	The number of births to girls aged 10-17 and in total, expressed as a proportion of all girls in the same age group.	In 2004, the number of babies born to girls under 18 years of age was 654.	There was a decrease from 2000, when the number of babies born to girls under 18 years of age was 777.	Vital Statistics	2004
Self-esteem	The proportion of children aged 8-17 who report feeling happy with the way they are.	51.1% of children aged 8-11 report to always feel happy with the way they are, compared with 25.5% of children aged 12-17.	More boys report being happy than girls. A higher percentage of younger children (8-11 years) report being happy than older ones.	KIDSCREEN	2005
Self-reported happiness	The proportion of children aged 10-17 who report being happy with their life at present.	In 2002, 89.5% of children reported that they were happy with their life at present.	In 2002, girls aged 10-11 were most likely to report being happy, while girls aged 15-17 were least likely to report this.	Health Behaviour in School-aged Children (HBSC) Survey	2002
Youth suicide	The number of suicides among children aged 10-17, expressed as a proportion of all children in the same age group.	In 2004, there were 18 suicides among children under 18. Youth suicide accounted for 22% of all deaths in the 10-17 age group.	The youth suicide rate is higher for boys (6 per 100,000) than for girls (1.8 per 100,000).	Vital Statistics	2004
Physical activity	The proportion of children aged 10-17 who report being physically active for at least 60 minutes per day on at least 2 days per week.	In 2002, 87.4% of children reported that they were active for at least 60 minutes per day on 2 days or more per week. This was higher for boys (91.1%) than for girls (84.7%).	Using the ages of 11, 13, and 15 only to draw international comparisons, Ireland ranked 9th among 34 WHO countries participating in the HBSC Survey. The average was 86.8.	Health Behaviour in School-aged Children (HBSC) Survey	2002
Physical activity	The proportion of children aged 10-17 who report being physically active for at least 60 minutes per day on more than 4 days per week.	In 2002, 47.4% of all children reported that they were active for at least 60 minutes per day on more than 4 days per week. This was higher for boys (57.5%) than for girls (39.9%).	Using the ages of 11, 13, and 15 only to draw international comparisons, Ireland ranked 2nd among 34 WHO countries participating in the HBSC Survey. The average was 36.7.	Health Behaviour in School-aged Children (HBSC) Survey	2002
Nutritional habits	The proportion of children aged 10-17 who report eating breakfast on 5 or more days per week.	In 2002, 77.3% of children reported eating breakfast 5 or more times per week. This was higher for boys (81.4%) than for girls (74.3%).	Using the ages of 11, 13, and 15 only to draw international comparisons, Ireland ranked 14th among 32 WHO countries participating in the HBSC Survey.	Health Behaviour in School-aged Children (HBSC) Survey	2002
Youth homelessness	The number of homeless children, expressed as a proportion of all children.	The total number of young people who appeared to the Health Service Executive (HSE) to be homeless in 2004 was 495. This was a rate of 45.8 per 100,000 children.	In 2004, almost half (43%; n = 210) of children known to the HSE to be homeless were in the Eastern Area Health Authority.	Childcare Interim Dataset	2004

XX

FORMAL AND INFORMAL SUPPORTS

Indicator	Measure	Description	Comparisons	Data Source	Year
Public expenditure on education for children and young people	Public expenditure on education, expressed as a percentage of GDP and GNI.	Real non-capital expenditure per student in Ireland increased by 112% for first level and by 91% for second level over the period 1996-2005 when measured in constant 2005 prices. In 2003, public expenditure on education as a percentage of GNI was similar to the EU average of 5.2% of GDP.	Ireland's expenditure on education, expressed as a percentage of GDP, was the 5th lowest among EU Member States in 2003.	Department of Education and Science; Eurostat	2005

Economic security

Indicator	Measure	Description	Comparisons	Data Source	Year
Relative poverty	The number of children living in households with a household income below the national 60% median, equivalised using the national equivalence scale, expressed as a proportion of all children.	In 2004, 22.7% of children under 18 were considered to be at risk of poverty.	In 2004, the number of persons under 16 living in households at a risk of poverty in Ireland (22%) was higher that the EU average (20%).	EU Survey on Income and Living Conditions (EU-SILC)	2004
Consistent poverty	The number of children living in households with a household income below the national 60% median, equivalised using the national equivalence scale, and experiencing basic deprivation, expressed as a proportion of all children.	9.7% of children under 18 experienced consistent poverty in 2004. Households with children had higher poverty rates than those without children.	Persons in households comprising a single adult with children had a consistent poverty rate of 31.1% in 2004.	EU Survey on Income and Living Conditions (EU-SILC)	2004
Availability of housing for families with children	The number of children in families on a local authority housing waiting list, expressed as a proportion of all children.	22,335 households with children were identified as being in need of social housing in the 2005 assessment of housing needs. In 2005, 61.4% of family households in need of social housing were households with one child, while 5.7% of households included 4 or more children.	There has been a 24.2% (n = 7,149) decrease in the number of households identified as being in need of social housing.	Triennial Assessment of Housing Needs	2005
Perceived safety in the community	The proportion of children aged 10-17 who report feeling safe in the area where they live.	In 2002, 87.4% of children reported that they felt safe in the area where they live.	Using the ages of 11, 13, and 15 only to draw international comparisons, Ireland ranked 11th among 16 WHO countries participating in the HBSC Survey. The average was 89.6.	Health Behaviour in School-aged Children (HBSC) Survey	2002

continued

FORMAL AND INFORMAL SUPPORTS (continued)

Indicator	Measure	Description	Comparisons	Data Source	Year
Environment and places	The proportion of children aged 10-17 who report there are good places in their area to spend their free time.	43.9% of children report that there are good places in their area to spend their free time.	Ireland ranked 14th among 15 WHO countries participating in the HBSC Survey. The percentages of children reporting that there are good places in their area to spend their free time are higher among younger children aged 10-11 (59.6%) compared with older children aged 15-17 (32.6%). Boys are more likely to report this (47.8%) than girls (41.0%).	Health Behaviour in School-aged Children (HBSC) Survey	2002
Referrals to the Garda Juvenile Diversion Programme	The number of children referred to the Garda Juvenile Diversion Programme, expressed as a proportion of all children.	A total of 17,517 children aged 7-17 were referred to the Garda Juvenile Diversion Programme in 2005. In the State as a whole, about 21% of children referred to the Programme were female.	The highest referral rate was in the 15-17 age group, with 15,430 referrals. This amounted to 884 referrals per 10,000 persons aged 15-17. The highest single cause of referrals in 2005 were alcohol-related offences.	Crime statistics	2005
Antenatal care	The distribution of timing of first antenatal visit by trimester for all women delivering live or stillborn babies.	In 2003, 64.8% of women presented for antenatal care in the first trimester; 22.2% in the second trimester; and 7.9% in the third trimester.		National Perinatal Reporting System (NPRS)	2003
Childhood immunisation	The percentage uptake of D3/P3/T3/Hib3/Polio3 and Meningococcal C3 vaccinations at (a) 12 months and (b) 24 months. The percentage uptake of MMR1 vaccinations at 24 months.	In 2004, overall, the level of uptake of immunisation for children was about 83% for 12-month-old infants and 89% for infants aged up to 24 months. In 2000, 78.9% of children aged up to 24 months had received their first dose of the MMR vaccine. This proportion dropped to 73.2% in 2001, but has increased since, rising to 81.1% in 2004.	There has been an increase since 2000 in level of uptake for children aged up to 12 months and also up to 24 months. The rate of completed vaccination for diphtheria, tetanus, pertussis and polio were the 3rd lowest in the EU in 2004.	Immunisation Uptake Statistics	2004

continued

xxii

FORMAL AND INFORMAL SUPPORTS (continued)

Indicator	Measure	Description	Comparisons	Data Source	Year
Screening for growth and development					
Public Health Nurse visit for newborns	The percentage of mothers of newborn children visited by a Public Health Nurse within 48 hours of discharge from hospital.	In 2004, the percentage of mothers of newborn babies contacted by a Public Health Nurse within 48 hours of discharge from hospital ranged from 59% (for a small number of areas in the former Eastern Regional Health Authority) to 95.5% in the former Western Health Board area.		National Health Services Performance Indicators	2004
Developmental screening	The percentage uptake of developmental screening at 7 to 9 months.	In 2003, the percentage uptake of Child Health Core Screening Programme at 7-9 months ranged from 68% in the former Western Health Board area to 0% in the former Southern Health Board area.		National Health Services Performance Indicators	2003
Accessibility of basic health services for children and young people	The number of children on hospital waiting lists.	In April 2006, 1,761 children were known to be on a hospital waiting list for treatment. 40% of these children were on the hospital waiting list for 3-6 months and 26% for one year or more.		Patient Treatment Register (PTR) (approx. 74% national coverage)	2006
Children and young people in care	The number of children who are in the care of the Health Service Executive (HSE), expressed as a proportion of all children. This can be subdivided by type of care arrangement: (a) foster care - general; (b) foster care - special; (c) foster care - relatives; (d) pre-adoptive placement; (e) residential - general; (f) residential - special; (g) at home under care order; and (h) other.	Over the period 2000-2004, the number of children in the care of the HSE rose from 4,424 to 5,060. In 2004, 18% of children were in care for less than one year. In 2004, almost 85% of all children in the care of the HSE lived in foster family homes.	Since 2000, there has been an increase in kinship care and a corresponding decrease in residential care.	Childcare Interim Dataset	2004
Mental health referrals	The number of admissions to psychiatric hospitals among children.	In 2005, there were 333 admissions to hospital for psychiatric care among children. Children aged 15-17 accounted for 85.9% (n = 286) of these admissions.	The number of admissions to hospital for psychiatric care has fallen since 2002, when there were 452 admissions.	National Psychiatric In-Patient Reporting System (NPIRS)	2005

SUMMARY OF MAIN FINDINGS

xxiii

INTRODUCTION

Ireland's first *State of the Nation's Children* report has been compiled by the Research Division of the Office of the Minister for Children (OMC) in association with the Central Statistics Office, the Statistics Division of the Department of Health and Children, and the Health Promotion Unit, National University of Ireland, Galway. The report is published in fulfilment of a commitment given in the National Children's Strategy (Department of Health and Children, 2000) that a regularly updated statement of key indicators of children's well-being would be made available. This commitment reflects a more global effort to measure and monitor child well-being (Ben-Arieh *et al*, 2001) and *State of the Nation's Children* reports are now a feature of a number of other countries, including Canada, the USA and UK.

This report aims to provide a description of the well-being of children and young people in Ireland and, as the first such report, sets out a benchmark for developments into the future. The report is based on a national set of child well-being indicators developed in 2005 and includes 48 indicator areas of children's lives, considered by multiple stakeholders, including children themselves, to be important (Hanafin and Brooks, 2005a). The development of the indicator set was conceptually driven by a holistic understanding of children's lives and guided by the definition of Andrews *et al* (2002, p. 103) of child well-being, as follows:

'healthy and successful individual functioning (involving physiological, psychological and behavioural levels of organisation), positive social relationships (with family members, peers, adult care-givers and community and societal institutions, for instance, school and faith and civic organisations), and a social ecology that provides safety (e.g. freedom from interpersonal violence, war and crime), human and civil rights, social justice and participation in civil society'.

This definition was used because it facilitated the inclusion of many different dimensions of children's lives, as well as highlighting the importance of children's relationships and formal and informal supports. This understanding of children's lives is coherent with the conceptualisation of the child as described in the 'whole child perspective' of the National Children's Strategy and is in line with the lifecycle framework set out in the recent Social Partnership Agreement, *Towards 2016: Ten-Year Framework Social Partnership Agreement 2006-2015* (Department of the Taoiseach, 2006).

There is general agreement that the identification of a small number of indicators is important for the following reasons:
- a small number of indicators keeps the report manageable and focused;
- a small number of indicators has a greater chance of acceptance in the policy arena and among the potential audience of policy-makers and politicians;
- a small number of indicators, which are readily understood, is more likely to become part of a generalised understanding of child well-being than a more exhaustive list.

An examination of indicators on children's lives in use elsewhere led to the identification of more than 2,500 individual indicators that could potentially have been used to describe children's lives. It was therefore necessary to distil these down to a much smaller number. This was done using a multi-stage incremental approach, which included:

- a background review and compilation of an inventory of indicators (Brooks and Hanafin, 2005);
- a feasibility study of data sources (Fitzgerald, 2004);
- a study on children's understandings of well-being (Nic Gabhainn and Sixsmith, 2005);
- a consensus process referred to as a Delphi Technique (Hanafin and Brooks, 2005a and 2005b).

These documents are available from the Office of the Minister for Children or are available on its website at www.omc.ie.

Overview of report

This *State of the Nation's Children* report is presented in four parts:

- **Part 1: Socio-demographics of children in Ireland.** This overview provides information on the number of children in the population, family structure, parental education level, child mortality, children seeking asylum, Traveller children and non-Irish national children. Data are drawn from perinatal statistics, the Census of Population and the Health Service Executive.
- **Part 2: Children's relationships with their parents and peers,** including levels of reported bullying and children's friendships. Data are drawn from various sources, including the 1998/2002 Health Behaviour in School-aged Children (HBSC) surveys and the 2000/2003 Programme for International Student Assessment (PISA) surveys.
- **Part 3: Outcomes of children's lives.** These are categorised according to health, education, and social, emotional and behavioural outcomes. Areas covered include the use of tobacco, alcohol and drugs; teenage pregnancy; chronic health conditions; educational attainment; and reported levels of happiness. A range of sources has been used, including data from the 2003 European Schools Project on Alcohol and Drugs (ESPAD) Survey, the National Intellectual Disability Database and the National Physical and Sensory Disability Database.
- **Part 4: Formal and informal supports for children.** These range across attendance at school, housing, antenatal care, immunisation, environmental supports and levels of economic security, including relative and consistent poverty.

Some considerations

Understandings of the purpose of indicators can range across a continuum, from 'number or a set of numbers' (New Policy Institute, 2002) to the provision of 'empirical, valid measurements of key dimensions of human well-being' (National Statistics Board, 2003). In this report, we aim to provide a description of the latter and in doing so, have taken account of a number of criteria considered internationally to be of importance (Moore, 1997). These criteria are set out below, with examples of data included in the report.

- **Comprehensiveness:** The report provides data on a number of areas of children's lives, ranging from 'abuse and maltreatment' to 'nutrition' and 'public expenditure'.
- **Inclusive of all ages:** Internationally, it is recognised that there is insufficient information about the period of middle childhood (6-10 years) and this is also the case with this report. With the exception of this age group, all other ages of children's lives are represented, including, for example, birth weight, numbers of children in early childcare settings and levels of smoking, alcohol and drug use among young people.
- **Positive and negative dimensions of children's lives:** Indicators that report on positive aspects of children's lives include the proportion of children who feel happy with the way they are and levels of participation in making school rules, while negative dimensions include the number of children referred to the Garda Juvenile Diversion Programme.
- **Reflective of social goals:** Indicators to support this area include the number of children absent from school for 20 or more days and the number of infants that were breastfed.
- **Objective and subjective:** A number of objective and subjective indicators are included, such as the number of children living in households where the income is below the national 60% median and the number of children aged 11, 13 and 15 who report to be happy with their lives.
- **Takes account of well-being and well-becoming:** This criterion recognises childhood as an important period in its own right, as well as recognising the importance of childhood as a preparation for adulthood. Indicators that reflect this include the percentage of children who report that there are good places in which to spend their free time (well-being) and the proportion of children who leave school before the statutory school-leaving age (well-becoming).

Although, in general, the report meets these criteria, there are some limitations. For certain indicator areas, there is a wealth of data that can be disaggregated according to a number of different aspects, including social class, geography, gender, age and time. For other indicator areas, however, only a basic description of the indicator is available, while for yet others only partial data are available. For example, the indicator area relating to expenditure on children's services includes only information about expenditure on children's education; similarly, the data on physical and sensory disability are based on the findings from 70% database coverage. Finally, due to a total absence of data, it is not possible to report on four indicator areas: pets and animals; nutritional outcomes; quality of early childhood care and education; and values and respect.

Some progress has, however, been made. For example, data on pets and animals have been collected in the 2006 HBSC Survey and will be available for inclusion in the next report. Discussions are also ongoing about the collection of data for the other three missing areas. In addition, data on 9-year-old children have been collected in the 2006 HBSC and while this will assist in understanding the middle childhood period, much remains to be done.

Besides data availability, other difficulties arise in relation to data sources, although these are common across a number of different countries and are not specific to Ireland. International comparison is hampered in some cases because of a lack of a common measure. Consistent poverty, for example, is a widely used measure in Ireland, but this does not have broad international comparability. This is also the case with the categorisation of antenatal care, where the timing of the first, second and third trimesters in Ireland differs from that used by the World Health Organization. Other issues also arise in an international context. Categorisation of social class, age and geographical location, for example, differs considerably across different data sources. When international survey data are collected, the imperative is often on gaining a robust comparison between countries rather than harmonisation with other data within individual countries. The PISA Survey in 2003, for example, categorises geographical location according to whether it is rural or urban, and has the following categories – village, hamlet or rural area (fewer than 3,000 people); small town (3,000 to about 15,000 people); town (15,000 to about 100,000 people); city (100,000 to about 1,000,000 people); and large city (with over 1,000,000 people). In addition, in the Irish context two further categories are included – 'close to Dublin city centre' and 'elsewhere in Dublin'. In contrast, the HBSC Survey provides a categorisation of geographical location across the 10 former health board areas (which have now been replaced by the HSE's regional structure, with only four categories). Thus, it is unlikely that a harmonisation of data categories across these two surveys will be feasible.

It has not been possible to draw on data that can provide a direct link between service provision and children's outcomes, although it is anticipated that, in time, data from the National Longitudinal Study of Children in Ireland will assist in filling this gap. This is an area that warrants development across a number of data sources and attention will be paid to this in future data developments. In terms of service provision, there is a need for data to be disaggregated to the most local level so that it can inform service developments. In a small number of cases, this is not possible because of the small population of Ireland relative to elsewhere. In this report, for example, the number of births to young people aged under 18 has decreased over the last five years. However, in some counties, there are insufficient numbers to present the data and, consequently, data from a number of counties have been combined together.

Conclusion

This first *State of the Nation's Children* report presents an overview of the well-being of children in Ireland and sets out a benchmark against which further developments can be compared. The approach taken to the development of the national set of child well-being indicators was evidence-based, systematic, comprehensive and inclusive of key stakeholders. Despite this, there will inevitably be areas that are underrepresented in the report, others where additional information is required and yet others where the social goals of today will not be those of tomorrow. The indicator set is flexible, dynamic and open to changes and development, and it is likely that future reports will take account of these issues. Nevertheless, this report is a first step in the process of ensuring that information about the lives of children living in Ireland is made available so that future developments in respect of children's lives can be benchmarked.

References

Andrews, A., Ben-Arieh, A., Carlson, M., Damon, W., Dweck, C., Earls, F., Garcia-Coll, C., Gold, R., Halfon, N., Hart, R., Lerner, R.M., McEwen, B., Meaney, M., Offord, D., Patrick, D., Peck, M., Trickett, B., Weisner, T. and Zuckerman, B. (2002) *Ecology of Child Well-Being: Advancing the Science and the Science-Practice Link.* Decatur, GA: Ecology Working Group, Center for Child Well-Being.

Ben-Arieh, A., Hevener-Kaufman, N., Bowers-Andrews, A., Goerge, R.M., Joo-Lee, B. and Aber, J.L. (2001) *Measuring and Monitoring Children's Well-Being.* Dordrecht: Kluwer Academic Publishers.

Brooks, A.M. and Hanafin, S. (2005) *Measuring Child Well-Being: An Inventory of Key Indicators, Domains and Indicator Selection Criteria to support the development of a National Set of Child Well-Being Indicators,* National Children's Office. Dublin: The Stationery Office.

Department of Health and Children (2000) *The National Children's Strategy: Our Children – Their Lives.* Dublin: The Stationery Office.

Department of the Taoiseach (2006) *Towards 2016: Ten-Year Framework Social Partnership Agreement 2006-2015.* Dublin: The Stationery Office.

Fitzgerald, E. (2004) *Counting Our Children: An Analysis of Official Data Sources on Children and Childhood in Ireland.* Dublin: Children's Research Centre, University of Dublin, Trinity College.

Hanafin, S. and Brooks, A.M. (2005a) *Report on the development of a National Set of Child Well-Being Indicators,* National Children's Office. Dublin: The Stationery Office.

Hanafin, S. and Brooks, A.M. (2005b) *The Delphi Technique: A Methodology to support the development of a National Set of Child Well-Being Indicators,* National Children's Office. Dublin: The Stationery Office.

Moore, K.A. (1997) 'Criteria for Indicators of Child Well-Being', in *Indicators of Children's Well-Being,* R.M. Hauser, B.V. Brown and W.R. Prosser (eds.). New York: Russell Sage Foundation, pp. 36-44.

National Statistics Board (2003) *Developing Irish Social and Equality Statistics to meet Policy Needs: Report of the Steering Group on Social and Equality Statistics.* Dublin: The Stationery Office.

New Policy Institute (2002) *Poverty Reduction Indicators: A Discussion Paper.* Dublin: Combat Poverty Agency.

Nic Gabhainn, S. and Sixsmith, J. (2005) *Children's Understanding of Well-Being,* National Children's Office. Dublin: The Stationery Office.

PART 1: SOCIO-DEMOGRAPHICS

Context

The National Children's Strategy, *Our Children – Their Lives,* was published in 2000, following extensive consultation with children, organisations and individuals providing care and support for children and young people. This 10-year plan provides the overarching strategic approach to improving the lives of children living in Ireland. Its vision is:

'An Ireland where children are respected as young citizens with a valued contribution to make and a voice of their own; where all children are cherished and supported by family and the wider society; where they enjoy a fulfilling childhood and realise their potential.'

This vision is consistent with that of the United Nations Convention on the Rights of the Child, ratified by Ireland in 1992 (UN, 1989). The Convention has four guiding principles:

- all children should be entitled to basic rights without discrimination;
- the best interests of the child should be the primary concern of decision-making;
- children have the right to life, survival and development;
- the views of children must be taken into account in matters affecting them.

A monitoring report on the implementation of the National Children's Strategy is published each year and can be accessed at www.nco.ie.

In December 2005, the Government took a decision to set up the Office of the Minister for Children (OMC) as part of the Department of Health and Children in order to bring greater coherence to policy-making for children. The Minister for Children can now attend all Government Cabinet meetings and is supported by the OMC in:

- implementing the National Children's Strategy;
- implementing the National Childcare Investment Programme 2006–2010;
- developing policy and legislation on child welfare and child protection;
- implementing the Children Act (Government of Ireland, 2001).

The OMC focuses on harmonising policy issues that affect children in areas such as early childhood care and education, youth justice, child welfare and protection, children and young people's participation, research on children and young people, and cross-cutting initiatives for children.

A commitment to investing in children in all areas of life has been given in the most recent Social Partnership Agreement (Department of the Taoiseach, 2006). Specific areas identified for investment include access to childcare services; improvements in educational outcomes; access to health, personal social services and suitable accommodation; recreational and cultural opportunities; and appropriate participation in local and national decision-making.

Significance

Basic information about the number, age and location of children is a necessary prerequisite to appropriate planning around children's lives. The number of children in any given location will, for example, determine the demand for schools, healthcare, childcare and other services. The demographic composition of a country is an important predictor of its social and economic state, and significant demographic differences are seen between low-income and more developed countries in this regard. In low-income countries, high birth rates, high infant and child mortality rates and high emigration rates are a feature of society. The opposite is true for more developed countries, where decreasing birth rates, comparatively low infant and child mortality rates and net immigration tend to be a feature. This has been the case for Ireland. There has been a decrease in the birth rate from 21.4 per 1,000 of the estimated population in the 1970s to 14.8 in 2005. Infant and child mortality rates have also decreased and there is now net immigration for the first time in Ireland's history.

In many low-income countries, 10%-20% of children die before reaching the age of 5. A key target of the United Nations Convention on the Rights of the Child, as stated in Article 24, is that State Parties should aim to 'diminish infant and child mortality' (UN, 1989). In recent decades, there has been a marked decline in infant and child mortality rates in both advanced economic and developing nations (Sloper and Quilgars, 2002) and it is clear that social, economic, technological and policy developments can make a significant difference to mortality rates.

In lesser developed countries, the most significant changes to mortality rates in infants can be made by improving sanitation, ensuring clean water supplies, improving maternal and child welfare services, and providing satisfactory nutrition for mothers as well as infants and children. As countries become more developed, the causes of death are more likely to be due to congenital abnormalities, infectious diseases and injury and poisoning. Policy interventions can also be successful in reducing infant and child mortality rates in these countries. In the early 1990s, for example, a Government-sponsored campaign, based on epidemiological research undertaken in the UK (ALSPAC), resulted in a decrease in the level of Sudden Infant Death Syndrome. The campaign focused on sleeping position, maternal and passive smoking around infants, and infant's temperature.

Historically, emigration was a feature of the demographic landscape of Ireland. But this has changed in recent years and increasing levels of immigration over the past decade has meant that social and cultural diversity have become significant features of Irish life. The importance of ensuring social inclusion measures and of providing a supportive environment for immigrants is well recognised (Immigrant Council of Ireland, 2004). In recent years, the Irish Government has worked to promote intercultural practices and tackle racism so as to facilitate the participation of migrants in Irish society. Children from different races and ethnicities can show lower levels of well-being in a number of areas, including health, mortality, school performance and achievement, and access to family and community resources. Irish research findings have highlighted the difficulties children of different races and ethnicities experience in integrating into schools (Keogh and Whyte, 2003) and communities (Guerin, 2003; Stavrou, 2003). Difficulties encountered included inadequate knowledge of the education system and educational entitlements, and inadequate language skills to access information.

A number of legislative and policy steps have been taken to support families and children who immigrate to Ireland. This includes the introduction of equality legislation (Government of Ireland, 1998, 2000 and 2004); the establishment of the National Consultative Committee on Racism and Interculturalism; the publication of the National Action Plan against Racism in 2004 (Department of Justice, Equality and Law Reform, 2004); the development of guidelines for intercultural education in primary and post-primary schools (National Council for Curriculum and Assessment, 2005 and 2006); and a commitment under the National Anti-Poverty Strategy, *Building an Inclusive Society 2002-2007,* to reducing poverty and exclusion of migrants (Department of Social and Family Affairs, 2002).

Data is now presented on the following three indicators:
- Child population
- Child mortality
- Non-Irish national children

CHILD POPULATION

Measure

The number of children under 18, expressed as a proportion of the total population.

Key findings

- In 2005, there were 1,027,880 children under 18 years of age living in Ireland. Of these, 527,389 were boys and 500,491 were girls *(see Table 1)*.
- In 2005, the percentage of children under 18 years accounted for almost one-quarter (24.9%) of the total population of Ireland.

Table 1: Population of Ireland under 18 years (2005)			
Years of age	Boys	Girls	Total
<1	31,493	29,573	61,066
1	31,884	30,299	62,183
2	31,683	29,892	61,575
3	28,274	27,553	55,827
4	29,096	27,618	56,714
5	29,304	28,139	57,443
6	29,626	28,205	57,831
7	29,203	27,395	56,598
8	28,758	26,792	55,550
9	27,705	26,083	53,788
10	27,180	25,736	52,916
11	27,027	25,815	52,842
12	28,073	26,204	54,277
13	28,635	27,608	56,243
14	30,148	28,289	58,437
15	29,261	27,997	57,258
16	29,478	27,825	57,303
17	30,561	29,468	60,029
Total population – under 18	527,389	500,491	1,027,880
Total population – all ages	2,058,952	2,071,770	4,130,722

Source: Population Projections, CSO

PART 1: SOCIO-DEMOGRAPHICS

- The percentage of children under 18 years of age has consistently decreased over the last 25 years, from 36.2% of the total population in 1981 to 24.9% in 2005 *(see Table 2)*.
- Despite an overall increase in the population over the same period, the number of children under 18 years has decreased from 1,246,443 in 1981 to 1,027,880 in 2005.
- In Ireland in 2005, boys under 18 years accounted for 25.6% of all males in the population and girls under 18 years accounted for 24.2% of all females in the population. The corresponding figures at EU25 level were 21.1% and 19.1% respectively.

Table 2: Population under 18 years, by gender (selected years 1981-2005)

Year	Boys	% of all males	Girls	% of all females	Total	% of all ages
1981	638,768	36.9	607,675	35.5	1,246,443	36.2
1986	630,985	35.7	599,165	33.8	1,230,150	34.7
1991	587,655	33.5	557,738	31.5	1,145,393	32.5
1996	550,389	30.6	521,583	28.6	1,071,972	29.6
2000	525,484	27.9	498,011	26.1	1,023,495	27.0
2001	522,049	27.3	494,683	25.6	1,016,732	26.4
2002	519,483	26.7	493,548	25.0	1,013,031	25.9
2003	520,837	26.3	495,344	24.7	1,016,181	25.5
2004	523,709	26.0	497,447	24.5	1,021,156	25.3
2005	527,389	25.6	500,491	24.2	1,027,880	24.9

Source: Census of the Population 2002 and Population Estimates, CSO

- In 2005, Ireland had a higher proportion of children under 18 years of age (25%) than any other EU Member State *(see Table 3 and Figure 1)*.

Table 3: Percentage of population under 18 years in EU25 (selected years 1995-2005)			
Country	1995	2000	2005
Austria	21.2	20.8	19.7
Belgium	21.7	21.2	20.8
Cyprus	29.5	27.8	23.6
Czech Republic	23.9	20.6	18.7
Denmark	20.9	21.5	22.3
Estonia	-	22.9	20.8
Finland	22.9	22.2	21.1
France	23.5	22.8	22.3
Germany	19.5	19.0	18.0
Greece	21.8	19.4	17.8
Hungary	23.0	20.7	19.3
Ireland	**30.3**	**27.2**	**25.0**
Italy	18.4	17.5	17.1
Latvia	24.8	22.6	19.6
Lithuania	26.1	24.8	21.8
Luxembourg	21.6	22.2	22.2
Malta	26.6	25.0	21.9
Netherlands	21.9	22.0	22.1
Poland	28.1	24.9	21.2
Portugal	22.6	20.2	19.0
Slovakia	28.3	24.7	21.6
Slovenia	23.1	20.2	18.1
Spain	21.7	18.7	17.6
Sweden	22.3	21.9	21.5
United Kingdom	23.0	22.8	22.2
EU25	**22.1**	**21.0**	**19.8**

Source: Eurostat

PART 1: SOCIO-DEMOGRAPHICS

13

Figure 1: Percentage of population under 18 years in EU25 (2005)

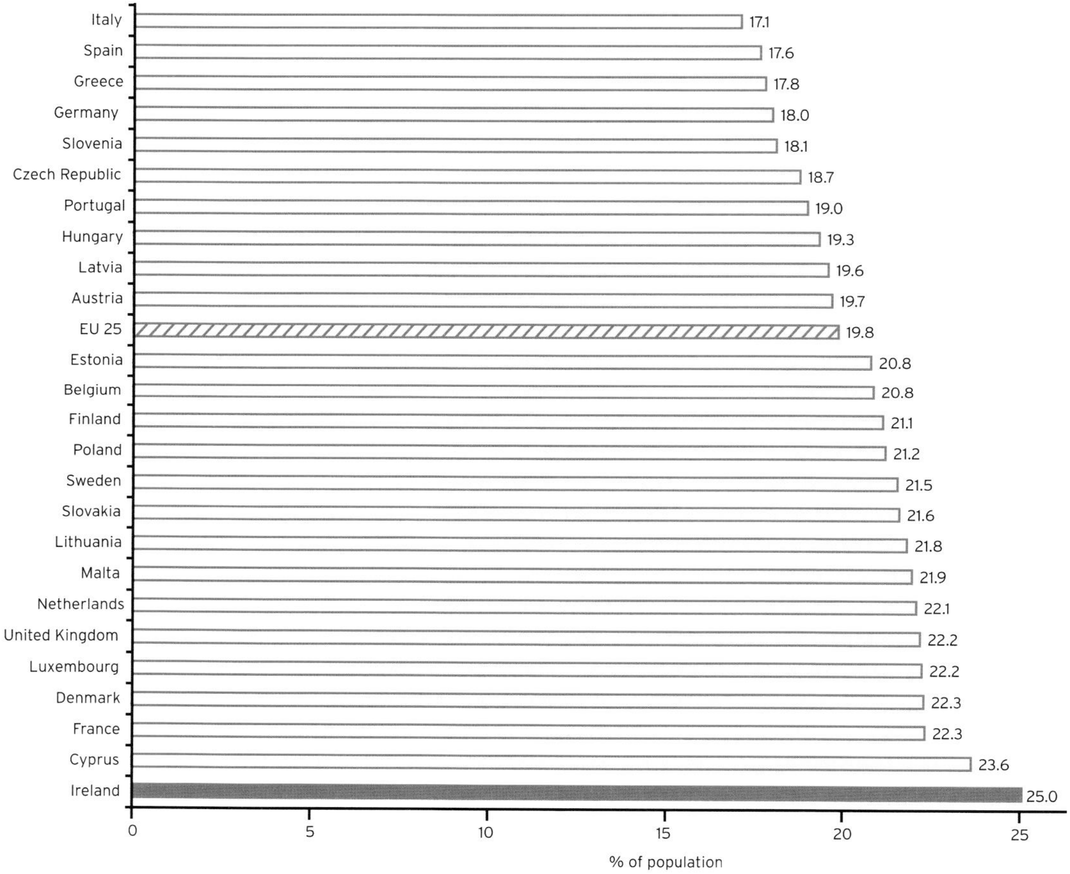

Country	%
Italy	17.1
Spain	17.6
Greece	17.8
Germany	18.0
Slovenia	18.1
Czech Republic	18.7
Portugal	19.0
Hungary	19.3
Latvia	19.6
Austria	19.7
EU 25	19.8
Estonia	20.8
Belgium	20.8
Finland	21.1
Poland	21.2
Sweden	21.5
Slovakia	21.6
Lithuania	21.8
Malta	21.9
Netherlands	22.1
United Kingdom	22.2
Luxembourg	22.2
Denmark	22.3
France	22.3
Cyprus	23.6
Ireland	25.0

% of population

Source: Eurostat

Technical notes

Population estimates are based on the de facto population present on Census night in any area, including visitors present at that time as well as those in residence. Usual residents who are temporarily absent from the area are excluded from the Census count.

CHILD MORTALITY

Measure

> **The number of deaths among children under 18, expressed as a proportion of all children. This may be subdivided by principal cause of death.**

Key findings

- The death rate of children under 18 years was 5.5 deaths per 10,000 in 2000. This rate declined to 4.6 deaths per 10,000 in 2004 *(see Table 4)*.
- The death rates were consistently higher for boys than for girls. In 2004, the death rate for boys was 5.3 per 10,000, compared to the death rate for girls of 3.8 per 10,000.

Table 4: Death rates (per 10,000) of children under 18, by gender (2000-2004)	2000	2001	2002	2003	2004
Boys	6.4	6.2	5.6	5.8	5.3
Girls	4.6	4.9	4.5	3.9	3.8
Total	5.5	5.6	5.1	4.9	4.6

Source: Vital Statistics, CSO

- The majority of deaths occur in the period of infancy (aged less than one year). Infant deaths accounted for 300 of the total of 465 deaths of children under 18 years in 2004. This represented a death rate of 48.7 per 10,000 children aged less than one year, compared to an overall rate of 4.6 per 10,000 children aged under 18 *(see Table 5)*.
- There has been a substantial decrease in infant mortality rates over the last 5 years. In 2000, this rate was 63 per 10,000; by 2004, it was 48.7 per 10,000.
- Similarly, there has been a decrease in the mortality rates among children aged 15-17 over the last 5 years. In 2000, this rate was 5.1 per 10,000; by 2004, it was 2.8 per 10,000.

Table 5: Number and rate (per 10,000) of deaths of children, by age group (2000-2004)	2000		2001		2002		2003		2004	
Years of age	No.	Rate	No.	Rate	No.	Rate	No.	Rate	No.	Rate
<1	338	63.0	331	60.1	305	56.0	326	53.8	300	48.7
1-4	45	2.1	78	3.6	59	2.6	49	2.2	48	2.1
5-9	39	1.5	36	1.4	28	1.1	29	1.1	35	1.3
10-14	43	1.5	43	1.5	50	1.8	42	1.5	33	1.2
15-17	100	5.1	78	4.1	74	4.0	50	2.7	49	2.8
Total	565	5.5	566	5.6	516	5.1	496	4.9	465	4.6

Source: Vital Statistics, CSO

■ Most deaths of children under 18 years were attributable to certain conditions in the perinatal period, congenital malformations, followed by injury and poisoning and Sudden Infant Death Syndrome *(see Table 6)*. In contrast, other conditions, such as cancer, cardiac and respiratory illnesses, are more prevalent among the causes of deaths in adults.

Table 6: Deaths of children under 18, by age group and main causes (2004)						
Main cause	<1	1-4	5-9	10-14	15-17	<18
Malignant neoplasm	0	8	10	9	9	36
Certain conditions in the perinatal period	124	1	0	0	0	125
Congenital malformations	112	3	2	4	0	121
Sudden Infant Death Syndrome	36	4	0	0	0	40
Injury and poisoning	3	7	7	11	29	57
Other	25	25	16	9	11	86
Total	300	48	35	33	49	465

Source: Vital Statistics, CSO

■ More boys than girls died in each category according to cause of death *(see Figure 2)*. This was particularly notable for the category 'Injury and poisoning', where more than three times as many deaths were recorded for boys than for girls.

Figure 2: Number of children under 18, by gender and main cause of death (2004)

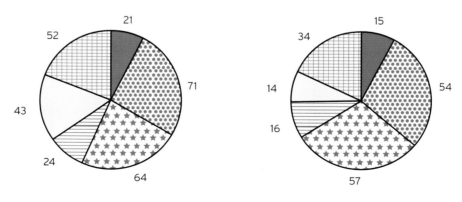

■ Malignant neoplasms ■ Certain conditions in the perinatal period ■ Congenital malformations
■ Sudden Infant Death Syndrome □ Injury and poisoning ■ Other

Source: Vital Statistics, CSO

- In 2004, the infant mortality rate in Ireland was 4.9 per 1,000 live births. This compared to the EU25 average of 4.0 per 1,000 live births *(see Table 7)*.
- Among the EU25, Latvia reported the highest infant mortality rate (9.4 per 1,000 live births), while Sweden reported the lowest infant mortality rate (3.1 per 1,000 live births).

Table 7: Infant mortality rate (per 1,000 live births) in EU25 (2004)	
Country	2004
Latvia	9.4
Lithuania	7.9
Poland	6.8
Slovakia	6.8
Hungary	6.6
Estonia	6.3
Malta	5.9
United Kingdom	5.1
Ireland	**4.9**
Austria	4.5
Denmark	4.4
Belgium	4.3
Germany	4.1
Italy	4.1
Netherlands	4.1
Portugal	4.0
EU25	**4.0**
Greece	3.9
Luxembourg	3.9
France	3.9
Czech Republic	3.7
Slovenia	3.7
Spain	3.5
Cyprus	3.5
Finland	3.3
Sweden	3.1

Source: Eurostat

PART 1: SOCIO-DEMOGRAPHICS

17

- With a small number of exceptions, the mortality rate per 10,000 of children in selected countries across the EU25 is higher for boys than for girls *(see Table 8)*.
- Mortality rates are also substantially higher in the 0-4 age group than for any other age group. The data show that Latvia has the highest mortality rate for boys in the 0-4 age group (29.8 per 10,000) and Slovenia has the lowest mortality rate (9.6 per 10,000).

Table 8: Rate (per 10,000) of deaths of children across selected countries in EU25, by age group and gender (2000-2004)								
	Boys				Girls			
	0-4	5-9	10-14	15-19	0-4	5-9	10-14	15-19
Czech Republic	10.7	1.5	1.6	6.2	8.6	1.1	1.2	2.6
Germany	10.3	1.1	1.2	4.9	8.7	0.9	0.8	2.3
Estonia	16.9	2.2	2.2	12.4	16.9	1.3	1.4	2.1
Greece	10.6	1.9	1.8	5.9	9.9	0.9	0.9	2.6
Spain	11.5	1.3	1.8	5.5	9.3	0.9	1.1	2.3
France	11.7	1.4	1.6	6.3	9.4	1.1	1.2	2.6
Ireland	**13.0**	**1.6**	**1.4**	**5.8**	**10.8**	**1.0**	**1.0**	**1.7**
Italy	11.6	1.7	1.7	5.7	9.5	0.9	1.1	2.1
Cyprus	11.6	3.6	1.8	9.1	13.4	2.3	1.5	2.2
Latvia	29.8	3.8	3.4	8.5	23.0	2.1	1.2	5.0
Lithuania	19.8	3.0	2.4	12.0	16.7	2.1	1.4	3.7
Hungary	17.2	1.7	2.2	5.6	13.7	1.4	1.1	2.5
Netherlands	11.4	1.1	1.5	4.0	8.9	0.9	0.9	1.7
Austria	10.8	1.3	1.3	7.7	9.6	1.2	1.2	3.7
Poland	16.9	1.8	2.1	6.1	13.7	1.2	1.4	2.5
Portugal	11.8	2.1	1.9	6.0	8.5	1.6	1.9	2.9
Slovenia	9.6	1.4	1.8	6.7	9.0	0.9	1.7	2.5
Finland	10.6	1.7	1.8	6.4	6.9	1.6	1.4	3.1
Sweden	9.8	1.0	1.1	3.9	6.7	0.7	0.9	3.0
United Kingdom	13.7	1.1	1.4	4.9	11.4	0.9	1.1	2.5

Source: Eurostat

Technical notes

Deaths are coded according to the 9th Revision of the International Statistical Classification of Diseases, Injuries and Causes of Death. Stillborn babies are excluded from infant mortality figures, which refer to deaths of children aged less than one year.

NON-IRISH NATIONAL CHILDREN

Measure

The number of non-Irish national children, expressed as a proportion of all children.

Key findings

■ In 2002, nearly 40,000 children under 18 years were non-Irish nationals, representing just under 4.0% of the total child population of Ireland *(see Table 9)*.

Table 9: Non-Irish national children, by age group and gender (2002)						
	Boys		Girls		Total	
Years of age	No.	%	No.	%	No.	%
0-4	4,166	2.9	4,131	3.1	8,297	3.0
5-9	6,583	4.9	6,296	4.9	12,879	4.9
10-14	6,373	4.4	6,339	4.6	12,712	4.5
15-17	2,956	3.1	2,994	3.3	5,950	3.2
Total	**20,078**	**3.9**	**19,760**	**4.0**	**39,838**	**4.0**

Source: Census of the Population 2002, CSO

■ Nearly one-quarter (9,250) of non-Irish national children lived in Dublin and a further 10.1% (4,004) in Cork *(see Figure 3)*.

Figure 3: Number of non-Irish national children, by county (2002)

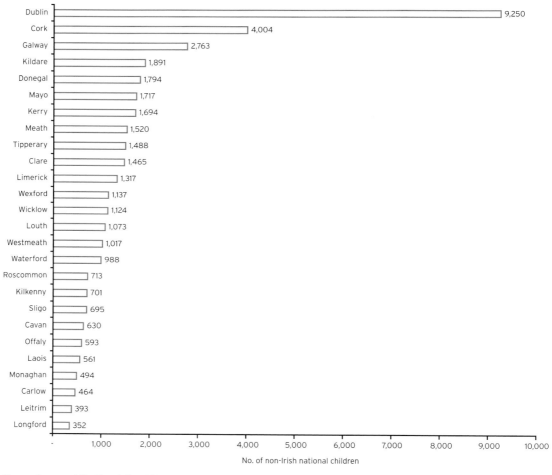

Source: Census of the Population 2002, CSO

- Over half (51.2%) of non-Irish nationals under 18 years reported their nationality as British or Northern Irish *(see Table 10)*. Americans were the next most common nationality (10.2% of the total), while the only other national minority with more than 5% of the total number of non-Irish national children was Nigerian.
- Those with Irish, not-stated and dual nationality (e.g. Irish-English or Irish-American) are excluded from all of the tables and graphs.

Table 10: Non-Irish national children, by nationality (2002)

Nationality	No.	%
United Kingdom	20,403	51.2
USA	4,073	10.2
Nigeria	2,314	5.8
Romania	916	2.3
South Africa	875	2.2
Germany	794	2.0
Pakistan	654	1.6
Australia	449	1.1
Canada	449	1.1
Russia	440	1.1
France	403	1.0
Netherlands	380	1.0
Other	7,688	19.3
Total	**39,838**	**100.0**

Source: Census of the Population 2002, CSO

Technical notes

The definition of children includes all people under 18 years of age when the data were collected. Figures refer to all people usually resident within the State on Census night in 2002. (Since that time, the diversity of the population in the State has probably increased.) Those with dual Irish, not-stated or dual Irish-Other nationality have been excluded from the figures in the tables and graphs.

PART 1: SOCIO-DEMOGRAPHICS

References

Department of Health and Children (2000) *The National Children's Strategy: Our Children – Their Lives.* Dublin: The Stationery Office.

Department of Justice, Equality and Law Reform (2004) *Planning for Diversity – The National Action Plan against Racism.* Dublin: The Stationery Office.

Department of Social and Family Affairs (2002) *Building an Inclusive Society 2002-2007.* Dublin: The Stationery Office.

Department of the Taoiseach (2006) *Towards 2016: Ten-Year Framework Social Partnership Agreement 2006-2015.* Dublin: The Stationery Office.

Government of Ireland (1998) *Employment Equality Act.* Dublin: The Stationery Office.

Government of Ireland (2000) *Equal Status Act.* Dublin: The Stationery Office.

Government of Ireland (2001) *Children Act.* Dublin: The Stationery Office.

Government of Ireland (2004) *Equality Act.* Dublin: The Stationery Office.

Guerin, P. (2003) *Building Solidarity across Communities.* Dublin: South West Inner City Network.

Immigrant Council of Ireland (2004) *Voices of Immigrants: The Challenges of Inclusion.* Dublin: Immigrant Council of Ireland.

Keogh, A.F., and Whyte, J. (2003) *Getting On: The Experiences and Aspirations of Immigrant Students in Second-level Schools linked to Trinity Access Programmes.* Dublin: Children's Research Centre, University of Dublin, Trinity College.

National Council for Curriculum and Assessment (2005) *Intercultural Education in Primary Schools: Guidelines for Schools.* Dublin: National Council for Curriculum and Assessment.

National Council for Curriculum and Assessment (2006) *Intercultural Education in Post-Primary Schools: Enabling students to respect and celebrate diversity, to promote equality and to challenge unfair discrimination.* Dublin: National Council for Curriculum and Assessment.

Sloper, P. and Quilgars, D. (2002) 'Mortality', in *The Well-Being of Children in the UK,* J. Bradshaw (ed.). York: Save the Children, pp. 27-44.

Stavrou, A. (2003) *The Provision of Services to Migrants in Cork City and County.* Cork: Southern Integrated Research Partnership.

UN (1989) *Convention on the Rights of the Child.* Geneva: United Nations Office of the High Commissioner for Human Rights. Available at www.ohchr.org

FAMILY STRUCTURE

Context

The family is recognised within the Irish Constitution as the most fundamental unit of the State. Although the majority of children continue to live in a two-parent family, the changing nature of family structures in Ireland has been one of the most striking demographic changes in recent years. The report on the *Commission on the Family* provided an in-depth analysis of the issues affecting families and made a number of wide-ranging recommendations across different policy areas (Department of Social and Family Affairs, 1998). The Family Support Agency was established in 2003 and has clearly defined functions and responsibilities in the area of family policy and services. Specifically, it brings together programmes and services introduced by Government since 1997, which are designed to:

- promote local family support;
- support ongoing parenting relationships for children;
- help prevent marital breakdown.

In Ireland, there is a long-standing Government commitment to supporting families parenting alone and up to the 1990s these supports were premised on the basis that women with children should remain in the home full time. In 1997, a new allowance was introduced called the One-Parent Family Payment. This is a means-tested payment made to men or women who are caring for a child or children without the support of a partner. In 2005, the expenditure on the one-parent family scheme was €770 million (Department of Social and Family Affairs, 2006).

Further developments are currently underway and these are predicated on the basis that employment is an important route out of poverty for all low-income families, including families parenting alone. In a 2005 discussion paper entitled *Proposals for supporting Lone Parents,* the Department of Social and Family Affairs presented a review of the issues facing lone parents and described the current supports that are in place, as well as the barriers to achieving economic independence (Department of Social and Family Affairs, 2006). This paper sets out a series of reforms to remove obstacles to employment for lone parents and consultation around these areas is currently taking place.

Significance

The *Commission on the Family* set out a number of areas for development of family policy, which are underpinned by an assumption that all families have some needs (Department of Social and Family Affairs, 1998). These areas include building strengths in families; supporting families in carrying out their functions in the care and nurturing of children; promoting continuity and stability in family life; and protecting and enhancing the position of children and vulnerable dependant family members. Families parenting alone are not a homogeneous group: within this group, there are differing income levels, educational experiences, household compositions and levels of parental involvement with children. Consequently, the needs and outcomes of this group are as diverse as all other family structures.

There is, however, some evidence that lone parents are considerably more likely to have a lower income than two-parent families. In 2004, for example, 31% of one-parent families in Ireland lived in consistent poverty, compared to 7% of the population as a whole (Layte *et al,* 2006). The Combat Poverty Agency (2006) notes that among the reasons why one-parent families are more likely to be poor are lower levels of educational achievement and difficulties in making the financial shift from welfare to work. A recent survey on indebtedness, commissioned by One Parent Exchange Network with the support of MABS and the Society of St. Vincent de Paul, found that lone-parent households report the lowest average household weekly income, but also report the lowest average debt to income ratio (Conroy, 2005). Findings from the Health Behaviour in School-aged Children Survey note that Irish children living with both parents are more likely to report 'excellent health' and 'feeling happy' about their lives, and less likely to report having been drunk or being current smokers, than those living with one parent (Molcho and Nic Gabhainn, 2005).

Measure

> **The number of children under 18 who live in family household units with only one parent or primary care-giver resident, expressed as a proportion of all children.**

Key findings

- In 2002, a total of 140,693 children under 18 years of age lived with a lone parent or guardian. This amounted to 14% of all children living in households with a single parent or guardian *(see Table 11).*

Table 11: Children under 18 living with lone parent, by age group and gender (2002)						
Years of age	Boys		Girls		Total	
	No.	%	No.	%	No.	%
0-4	16,734	11.8	16,028	11.9	32,762	11.9
5-9	18,986	14.0	17,847	14.0	36,833	14.0
10-14	21,631	14.9	20,710	14.9	42,341	14.9
15-17	14,570	15.3	14,187	15.8	28,757	15.6
Total	71,921	13.9	68,772	14.0	140,693	14.0

Source: Census of the Population 2002, CSO

- In 2002, one in 3 children in lone-parent families were resident in the Dublin area and one in 9 in Cork *(see Table 12)*.
- Less than one in 10 children living in counties Cavan, Leitrim, Meath and Roscommon lived in one-parent families.

Table 12: Children under 18 living with lone parent, by county (2002)			
County	No.	% within county	% within State
Carlow	1,838	14.8	1.3
Cavan	1,346	8.5	1.0
Clare	3,412	12.3	2.4
Cork	15,273	13.4	10.9
Donegal	4,981	12.6	3.5
Dublin	46,996	18.0	33.4
Galway	6,043	11.4	4.3
Kerry	3,812	11.6	2.7
Kildare	5,615	12.0	4.0
Kilkenny	2,353	10.7	1.7
Laois	1,841	11.0	1.3
Leitrim	634	9.4	0.5
Limerick	6,387	14.6	4.5
Longford	1,213	14.0	0.9
Louth	4,816	17.3	3.4
Mayo	3,303	10.5	2.3
Meath	3,626	9.4	2.6
Monaghan	1,545	10.5	1.1
Offaly	1,987	10.9	1.4
Roscommon	1,315	9.2	0.9
Sligo	1,888	12.6	1.3
Tipperary	4,736	12.5	3.4
Waterford	4,186	15.9	3.0
Westmeath	2,659	13.3	1.9
Wexford	4,515	14.0	3.2
Wicklow	4,373	14.1	3.1
State	140,693	14.0	100.0

Source: Census of the Population 2002, CSO

PART 1: SOCIO-DEMOGRAPHICS

25

■ In 2002, 26% (32,762) of children in lone-parent families were aged 0-4; 23% (36,833) were aged 5-9; 31% (42,341) were aged 10-14; and the remaining 20% (28,757) were aged 15-17 *(see Figure 4)*.

Figure 4: Percentage of children in lone-parent families, by age group (2002)

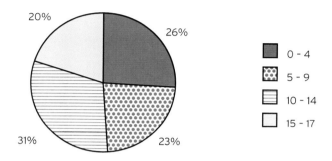

Source: Census of the Population 2002, CSO

Technical notes

Figures are based on place of usual residence rather than de facto presence on Census night.

References

Combat Poverty Agency (2006) *Fact Sheet: Lone Parent Families and Poverty.* Dublin: Combat Poverty Agency.

Conroy, P. (2005) *Do the poor pay more? An OPEN Report on Lone Parents and Credit.* Dublin: One Parent Exchange Network.

Department of Social and Family Affairs (1998) *Commission on the Family: Strengthening Families for Life.* Dublin: The Stationery Office.

Department of Social and Family Affairs (2006) *Proposals for supporting Lone Parents – Discussion Document.* Dublin: Department of Social and Family Affairs.

Layte, R., Maître, B., Nolan, B. and Whelan, C.T. (2006) *Day In, Day Out: Understanding the Dynamics of Child Poverty.* Dublin: Combat Poverty Agency.

Molcho, M. and Nic Gabhainn, S. (2005) *Family Structure among Irish School Children. Research Fact Sheet No. 2. Health Behaviour in School-aged Children Survey.* Galway: Department of Health Promotion, National University of Ireland, Galway.

PARENTAL EDUCATION LEVEL

Context

Education in Ireland is compulsory by law from the age of 6 to 16, or until students have completed 3 years of second-level education. The numbers of students completing first, second and third-level education in Ireland have increased steadily over the last 40 years. In 1965, for example, only 20% of students completed second-level education; this compares with almost 80% in 2004 (Department of Education and Science, 2005a).

The mission of the Department of Education and Science (2005b) is to provide for high-quality education, which will:
- enable individuals to achieve their full potential and to participate fully as members of society;
- contribute to Ireland's social, cultural and economic development.

Within this mission, there is a commitment to ongoing education. In 2000, Ireland's first *White Paper on Adult Education* was published (Department of Education and Science, 2000). It set out lifelong learning as the governing principle of educational policy in Ireland and recommended that adult education should be underpinned by three core principles, namely:
- a systemic approach that recognises that the interfaces between the different levels of educational provision and the quality of the early school experience have a critical influence on learners' motivation and ability to access and progress in adult education and training;
- equality of access, participation and outcome for participants in adult education;
- the development of interculturalism or the need to frame educational policy and practice in the context of serving a diverse population, as opposed to a uniform one, and the development of curricula, materials, training and in-service modes of assessment and delivery methods, which accept such diversity as the norm.

Compared with elsewhere, Ireland has a high level of educational attainment among the adult population (age group 25-64) and in a recent report was ranked 8th of 32 countries for this indicator (OECD, 2005).

Significance

Education is a key predictor of economic and social success for individuals, employers and countries. In cross-country comparisons, formal schooling has been found to play an important role in enhancing economic growth, raising labour market earnings, improving employment probabilities, enhancing health outcomes, reducing crime and improving social capital (Machin, 2006). It is not surprising, therefore, that strong links between parental education level and children's outcomes have been identified. Findings from the Canadian National Longitudinal Study of Children, for example, found that the educational level of the mother in particular has a significant impact on child development (Government of Canada, 2003). Mothers who had completed more than a secondary school education were less likely to have toddlers with problematic personal and social behaviours, and were more likely to have toddlers with advanced language skills.

In an examination of the impact of parental income and education on the schooling of children, Chevalier *et al* (2005) reported that there were stronger effects for maternal education than paternal and stronger effects on sons than daughters. Areas examined were decisions by children to participate in post-compulsory schooling and the achievement of five or more GCSEs (at Grade A-C). The level of parental education attainment is, therefore, an important factor in supporting children's development.

Measure

> **The number of children under 18 whose parents have attained (a) primary,**
> **(b) lower secondary, (c) upper secondary or (d) third-level education,**
> **expressed as a proportion of all children.**

Key findings

- In 2002, just over one-quarter of children under 18 years of age lived in families where the head of the household had a third-level degree or higher educational qualification *(see Table 13)*. This proportion varied from 32.9% where the household contained children aged 0-4 to 19.9% for households with children aged 13-17.
- Almost 59% of children under 18 lived in families where the highest level of education attained by the head of the household was a lower secondary or upper secondary education.
- Only 13.1% of children lived in families where the head of the household had either no formal education or primary education only.

Table 13: Percentage of children under 18, by age group and educational attainment of head of household (2002)				
Highest level of education attained	0-4	5-12	13-17	Total <18 years
Primary (including no formal education)	6.7	11.7	20.6	13.1
Lower secondary	25.5	30.1	30.0	28.9
Upper secondary	32.6	30.5	26.8	29.9
Third level (Degree or higher)	32.9	25.3	19.9	25.6
Not stated/not available	2.4	2.4	2.7	2.5
Total	100.0	100.0	100.0	100.0
Total by age group	250,735	414,839	290,474	956,048

Source: Census of the Population 2002, CSO

28

- Regional differences are apparent *(see Table 14 and Figure 5)*. In 2002, in Donegal, for example, 22.6% of children lived in families where the head of the household had either no formal education or primary education only, compared with 10.1% of children in Kildare.

County	Primary (including no formal education)	Lower secondary	Upper secondary	Third level (Degree or higher)	Not stated/ not available	Total
Carlow	945	2,007	1,716	1,247	155	6,070
Cavan	1,392	2,238	1,980	1,262	173	7,045
Clare	1,481	3,371	4,528	3,635	243	13,258
Cork	5,853	15,630	17,120	15,114	1,196	54,913
Donegal	3,984	5,459	4,429	3,346	434	17,652
Dublin	15,368	30,310	36,297	38,633	4,473	125,081
Galway	3,384	6,067	7,411	6,930	568	24,360
Kerry	2,095	4,693	4,941	3,476	273	15,478
Kildare	2,321	5,720	7,440	6,893	581	22,955
Kilkenny	1,342	3,198	3,257	2,367	198	10,362
Laois	1,202	2,455	2,458	1,481	152	7,748
Leitrim	401	989	991	612	82	3,075
Limerick	3,000	5,950	6,440	5,098	364	20,852
Longford	738	1,199	1,185	676	152	3,950
Louth	2,085	4,158	3,755	3,180	298	13,476
Mayo	2,352	4,065	4,736	2,870	228	14,251
Meath	2,144	5,065	5,856	5,158	347	18,570
Monaghan	1,224	2,351	1,777	1,133	184	6,669
Offaly	1,377	2,702	2,451	1,422	299	8,251
Roscommon	893	2,046	2,251	1,302	88	6,580
Sligo	853	1,887	2,197	1,894	147	6,978
Tipperary	2,545	5,614	5,782	3,473	431	17,845
Waterford	1,672	3,940	3,871	3,038	304	12,825
Westmeath	1,242	2,770	2,918	2,226	208	9,364
Wexford	2,630	5,131	4,427	2,843	222	15,253
Wicklow	1,702	3,888	4,581	4,605	313	15,089
State	64,225	132,903	144,795	123,914	12,113	477,950

Table 14: Number of children under 18, by county and educational attainment of head of household (2002)

Source: Census of the Population 2002, CSO

Figure 5: Percentage of children under 18 living in households where head of household has no formal education or primary education only, by county (2002)

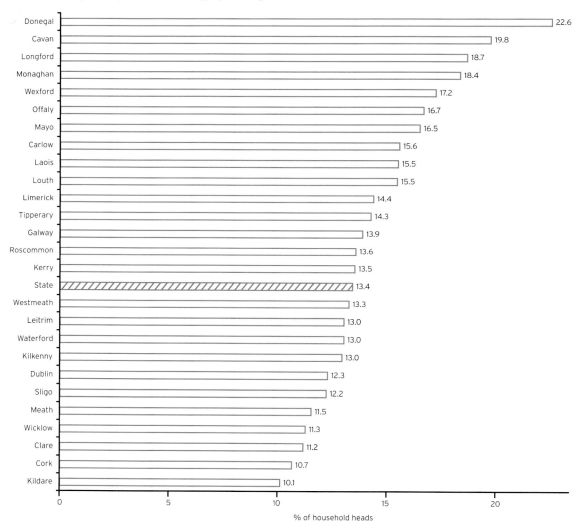

Source: Census of the Population 2002, CSO

30

Technical notes

The educational attainment of the head of the household refers to the highest standard reached by the head of the household (whether male or female, lone parent or couple). The household is defined as either one person living alone or a group of related/unrelated people living at the same address with common housekeeping arrangements, i.e. sharing at least one meal a day or sharing a living room or sitting room. The figures are based on responses to Question 21 of the 2002 Census, which distinguishes between four main categories:

(1)   No formal education or just primary education.
(2)   Lower secondary: Junior, Intermediate/Group Certificate, 'O' levels/GCSEs, NCVA Foundation Certificate, Basic Skills Training Certificate or equivalent.
(3)   Upper secondary: Leaving Certificate, 'A' levels, NCVA Level 1 Certificate or equivalent, Technical or Vocational qualification, both Upper Secondary and Technical or Vocational qualification.
(4)   Third level: Non-degree, primary degree, Professional qualification (of Degree status at least), both a Degree and a Professional qualification, post-graduate Certificate or Diploma, post-graduate Degree (Masters) or Doctorate (PhD).

The data are also based on the concept of usual residence rather than the defacto residence of household on Census night.

References

Chevalier, A., Harmon, C., O'Sullivan, V. and Walker, I. (2005) *The Impact of Parental Income and Education on the Schooling of their Children. IFS Working Papers, W05/05.* Warwick: The Institute for Fiscal Studies, University of Warwick.

Department of Education and Science (2000) *Learning for Life: White Paper on Adult Education.* Dublin: The Stationery Office.

Department of Education and Science (2005a) *Statistical Report 2005.* Dublin: The Stationery Office.

Department of Education and Science (2005b) *Statement of Strategy 2005-2007.* Dublin: The Stationery Office.

Government of Canada (2003) *The Well-Being of Canada's Young Children: Government of Canada Report.* Ottawa: Human Resources Development Canada and Health Canada.

Machin, S. (2006) *Social Disadvantage and Education Experiences: OECD Social Employment and Migration Working Papers.* Paris: Organisation for Economic Cooperation and Development.

OECD (2005) *Education at a Glance.* Paris: Organisation for Economic Cooperation and Development.

PART 1: SOCIO-DEMOGRAPHICS

SEPARATED CHILDREN SEEKING ASYLUM

Context

A separated child, also referred to as an unaccompanied minor, is defined as 'a child or young person under 18 years of age who is outside their country of origin and separated from both parents, or legal or customary primary care-giver' (McNeice and Almirall, 1999, p. 8). The 1951 UN Geneva Convention relating to the Status of Refugees is the main international instrument overseeing the right of asylum-seekers, including separated children, to apply for refugee status (UN, 1951). This Convention has been incorporated into Irish law through the Refugee Act (Government of Ireland, 1996), as amended by the Immigration Act (Government of Ireland, 1999) and the Illegal Immigrants (Trafficking) Act (Government of Ireland, 2000). Under the provisions of the Refugee Act, an Immigration Officer is required to inform the relevant Health Authority if a person under 18 years of age, who is not in the custody of another person, arrives at the frontiers or in the State. In addition to this legislation, there are a number of specific responsibilities placed on the Health Service Executive under the Child Care Act (Government of Ireland, 1991), including a responsibility to apply for asylum on the child's behalf.

Significance

While separated children seeking asylum are not a homogeneous group, there are, nevertheless, a number of areas that can influence their well-being. Most fundamentally, they do not have parental or family support in their day-to-day lives. In addition, they may experience difficulties around language, culture, religion, social norms and oppression (Thomas and Byford, 2003). They may also have additional health and social needs. Burnett and Peel (2001), for example, have suggested that although the basic health needs of asylum-seekers are broadly similar to those of the host population, previous poor access to services may have led to certain conditions being untreated. In addition, attitudes to reproductive health tend to be influenced by the country and region of origin rather than the destination country and, consequently, attitudes of separated children seeking asylum may differ significantly from those of their Irish peers.

In a recent study on separated children seeking asylum, carried out in the former East Coast Area Health Board (where there are the largest number of such children), several additional needs were identified with this group, including specific difficulties in integrating with those outside their own ethnic peer group (Conroy and Fitzgerald, 2005). In addition, separated children have many health risks that arise from both the smuggling and trafficking of children.

Measure

> **The number of separated children seeking asylum, expressed as a proportion of all children.**

Key findings

■ Overall, the number of separated children seeking asylum has fallen over the period 2002 to 2004 *(see Table 15)*. In 2002, there were 779 separated children seeking asylum. By 2004, this figure had fallen to 679 children.

■ The majority of separated children seeking asylum are found in the former Eastern Regional Health Authority area. In 2004, over 90% (619) of separated children seeking asylum were in this area.

■ Of the 679 separated children seeking asylum in 2004, 324 were boys and 355 were girls.

Table 15: Number of separated children seeking asylum, by gender and former health board area (2002-2004)

	2002			2003			2004		
	Boys	Girls	Total	Boys	Girls	Total	Boys	Girls	Total
Eastern Regional Health Authority	358	341	699	394	399	793	294	323	617
Midland Health Board	0	0	0	0	0	0	0	0	0
Mid-Western Health Board	18	4	22	4	3	7	2	1	3
North-Eastern Health Board	12	3	15	0	0	0	6	10	16
North-Western Health Board	0	1	1	2	0	2	1	3	4
South-Eastern Health Board	4	2	6	6	1	7	5	6	11
Southern Health Board	17	15	32	28	15	43	10	7	17
Western Health Board	3	1	4	2	4	6	6	5	11
State	412	367	779	436	422	858	324	355	679

Source: Childcare Interim Dataset 2002-2004, Department of Health and Children

■ In 2004, 66% (450) of the separated children seeking asylum were reunited with their families; 26% (176) were placed in the care of the former health boards; 2% (13) were found not to be minors; and the outcomes for the remaining 6% (40) were not classified *(see Figure 6)*.

PART 1: SOCIO-DEMOGRAPHICS

33

Figure 6: Outcomes for separated children seeking asylum (2004)

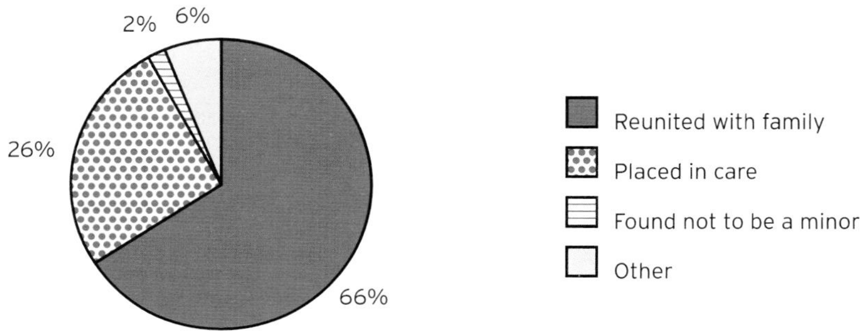

2% 6%
26%
66%

Reunited with family
Placed in care
Found not to be a minor
Other

Source: Childcare Interim Dataset 2002-2004, Department of Health and Children

References

Burnett, A. and Peel, M. (2001) 'Health Needs of Asylum Seekers and Refugees in Britain', *British Medical Journal,* No. 322, pp. 544-47.

Conroy, P. and Fitzgerald, F. (2005) *Separated Children seeking Asylum: Health and Educational Needs.* Wicklow: Health Service Executive.

Government of Ireland (1991) *Child Care Act.* Dublin: The Stationery Office.

Government of Ireland (1996) *Refugee Act.* Dublin: The Stationery Office.

Government of Ireland (1999) *Immigration Act.* Dublin: The Stationery Office.

Government of Ireland (2000) *Illegal Immigrants (Trafficking) Act.* Dublin: The Stationery Office.

McNeice, S. and Almirall, L. (1999) *Separated Children in Ireland: A Report on Legal and Social Conditions.* Dublin: Irish Refugee Council.

Thomas, S. and Byford, S. (2003) 'Research with Unaccompanied Children seeking Asylum', *British Medical Journal,* No. 327, pp. 1400-02.

UN (1951) *Convention and Protocol relating to the Status of Refugees.* New York: United Nations High Commissioner for Refugees.

TRAVELLER CHILDREN

Context

Travellers are a distinct minority group of Irish people who differ from the general population in many respects, including their lifestyle, culture and treatment by society (Department of Health and Children, 2002, p. 2). Since 1998, four pieces of legislation have supported the rights of minority communities, including Travellers, in areas such as education and employment. The Education Act (Government of Ireland, 1998a) legally obliges schools to provide for a diversity of needs, values, beliefs, tradition, languages and ways of life in society, while the Education (Welfare) Act (Government of Ireland, 2000a) safeguards every child's entitlement to remain at school until reaching the age of 16 or until completion of 3 years of post-primary education. The Employment Equality Act (Government of Ireland, 1998b) and the Equal Status Act (Government of Ireland, 2000b) include provisions to prohibit discrimination on the grounds of being a member of the Traveller community. Section 7(2) of the Equal Status Act relates specifically to educational institutions. The Department of Education and Science (2002a and 2002b) has issued guidelines on Traveller education in primary and post-primary schools and a Strategy for Traveller Education is currently being drafted by the same Department.

In 2002, the Department of Health and Children launched a Traveller Health Strategy, which set out 122 actions ranging across increasing awareness for health personnel in respect of Traveller culture, initiatives to make services more accessible and the establishment of partnerships between Travellers and formal structures at local and national levels. A need for improved coordination at national level is reiterated in the report of the High Level Group on Traveller Issues (Department of Justice, Equality and Law Reform, 2005), along with a recognition of the need for more robust data on Traveller outcomes. A study on Traveller health needs, currently being commissioned and funded by the Department of Health and Children, may assist in bridging this gap.

Significance

Although there is a lack of up-to-date information on the lives of Traveller children, there is nevertheless some indication that children from the Travelling community have significantly poorer outcomes than children in the general population. The 2002 Census report on the Travelling community, for example, showed considerable demographic differences compared with the settled community, including a higher birth rate, lower life expectancy and larger family size (CSO, 2004). Travellers of all ages have higher mortality rates than people in the general population: Traveller women live on average 12 years less than women in the general population and Traveller men, 10 years less.

The Department of Health and Children (2002) reported that the infant mortality rate for Travellers was 18.1 per 1,000 live births, compared with a national figure of 7.4 in 1987. In 1999, the occurrence of Sudden Infant Death Syndrome among Traveller families was 12 times higher than that of the national figure. In the 2002 Census, 38% of Traveller households were found to be living in temporary housing units. A recent *Survey of Traveller Education Provision* found that Traveller children living on unofficial halting sites had lower levels of school attendance rates (on average 68%) than those living on official halting sites (on average 78%) or in houses (on average 82%); the same survey found a learning disability rate of 15%, which is considered to be some 7% higher than the overall school-going population (Department of Education and Science, 2006).

Measure

The number of Traveller children, expressed as a proportion of all children.

Key findings

- In 2002, there were 23,681 Travellers living in Ireland. Of these, 49.5% (11,725) were under 18 years of age *(see Table 16)*.
- Overall, in 2002, Traveller children accounted for 1.2% of the total child population.

Table 16: Population of Travellers under 18 years, by age group and gender (2002)			
Years of age	Boys	Girls	Total
0-4	1,786	1,622	3,408
5-9	1,727	1,648	3,375
10-14	1,575	1,643	3,218
15-17	893	831	1,724
Total Traveller population – under 18	5,981	5,744	11,725
Total Traveller population – all ages	11,708	11,973	23,681

Source: Census of the Population 2002, CSO

- In 2002, Traveller children accounted for 1.2% (3,408) of the 0-4 age group of children living in Ireland; 1.3% (3,375) of the 5-9 age group; 1.1% (3,218) of the 10-14 age group; and 0.9% (1,724) of the 15-17 age group.
- In 2002, more Traveller children lived in Dublin and Galway than in any other county. However, the counties with the highest proportion of Travellers compared to the total population were Longford (3.5%) and Galway (3.0%) *(see Table 17)*.

36

Table 17: Irish Travellers under 18 years, by county (2002)			
County	No. of Travellers	Total population of county	% Travellers within county
Carlow	139	12,345	1.1
Cavan	83	15,845	0.5
Clare	401	27,931	1.4
Cork	849	114,833	0.7
Donegal	153	39,595	0.4
Dublin	2,828	262,048	1.1
Galway	1,582	53,293	3.0
Kerry	338	33,110	1.0
Kildare	201	46,899	0.4
Kilkenny	205	22,310	0.9
Laois	229	16,669	1.4
Leitrim	70	6,764	1.0
Limerick	637	44,166	1.4
Longford	298	8,636	3.5
Louth	287	27,949	1.0
Mayo	459	31,676	1.4
Meath	345	38,428	0.9
Monaghan	113	14,737	0.8
Offaly	316	18,214	1.7
Roscommon	182	14,302	1.3
Sligo	202	15,018	1.3
Tipperary	470	37,938	1.2
Waterford	255	26,616	1.0
Westmeath	318	20,147	1.6
Wexford	514	32,239	1.6
Wicklow	251	31,323	0.8
State	11,725	1,013,031	1.2

Source: Census of the Population 2002, CSO

Technical notes

Travellers are identified as those answering 'Yes' to Question 13 of the 2002 Census, which asks 'Are you a member of the Irish Traveller community?'

PART 1: SOCIO-DEMOGRAPHICS

References

CSO (2004) *Irish Traveller Community: A Census 2002 Report.* Dublin: Central Statistics Office.

Department of Education and Science (2002a) *Guidelines on Traveller Education in Primary Schools.* Dublin: The Stationery Office.

Department of Education and Science (2002b) *Guidelines on Traveller Education in Second-level Schools.* Dublin: The Stationery Office.

Department of Education and Science (2006) *Survey of Traveller Education Provision, Survey and Evaluation Unit of the Inspectorate of the Department of Education and Science.* Dublin: The Stationery Office.

Department of Health and Children (2002) *Traveller Health Strategy.* Dublin: The Stationery Office.

Department of Justice, Equality and Law Reform (2005) *High Level Group on Traveller Issues, Monitoring Report.* Dublin: The Stationery Office.

Government of Ireland (1998a) *Education Act.* Dublin: The Stationery Office.

Government of Ireland (1998b) *Employment Equality Act.* Dublin: The Stationery Office.

Government of Ireland (2000a) *Education (Welfare) Act.* Dublin: The Stationery Office.

Government of Ireland (2000b) *Equal Status Act.* Dublin: The Stationery Office.

PART 2: RELATIONSHIPS

'Children affect and in turn are affected by the relationships around them.'

(National Children's Strategy, 2000, p. 25)

covering
RELATIONSHIPS WITH PARENTS
and
RELATIONSHIPS WITH PEERS

RELATIONSHIPS WITH PARENTS

Context

The family is acknowledged as the most fundamental unit of the State and has traditionally received special protection, both in legislation and in policy. Since the publication of the report on the *Commission on the Family* (Department of Social and Family Affairs, 1998), a number of changes have taken place in Irish family policy, including the consolidation of existing family policy; the introduction of a range of measures designed to reconcile work and family life, and to raise the level of support of carers; and thirdly, the development of services to support families, including those that focus on families in need and those that provide counselling and mediation for couples experiencing difficulties (Daly and Clavero, 2002).

Decreased family time together, as a consequence of commuting and parental participation in the workforce, was identified as a key factor influencing family life in a recent report (Daly, 2004). Increasingly, family-friendly work arrangements are becoming an essential part of ensuring that workers can combine their personal life and caring responsibilities with their employment (Drew *et al,* 2004). There are a number of legislative measures in place to assist in family-friendly working arrangements, including the Protection of Employees (Part-time Work) Act, Maternity Protection Act, Parental Leave Act, Force Majeure Leave Act, Adoptive Leave Act and Carer's Leave Act. Other non-statutory leave can also be made available to families, including flexi-working, term-time working, paternity leave and compassionate leave (National Framework Committee for Work – Life Balance Policies, 2005). Currently, there is no legal entitlement to paternity leave in Ireland and it is provided only at the employer's discretion.

Significance

The family is one of the most important contexts for the development of the young child, the context in which social behaviour and attitudes are first adopted (Pederson *et al*, 2001). By providing the primary social environment, the family plays an important role in the development of the individual's communication skills, attitudes and behavioural patterns. A large body of literature exists in relation to the influence of parenting styles, family communication and parent-child relations on life skills, psycho-social adjustment, mental health and health behaviour (e.g. Galambos and Ehrenberg, 1997; Ryan *et al*, 1994; Field *et al,* 1994; Settertobulte, 2000).

The relationships between parents and children are of great importance to the life of the child. Poor parent-child relationships are associated with delinquent behaviour (Youniss *et al,* 1997; Lapsley and Edgerton, 2002; Bogard, 2005), depression (Young *et al,* 2005) and psychosomatic symptoms (Murberg and Bru, 2004). Adolescence, however, is a period when conflicts with parents tend to arise. These are considered by some as an integral component of parent-adolescent relationships and, despite such conflicts, parents remain an important source of support (Laursen, 1995).

44

The importance of support from both fathers and mothers to the lives of children has been previously acknowledged (Tamis-LeMonda and Carera, 2002; Luthar and Becker, 2002). In the Canadian National Longitudinal Study of Children, findings suggest that the amount of time parents interact directly with their children is positively related to child outcomes, although the importance of time is not measured only by the actual number of hours the parents spend with the child, but rather the 'quality' of that time (Government of Canada, 2003).

Data is now presented on several indicators that examine the relationship children have with their parents, including the number of children who report that they find it easy to talk to their parents if something is really bothering them and the number of children whose parents discuss with them how well they are doing at school on a weekly basis.

PART 2: RELATIONSHIPS

Relationship with mothers

Measure

> **The proportion of children aged 10-17 who report that they find it easy to talk to their mother when something is really bothering them.**

Key findings

- In 2002, 77.6% of children aged 10-17 reported that they found it easy to talk to their mother when something was really bothering them. This compares with results from 1998, when 74.0% of children reported this *(see Table 18)*.

Differences by age, social class and gender

- In 2002, the percentage of children reporting that they found it easy to talk to their mother when something was really bothering them was higher among girls, younger children and children from lower social classes:
  - 79.1% of girls reported this, compared to 75.5% of boys;
  - 86.7% of 10-11 year-olds reported this, compared with 71.1% of 15-17 year-olds;
  - 80.1% of children from social class 5-6 reported this, compared to 76.2% of children from social class 1-2.

Table 18: Percentage of children who report that they find it easy to talk to their mother when something is really bothering them, by age, social class and gender (1998 and 2002)

	1998			2002		
	Boys	Girls	Total	Boys	Girls	Total
Total	70.9	76.9	74.0	75.5	79.1	77.6
Years of age						
10-11	77.3	84.3	81.2	85.4	87.8	86.7
12-14	73.9	78.9	76.4	76.6	81.9	79.6
15-17	61.7	68.3	65.0	68.9	72.5	71.1
Social class						
SC 1-2	69.1	73.9	71.6	74.0	77.7	76.2
SC 3-4	70.7	79.2	75.0	76.4	80.0	78.5
SC 5-6	73.2	77.6	75.6	79.5	80.6	80.1

Source: HBSC Survey

46

Differences by geographical area

- In 2002, the highest percentage of children who reported that they found it easy to talk to their mothers when something was really bothering them lived in the former Western Health Board area (79.7%) and the lowest percentage in the former Southern Health Board area (74.8%) *(see Table 19)*.

Table 19: Percentage of children aged 10-17 who report that they find it easy to talk to their mother when something is really bothering them, by former health board area (1998 and 2002)		
	1998	2002
Eastern Regional Health Authority	77.1	79.3
Western Health Board	75.4	79.7
South-Eastern Health Board	74.5	75.8
Midland Health Board	73.7	77.7
North-Western Health Board	73.4	77.0
North-Eastern Health Board	73.1	77.9
Mid-Western Health Board	72.8	75.4
Southern Health Board	69.5	74.8
Mean average	74.0	77.6

Source: HBSC Survey

International comparisons

- From the 2002 HBSC Survey, using the ages of 11, 13 and 15 only to draw international comparisons, 79.4% of Irish children reported that they found it easy to talk to their mother when something was really bothering them *(see Figure 7)*. The HBSC average was 82.7%.
- Among all 35 countries that used this HBSC item, the lowest percentage for this indicator was found among Belgian (French) children (69.2%) and the highest among Slovenian children (92.7%).
- Overall, Irish 11-year-old children were ranked 31st, Irish 13-year-old children were ranked 25th and Irish 15-year-old children were ranked 24th.

Figure 7: Percentage of children who report that they find it easy to talk to their mother when something is really bothering them, by country (2002)

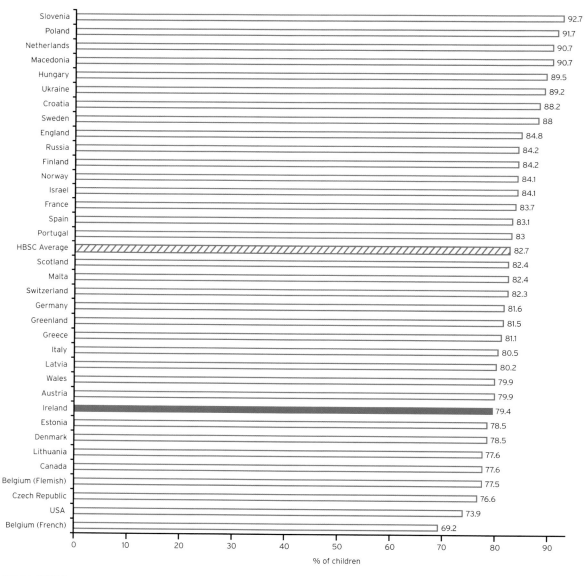

Country	%
Slovenia	92.7
Poland	91.7
Netherlands	90.7
Macedonia	90.7
Hungary	89.5
Ukraine	89.2
Croatia	88.2
Sweden	88
England	84.8
Russia	84.2
Finland	84.2
Norway	84.1
Israel	84.1
France	83.7
Spain	83.1
Portugal	83
HBSC Average	82.7
Scotland	82.4
Malta	82.4
Switzerland	82.3
Germany	81.6
Greenland	81.5
Greece	81.1
Italy	80.5
Latvia	80.2
Wales	79.9
Austria	79.9
Ireland	79.4
Estonia	78.5
Denmark	78.5
Lithuania	77.6
Canada	77.6
Belgium (Flemish)	77.5
Czech Republic	76.6
USA	73.9
Belgium (French)	69.2

% of children

Source: HBSC Survey

Relationship with fathers

Measure

> The proportion of children aged 10-17 who report that they find it easy to talk to their father when something is really bothering them.

Key findings

- In 2002, 56.2% of children aged 10-17 reported that they found it easy to talk to their father when something was really bothering them. This compares with results from 1998, when 48.1% of children reported this *(see Table 20)*.

Differences by age, social class and gender
- In 2002, the percentage of children reporting that they found it easy to talk to their father when something was really bothering them was higher among boys and younger children:
  - 64.0% of boys reported this, compared to 50.4% of girls;
  - 71.3% of 10-11 year-olds reported this, compared with 57.8% of 12-14 year-olds and 47.5% of 15-17 year-olds.

Table 20: Percentage of children who report that they find it easy to talk to their father when something is really bothering them, by age, social class and gender (1998 and 2002)

	1998			2002		
	Boys	Girls	Total	Boys	Girls	Total
Total	54.3	42.0	48.1	64.0	50.4	56.2
Years of age						
10-11	67.3	54.4	60.2	79.7	64.4	71.3
12-14	57.0	43.0	50.0	66.1	51.4	57.8
15-17	41.7	31.7	36.7	53.2	43.7	47.5
Social class						
SC 1-2	49.6	39.2	44.1	63.2	51.4	56.1
SC 3-4	54.5	43.9	49.2	64.7	50.9	56.8
SC 5-6	54.8	41.7	47.9	65.3	49.0	56.4

Source: HBSC Survey

Differences by geographical area

■ There was an increase between 1998 and 2002 across all former health board areas in the percentage of children who reported that they found it easy to talk to their father when something was really bothering them *(see Table 21)*. The highest percentage difference was found in the former Mid-Western Health Board area, which was 42.5% in 1998 and 56.3% in 2002.

Table 21: Percentage of children aged 10-17 who report that they find it easy to talk to their father when something is really bothering them, by former health board area (1998 and 2002)		
	1998	2002
North-Eastern Health Board	45.3	58.5
North-Western Health Board	48.4	58.2
Eastern Regional Health Authority	52.9	57.7
Mid-Western Health Board	42.5	56.3
Western Health Board	49.8	55.8
Midland Health Board	48.5	54.7
South-Eastern Health Board	45.3	54.1
Southern Health Board	45.8	52.7
Mean average	48.1	56.2

Source: HBSC Survey

International comparisons

■ From the 2002 HBSC Survey, using the ages of 11, 13 and 15 only to draw international comparisons, 58.7% of Irish children reported that they found it easy to talk to their father when something was really bothering them *(see Figure 8)*. The HBSC average was 64.2%.

■ Among all 35 countries that used this HBSC item, the lowest percentage for this indicator was found among Belgian (French) children (49.8%) and the highest among Slovenian children (83.6%).

■ Overall, Irish 11-year-old children were ranked 26th, Irish 13-year-old children were ranked 22nd and Irish 15-year-old children were ranked 28th.

Figure 8: Percentage of children who report that they find it easy to talk to their father when something is really bothering them, by country (2002)

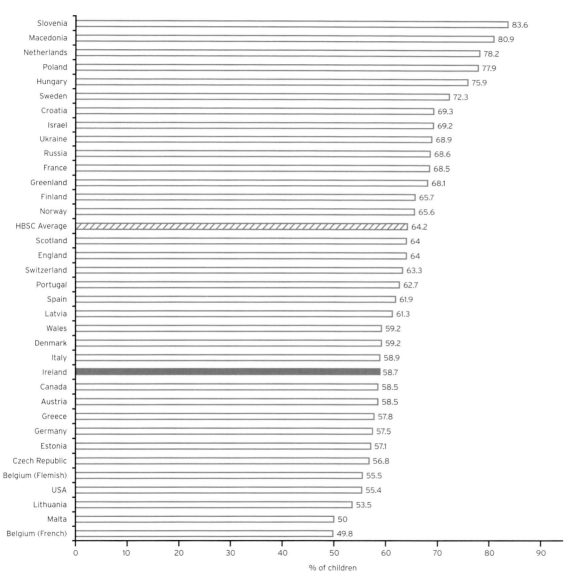

% of children

Source: HBSC Survey

Talking to parents

Measure

The proportion of children aged 15 who report that their parents spend time just talking with them several times a week.

Key findings

■ In 2000, 61.6% of children aged 15 reported that their parents spend time just talking with them several times a week *(see Table 22)*.

Differences by age, social class and gender

■ The percentage of children reporting that their parents spend time just talking with them several times a week was higher among girls – 70.3% of girls, compared to 52.8% of boys.

■ There were few social class differences found. However, children from the lowest social class category were marginally less likely to report that their parents spend time just talking to them several times a week (60.4%).

Table 22: Percentage of children aged 15 who report that their parents spend time just talking with them several times a week, by gender, social class and area (2000)	
Total	61.6
Gender	
Boys	52.8
Girls	70.3
Social class	
High SES	62.3
Medium SES	61.9
Low SES	60.4
Area	
Village, hamlet or rural area (population <3,000)	59.3
Town (population 3,000 to about 15,000)	62.0
Large town/small city (population 15,000 to about 100,000)	62.6
Large city (population 100,000 to 1,000,000)	66.4
Close to Dublin city centre	63.8
Elsewhere in Dublin city	60.5

Source: PISA Survey

Differences by geographical area

■ Children living in areas of population less than 3,000 people were least likely to report that their parents spend time just talking with them several times a week (59.3%), while children living in large cities other than Dublin were most likely (63.8%) to report this *(see Table 22)*.

International comparisons

■ From the 2000 PISA Survey, 61.6% of Irish children reported that their parents spend time just talking with them several times a week (see Figure 9). This compared with the OECD average of 59.6%.

■ Among all 27 OECD countries that used this PISA item, the lowest percentage for this indicator was found among German children (41.8%) and the highest among Hungarian children (90.3%). Irish children ranked 11th.

Figure 9: Percentage of children aged 15 who report that their parents spend time just talking with them several times a week, by country (2000)

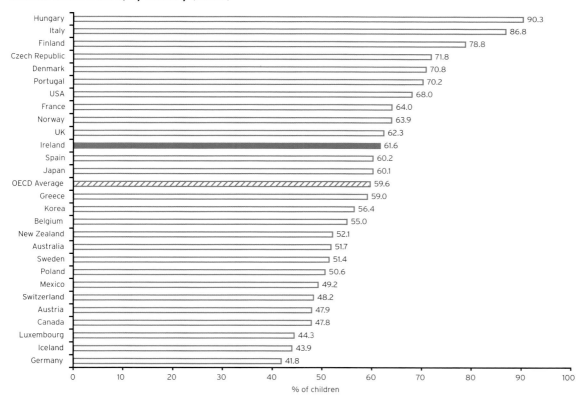

Country	%
Hungary	90.3
Italy	86.8
Finland	78.8
Czech Republic	71.8
Denmark	70.8
Portugal	70.2
USA	68.0
France	64.0
Norway	63.9
UK	62.3
Ireland	61.6
Spain	60.2
Japan	60.1
OECD Average	59.6
Greece	59.0
Korea	56.4
Belgium	55.0
New Zealand	52.1
Australia	51.7
Sweden	51.4
Poland	50.6
Mexico	49.2
Switzerland	48.2
Austria	47.9
Canada	47.8
Luxembourg	44.3
Iceland	43.9
Germany	41.8

% of children

Source: PISA Survey

PART 2: RELATIONSHIPS

53

Parental involvement in schooling

Measure

> **The proportion of children aged 15 who report that their parents discuss with them how well they are doing at school several times a week.**

Key findings

■ In 2000, 47.9% of children aged 15 reported that their parents discuss with them how well they are doing at school several times a week *(see Table 23)*.

Differences by age, social class and gender

■ The percentage of children reporting that their parents discuss with them how well they are doing at school several times a week was similar for boys and girls – 50.0% of girls, compared to 45.7% of boys.

■ 51.3% of children from the highest social class category reported that their parents discuss with them how well they are doing at school several times a week, compared to 45.1% of children from the lowest social class category.

Table 23: Percentage of children aged 15 who report that their parents discuss with them how well they are doing at school several times a week, by gender, social class and area (2000)	
Total	47.9
Gender	
Boys	45.7
Girls	50.0
Social class	
High SES	51.3
Medium SES	46.7
Low SES	45.1
Area	
Village, hamlet or rural area (population <3,000)	42.2
Town (population 3,000 to about 15,000)	51.1
Large town/small city (population 15,000 to about 100,000)	49.9
Large city (population 100,000 to 1,000,000)	49.5
Close to Dublin city centre	48.2
Elsewhere in Dublin city	48.3

Source: PISA Survey

54

Differences by geographical area

■ Children living in areas of population less than 3,000 people were least likely to report that their parents discuss with them how well they are doing in school several times a week (42.2%), while children living in towns (3,000 to 15,000 people) were most likely (51.1%) to report this *(see Table 23)*.

International comparisons

■ From the 2000 PISA Survey, 47.9% of Irish children aged 15 reported that their parents discuss with them how well they are doing in school several times a week (see Figure 10). This is less than the OECD average of 52.3%.

■ Among all 27 OECD countries that used this PISA item, the lowest percentage for this indicator was found among Finnish children (28.6%) and the highest among Italian children (83.4%). Irish children ranked 14th.

Figure 10: Percentage of children aged 15 who report that their parents discuss with them how well they are doing in school several times a week, by country (2000)

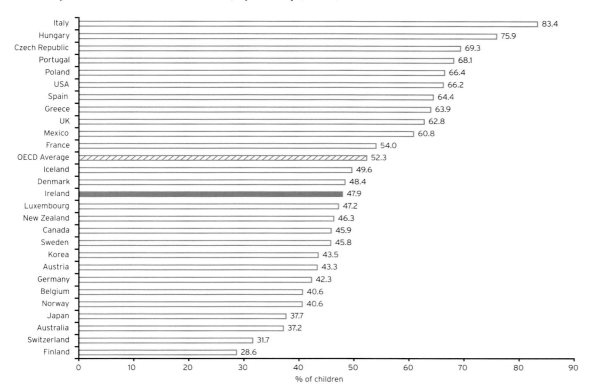

Source: PISA Survey

Eating a main meal together

Measure

> **The proportion of children aged 15 who report that their parents eat a main meal with them around a table several times a week.**

Key findings

■ In 2000, 77.1% of children aged 15 reported that their parents eat a main meal with them around a table several times a week *(see Table 24).*

Differences by age, social class and gender

■ Children from the medium and high social class categories (78.6% and 78.5% respectively) were most likely to report that their parents eat a main meal with them around a table several times a week, compared with children from the lowest (73.5%) social class category.

Table 24: Percentage of children aged 15 who report that their parents eat a main meal with them around a table several times a week, by gender, social class and area (2000)	
Total	77.1
Gender	
Boys	77.6
Girls	76.5
Social class	
High SES	78.5
Medium SES	78.6
Low SES	73.5
Area	
Village, hamlet or rural area (population <3,000)	77.8
Town (population 3,000 to about 15,000)	81.6
Large town/small city (population 15,000 to about 100,000)	73.9
Large city (population 100,000 to 1,000,000)	80.2
Close to Dublin city centre	68.6
Elsewhere in Dublin city	72.1

Source: PISA Survey

Differences by geographical area

■ In general, children from large cities other than Dublin were most likely to report that their parents eat a main meal with them around a table several times a week (80.2%). Children living close to Dublin city centre, however, were least likely (68.6%) to report this.

International comparisons

■ From the 2000 PISA Survey, 77.1% of Irish children reported that their parents eat a main meal with them around a table several times a week (see Figure 11). This is just below the OECD average of 78.9%.

■ Among all 27 OECD countries that used this PISA item, the lowest percentage for this indicator was found among Finnish children (60.0%) and the highest among Italian children (93.6%). Irish children ranked 16th.

Figure 11: Percentage of children aged 15 who report that their parents eat a main meal with them around a table several times a week, by country (2000)

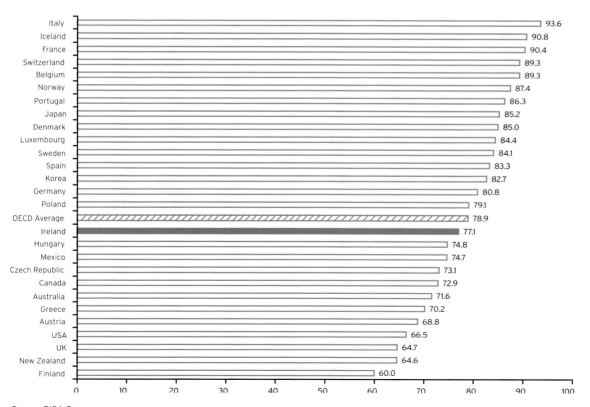

Source: PISA Survey

PART 2: RELATIONSHIPS

57

Technical notes

These data are drawn from the HBSC Survey from 1998 and 2002, and from the PISA Survey from 2000. Although this information is the most up-to-date available, it may not necessarily reflect the current situation. All data presented are drawn from self-report, self-completion questionnaires completed by children in schools. Thus, they are subject to potential biases in relation to self-presentation and memory. These measures may suffer from social desirability bias.

Percentage differences are presented for descriptive purposes only and may not reflect a statistically significant finding.

References

Bogard, L. (2005) 'Affluent Adolescents, Depression and Drug Use: The role of adults in their lives', *Adolescence*, Vol. 40, No. 158, pp. 281-306.

Daly, M. (2004) *Families and Family Life in Ireland: Report of Public Consultation Fora*, Department of Social and Family Affairs. Dublin: The Stationery Office.

Daly, M. and Clavero, S. (2002) *Contemporary Family Policy: A Comparative Review of Ireland, France, Germany and the UK*. Dublin: Institute of Public Administration.

Department of Social and Family Affairs (1998) *Commission on the Family: Strengthening Families for Life*. Dublin: The Stationery Office.

Drew, E., Humphries, P. and Murphy, C. (2004) *Off the Treadmill: Achieving Work – Life Balance*. Dublin: National Framework Committee for Work – Life Balance Policies, Department of Enterprise, Trade and Employment.

Field, T., Lang, C., Yando, R. and Bendell, D. (1995) 'Adolescents' Intimacy with Parents and Friends', *Adolescence*, Vol. 30, No. 117, pp. 113-40.

Galambos, N.L. and Ehrenberg, M.F. (1997) 'The Family as Health Risk and Opportunity: A Focus on Divorce and Working Families', in *Health Risks and Developmental Transitions during Adolescence*, J. Schulenberg, J.L. Maggs and K. Hurrelmann (eds.). Cambridge: Cambridge University Press.

Government of Canada (2003) *The Well-Being of Canada's Young Children: Government of Canada Report*. Ottawa: Human Resources Development Canada and Health Canada.

Lapsley, K. and Edgerton, J. (2002) 'Separation-Individuation, Adult Attachment Style, and College Adjustment', *Journal of Counselling and Development,* No. 80, pp. 484-92.

Laursen, B. (1995) 'Conflict and Social Interaction in Adolescent Relationships', *Journal of Research on Adolescence,* Vol. 5, No. 1, pp. 55-70.

Luthar, S.S. and Becker, B. (2002) 'Privileged but Pressured? A Study of Affluent Youth', *Child Development,* No. 73, pp. 1593-1610.

Murberg, T.A. and Bru, E. (2004) 'School-related Stress and Psychosomatic Symptoms among Norwegian Adolescents', *School Psychology International,* Vol. 25, No. 3, pp. 317-22.

National Framework Committee for Work – Life Balance Policies (2005) *Work Arrangements*. Available at: www.worklifebalance.ie/index.asp?locID=40&docID=-1 (accessed 4 September 2006).

Pederson, M., Granado Alcón, M.C., Borup, I., Zaborskis, A., Vollebergh, W., Smith, R. and Marklund, U. (2001) 'Focus Area Rationale: Family Culture', in *Health Behaviour in School-aged Children: A World Health Organization Cross-national Study: Research Protocol for the 2001/02 Survey,* C. Currie, O. Samdal, W. Boyce and R. Smith (eds.). Edinburgh: Child and Adolescent Health Research Unit, University of Edinburgh.

Ryan, R.M., Stiller, J. and Lynch, J.H. (1994) 'Representations of Relationships to Teachers, Parents and Friends as Predictors of Academic Motivation and Self-Esteem', *Journal of Early Adolescence,* Vol. 14, No. 2, pp. 226-49.

Settertobulte, W. (2000) 'Family and Peer Relations', in *Health and Health Behaviour among Young People,* C. Currie, K. Hurrelmann, W. Settertolute, R. Smith and J. Todd (eds.). Copenhagen: WHO-Europe.

Tamis-LeMonda, C.S. and Cabrera, N. (2002) *Handbook of Father Involvement: Multidisciplinary Perspectives.* Mahwah, NJ: Erlbaum.

Young, J.F., Berenson, K., Cohen, P. and Garcia, J. (2005) 'The Role of Parent and Peer Support in predicting Adolescent Depression: A Longitudinal Community Study', *Journal of Research on Adolescence,* Vol. 15, No. 4, pp. 407-23.

Youniss, J., Yates, M. and Su, Y. (1997) 'Social Integration, Community Service and Marijuana Use in High School Seniors', *Journal of Adolescent Research,* Vol. 12, No. 2, pp. 245-62.

PART 2: RELATIONSHIPS

RELATIONSHIPS WITH PEERS

Friendships

Context

While the Irish Constitution recognises that the family unit is the fundamental unit of the State, there is also a recognition that other relationships impact on a child. Within the National Children's Strategy (Department of Health and Children, 2000), there is an explicit recognition that the relationships around children extend beyond the family. Specifically, the Strategy notes that 'childhood is a complex set of dynamic relationships which interact in ways which are, as yet, not fully understood, but are recognised as essential to a satisfying and successful childhood'.

Peer relationships are considered to be of particular importance. This is particularly visible within the education sector, where the issue of friendships also receives attention through the implementation of Social, Personal and Health Education (SPHE) in primary and post-primary schools (Department of Education and Science, 2001). This SPHE programme is part of the curriculum and supports the personal development, health and well-being of young people and helps them to create and maintain supportive relationships. The Education Act emphasises that schools should promote the social and personal development of students and provide health education for them (Government of Ireland, 1998).

Peer relationships also take place outside the educational setting There is an increasing acknowledgement that national policy should take account of the need of children and young people to interact with each other in informal settings. This is being addressed in the forthcoming National Recreation Policy being developed by the Office of the Minister for Children (OMC, 2006). There are a number of examples of good practice in this area, including the Gaf Café initiative in Galway which was the result of a number of agencies getting together to create an alternative space where young people could 'hang out', get involved in a range of activities and access health services. The success of this initiative has led to similar cafés being set up in several other areas, including Waterford, Letterkenny and Sligo.

Significance

Adolescence is a time when peer relationships become more intense and extensive. Teenagers begin to encounter many new demands and expectations in social situations. They may begin dating, spending time with different groups of friends without adult supervision and collaborating on various tasks with others (Coleman and Hendry, 1999). Peers become crucial in defining their identities and developing personal and social competencies (Steinberg, 1996). About 90% of teenagers name at least one peer whom they consider to be a close friend; when they are asked to name more than one, most name someone who, in turn, also names him or her as a close friend (Brown, 2004). Friendship is thus a dyadic construct.

The importance of peer relationships is widely recognised by experts, educators and parents. Peer relationships can help satisfy different types of social needs (Baumister and Leary, 1995); can help develop skills, such as empathy, communication, cooperation and the management and resolution of conflicts (Hartup, 1989; Bender and Losel, 1997); and can provide a supportive context in which self-exploration, emotional growth and moral development can occur (Asher *et al*, 1996). Peer relationships, however, can also be linked with peer pressure to engage in negative behaviour. There is evidence that certain undesirable, anti-social or delinquent behaviours are performed by all, or almost all, members of a group of teenagers (Bender and Losel, 1997; Berndt 2002), even if peer pressure or influence is frequently more positive than negative (Brown *et al*, 1986; Berndt, 1996).

Measure

> **The proportion of children aged 10-17 who report to have 3 or more friends of the same gender.**

Key findings

■ In 2002, 85.3% of children aged 10-17 reported they had 3 or more friends of the same gender *(see Table 25).*

Differences by age, social class and gender
■ There were no significant differences across gender, age or social class.

Table 25: Percentage of children who report to have 3 or more friends of the same gender, by age, social class and gender (2002)			
	Boys	Girls	Total
Total	83.5	86.9	85.3
Years of age			
10-11	85.4	85.0	85.1
12-14	83.2	87.6	85.7
15-17	83.4	87.4	85.7
Social class			
SC 1-2	84.1	88.5	86.8
SC 3-4	85.0	87.2	86.2
SC 5-6	83.7	85.1	84.5

Source: HBSC Survey

Differences by geographical area

■ Some differences were identified according to geographical location *(see Table 26)*. More children in the former Eastern Regional Health Authority area reported having 3 or more friends than anywhere else (88%), while children in the former Southern Health Board area were least likely (81.7%) to report this.

Table 26: Percentage of children aged 10-17 who report to have 3 or more friends of the same gender, by former health board area (2002)	
Eastern Regional Health Authority	88.0
Midland Health Board	83.6
Mid-Western Health Board	82.3
North-Eastern Health Board	86.1
North-Western Health Board	86.2
South-Eastern Health Board	84.3
Southern Health Board	81.7
Western Health Board	85.9
Mean average	**85.3**

Source: HBSC Survey

International comparisons

■ From the 2002 HBSC Survey, using the ages of 11, 13 and 15 only to draw international comparisons, 90.3% of Irish children reported that they had 3 or more friends of the same gender. This compared with the HBSC average of 78.8% *(see Figure 12)*.

■ Among all 35 countries that used this HBSC item, the lowest percentage for this indicator was found among Spanish children (60.4%) and the highest among Irish children (90.3%).

■ Overall, Irish 11-year-old children were ranked 5th, Irish 13-year-old children were ranked 1st and Irish 15-year-old children were ranked 3rd.

Figure 12: Percentage of children who report to have 3 or more friends of the same gender, by country (2002)

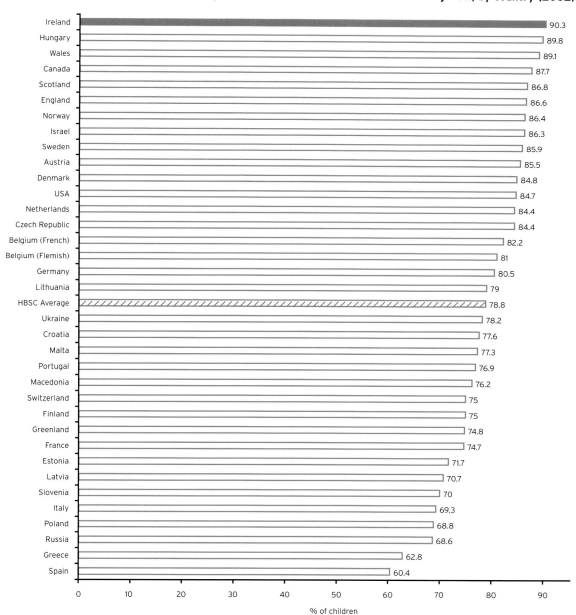

Country	%
Ireland	90.3
Hungary	89.8
Wales	89.1
Canada	87.7
Scotland	86.8
England	86.6
Norway	86.4
Israel	86.3
Sweden	85.9
Austria	85.5
Denmark	84.8
USA	84.7
Netherlands	84.4
Czech Republic	84.4
Belgium (French)	82.2
Belgium (Flemish)	81
Germany	80.5
Lithuania	79
HBSC Average	78.8
Ukraine	78.2
Croatia	77.6
Malta	77.3
Portugal	76.9
Macedonia	76.2
Switzerland	75
Finland	75
Greenland	74.8
France	74.7
Estonia	71.7
Latvia	70.7
Slovenia	70
Italy	69.3
Poland	68.8
Russia	68.6
Greece	62.8
Spain	60.4

% of children

Source: HBSC Survey

Technical notes

The indicator presented here provides information only with respect to the size of the student's peer group, but does not provide information about the characteristics of the peer group, about the time spent together and about the activities in which the group is involved. In addition, this indicator is derived from self-report data and may be susceptible to social desirability bias.

Percentage differences are presented for descriptive purposes only and may not reflect a statistically significant finding.

References

Asher, S.R., Parker, J.G. and Walker, D.L. (1996) 'Distinguishing friendship from acceptance: Implications for intervention and assessment', in *The Company they Keep: Friendship in Childhood and Adolescence,* W.M. Bukowski, A.F. Newcomb and W.W. Hartup (eds.). Cambridge: Cambridge University Press.

Baumister, R. and Leary, M.R. (1995) 'The need to belong: Desire for interpersonal attachments as a fundamental human motivation', *Psychological Bulletin,* No. 117, pp. 497-529.

Bender, D. and Losel, F. (1997) 'Protective and risk effects of peer relations and social support on anti-social behaviour in adolescents from multi-problem milieus', *Journal of Adolescence,* No. 20, pp. 661-78.

Berndt, T.J. (1996) 'Transitions in friendship and friends' influence', in *Transition Through Adolescence: Interpersonal Domains and Context,* J.A. Graber, J. Brook-Gunn and A.C. Petersen (eds.). Mahwah, NJ: Erlbaum.

Berndt, T.J. (2002) 'Friendship quality and social development', *Current Directions in Psychological Science,* Vol. 11, No. 1, pp. 7-10.

Brown, B.B. (2004) 'Adolescents' relationships with peers', in *Handbook of Adolescent Psychology,* R.M. Lerner and L. Steinberg (eds.). New York: Wiley.

Brown, B.B., Clasen, D.R. and Eicher, S.A. (1986) 'Perception of peer pressure, peer conformity dispositions, and self-reported behaviour among adolescents', *Developmental Psychology,* Vol. 22, No. 4, pp. 521-30.

Coleman, J.C. and Hendry, L. (1999) *The Nature of Adolescence. 2nd Edition.* London: Routledge.

Department of Education and Science (2001) *Social, Personal and Health Education: Guidelines for Teachers.* Dublin: The Stationery Office.

Department of Health and Children (2000) *The National Children's Strategy: Our Children – Their Lives.* Dublin: The Stationery Office.

Government of Ireland (1998) *Education Act.* Dublin: The Stationery Office.

Hartup, W.W. (1989) 'Social relationships and their development significance', *American Psychologist,* Vol. 44, No. 2, pp. 120-26.

OMC (2006) *Report of the Public Consultation for the Development of the National Recreation Policy for Young People,* Office of the Minister for Children. Dublin: The Stationery Office.

Steinberg, L. (1996) *Adolescence. 2nd Edition.* New York: McGraw-Hill.

Bullying

Context

Schools acknowledge the right of each member of the community to enjoy school in a secure environment. Tackling bullying and its negative impact has been on the agenda of the Department of Education and Science for some time: it has been included in a range of strategy, policy and guidance documents, including the guidelines for schools on countering bullying behaviour (Department of Education and Science, 1993; Guerin, 2001). These guidelines aimed to improve school ethos, raise awareness, ensure supervision and monitoring, and develop procedures for noting, reporting, investigating and dealing with incidents of bullying behaviour.

Subsequent child protection guidelines and procedures acknowledged that bullying in schools is an increasing problem (Department of Education and Science, 2001). These highlight the importance of boards of management in implementing policies to deal with bullying and in ensuring that teachers are aware of such policies and guidelines. Where the bullying is regarded as potentially abusive, the school is required to consult the relevant health authorities in an effort to deal with the situation. Following the publication of the final *Report of the Task Force on Student Behaviour in Second-level Schools,* a number of new measures have been announced to assist schools in dealing with behavioural difficulties (Department of Education and Science, 2006). These include:

■ new regional Behaviour Support Teams to work with schools that have significant discipline problems;

■ Behaviour Support classrooms to be piloted in schools.

Significance

Bullying is a form of teenage violence and is considered to be a relationship problem. It involves negative physical or verbal action, which has hostile intent, results in distress to the victim, is repeated over time and involves a power difference between the bullies and the victim (Olweus, 1991). Bullying is a subset of aggressive behaviours, characterised by a power imbalance. With repeated bullying, the power relationships between bullies and their victims become consolidated: bullies increase in power and victims lose power. In such a relationship, young people who are being bullied become increasingly powerless to defend themselves. Pepler and Craig (2000) have examined bullying from a developmental perspective and argue that this type of aggressive behaviour merits attention because it underlies many problems related to interpersonal violence. From this perspective, the lessons learnt in bullying within peer relationships can be applied to other developmentally significant relationships. The use of power and aggression found in playground bullying is an indicator of future sexual harassment, marital aggression, child abuse and elder abuse (Pepler *et al,* 1997).

Victims of bullying also experience a range of problem behaviours, such as depression and anxiety, even suicide in extreme cases (Craig, 1998; Olweus, 1991; Mills *et al*, 2004). Victims often miss a lot of school, become under-achievers, display poor self-concepts and run away from home (Olweus, 1994). Thus, understanding and preventing bullying during adolescence has important implications for the immediate health of young people, as well as long-term societal health (O'Moore, 2000).

Measure

> **The proportion of children aged 10-17 who report to have been bullied at school.**

Key findings

■ In 2002, approximately one-quarter of children aged 10-17 (23.3%) reported to have been bullied at school at least once in the last couple of months *(see Table 27)*.

Differences by age, social class and gender
■ Boys (26.4%) were more likely to report being bullied than girls (21.0%).
■ There was a consistent downward trend in the percentage of children who report being bullied at school by age. In 2002, 28.3% of children aged 10-11 reported to have been bullied, compared with 18.2% of 15-17 year-olds.
■ There was little difference across social class categories.

Table 27: Percentage of children who report to have been bullied in school (in the past couple of months), by age, social class and gender (1998 and 2002)

	1998			2002		
	Boys	Girls	Total	Boys	Girls	Total
Total	29.5	19.9	24.6	26.4	21.0	23.3
Years of age						
10-11	36.2	27.2	31.2	26.8	29.5	28.3
12-14	30.5	20.1	25.2	29.9	22.6	25.8
15-17	23.7	14.0	18.8	21.7	15.8	18.2
Social class						
SC 1-2	26.7	17.4	21.8	27.6	19.9	23.0
SC 3-4	29.8	21.0	25.4	24.8	21.6	22.9
SC 5-6	29.8	19.4	24.3	26.6	20.3	23.1

Source: HBSC Survey

Differences by geographical area

■ In 2002, children in the former Mid-Western Health Board area were most likely (29.5%) to report being bullied at school *(see Table 28)*. This represents a significant increase over the 1998 findings (18.8%). Children in the former Midland Health Board area were least likely (21.1%) to report being bullied.

Table 28: Percentage of children aged 10-17 who report to have been bullied in school (in the past couple of months), by former health board area (1998 and 2002)		
	1998	2002
Mid-Western Health Board	18.8	29.5
North-Eastern Health Board	22.5	27.0
Southern Health Board	25.0	23.8
South-Eastern Health Board	21.7	23.4
North-Western Health Board	29.3	23.3
Western Health Board	26.7	22.1
Eastern Regional Health Authority	27.6	21.7
Midland Health Board	21.9	21.1
Mean average	24.6	23.3

Source: HBSC Survey

International comparisons

■ From the 2002 HBSC Survey, using the ages of 11, 13 and 15 only to draw international comparisons, 25.9% of Irish children reported that they had been bullied at school *(see Figure 13)*. This compared with the HBSC average of 33.5%.

■ Among all 35 countries that used this HBSC item, the lowest percentage for this indicator was found among Swedish children (14.9%) and the highest among Lithuanian children (64.3%).

■ Overall, Irish 11-year-old children were ranked 26th, Irish 13-year-old children were ranked 25th and Irish 15-year-old children were ranked 26th.

Figure 13: Percentage of children who report to have been bullied in school (in the past couple of months), by country (2002)

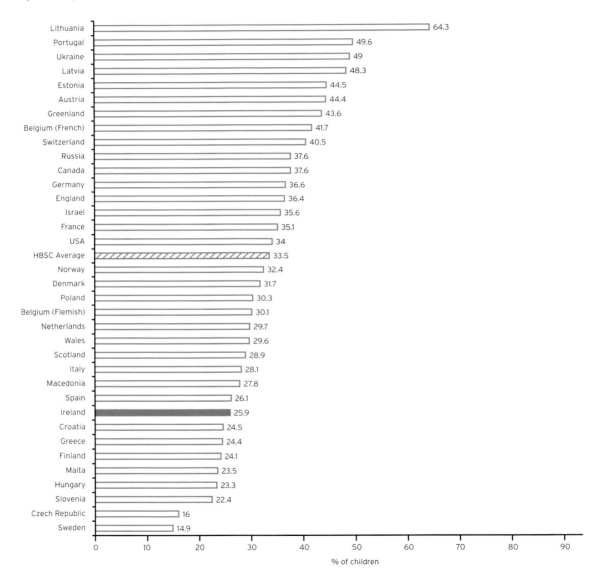

Country	%
Lithuania	64.3
Portugal	49.6
Ukraine	49
Latvia	48.3
Estonia	44.5
Austria	44.4
Greenland	43.6
Belgium (French)	41.7
Switzerland	40.5
Russia	37.6
Canada	37.6
Germany	36.6
England	36.4
Israel	35.6
France	35.1
USA	34
HBSC Average	33.5
Norway	32.4
Denmark	31.7
Poland	30.3
Belgium (Flemish)	30.1
Netherlands	29.7
Wales	29.6
Scotland	28.9
Italy	28.1
Macedonia	27.8
Spain	26.1
Ireland	25.9
Croatia	24.5
Greece	24.4
Finland	24.1
Malta	23.5
Hungary	23.3
Slovenia	22.4
Czech Republic	16
Sweden	14.9

% of children

Source: HBSC Survey

Technical notes

The measure of bullying presented here is a self-report item. Although the bullying items are broadly used and have been carefully validated (Olweus 1992 and 1994), self-report items are always susceptible to differences in interpretation. This limitation was approached by using a comprehensive introduction to the question.

Percentage differences are presented for descriptive purposes only and may not reflect a statistically significant finding.

References

Craig, W.M. (1998) 'The Relationship among Bullying, Victimization, Depression, Anxiety and Aggression in Elementary School Children', *Personality and Individual Differences,* No. 24, pp. 123-30.

Department of Education and Science (1993) *Guidelines on countering Bullying Behaviour in Primary and Post-Primary Schools.* Dublin: The Stationery Office.

Department of Education and Science (2001) *Child Protection: Guidelines and Procedures.* Dublin: The Stationery Office.

Department of Education and Science (2006) *School Matters: Report of the Task Force on Student Behaviour in Second-level Schools.* Dublin: The Stationery Office.

Guerin, S. (2001) *Examining Bullying in School: A Pupil-based Approach* (unpublished PhD manuscript). Dublin: Department of Psychology, University College Dublin.

Mills, C., Guerin, S., Daly, I., Lynch, F. and Fitzpatrick, C. (2004) 'The Relationship between Bullying, Depression and Suicidal Thoughts/Behaviours in Irish Adolescents', *Irish Journal of Psychological Medicine,* Vol. 21, No. 4, pp. 112-16.

O'Moore, A.M. (2000) 'Critical Issues for Teacher Training to counter Bullying and Victimisation in Ireland', *Aggressive Behaviour,* No. 26, pp. 99-111.

Olweus, D. (1991) 'Bully/Victim Problems among School Children: Some basic facts and effects of a school-based intervention program', in *The Development and Treatment of Childhood Aggression*, D. Pepler and K. Rubin (eds.). Mahwah, NJ: Erlbaum.

Olweus, D. (1992) 'Bullying among School Children: Intervention and Prevention', in *Aggression and Violence throughout the Life Span,* R.D. Peters, R.J. McMahon and V.L. Quinsey (eds.). Newbury Park: Sage.

Olweus, D. (1994) 'Bullying at School: Long-term outcomes for the victims and an effective school-based intervention program', in *Aggressive Behaviour: Current Perspectives,* L.R. Huesman (ed.). New York: Plenum Press.

Pepler, D. and Craig, W. (2000) *Making a Difference in Bullying. LaMarsh Report.* Toronto: LaMarsh Centre for Research on Violence and Conflict Resolution, York University.

Pepler, D.J., Craig, W.M., and Connolly, J. (1997) *Bullying and Victimization: The problems and solutions for school-aged children. Fact Sheet prepared for the National Crime Prevention Council of Canada.* Toronto: National Crime Prevention Council.

PART 3: CHILDREN'S OUTCOMES

'The attainments of individual children will reflect both their own capacity and the resources, supports and services available to them.'

(National Children's Strategy, 2000; p. 25)

covering
EDUCATION
HEALTH
SOCIAL, EMOTIONAL AND BEHAVIOURAL OUTCOMES

EDUCATION

Early childhood care and education

Context

The Office of the Minister for Children has overall responsibility for ensuring the implementation of the National Childcare Strategy 2006-2010, which aims to improve the availability and quality of childcare and to meet the needs of children and their parents. The Strategy builds on the Government's Equality Opportunities Childcare Programme 2000-2006, which is expected to produce 40,000 new childcare places. The new National Childcare Investment Programme 2006-2010 is expected to create a further 50,000 places. There is a network of 33 local city and county childcare committees and these provide a valuable resource for parents and others seeking information.

Síolta, a national quality framework for early childhood education, was developed through extensive consultation with multiple stakeholders and has recently been published by the Centre for Early Childhood Development and Education (2006). This framework will provide a mechanism through which improvements in the area of early childhood care and education can be made. It is intended that this framework will provide:

■ a support for individual professional practice and development;
■ a focus for team work and team development;
■ a tool for management, strategic planning and policy development;
■ a common base for the interactions of a varied team of professionals.

Early childhood care and education settings are regulated through the Child Care (Pre-School Services) Regulations and the Child Care (Pre-School Services) (Amendment) Regulations (Government of Ireland, 1996 and 1997). A pre-school inspectorate, comprising public health nurses and environmental health officers, undertakes inspections.

Significance

The period of childhood is a time of rapid growth and development. Across the developed world today, children spend an increasing part of their early childhood in out-of-home settings and for some children, these may be multiple settings with many different care-givers (OECD Directorate for Education, 2004). This is also the case in Ireland where, in recent years, there has been a significant increase in female participation in the workforce, with some 47% of mothers being economically active in 2004 (CSO, 2004).

There is strong evidence that positive or negative consequences of care and education can last well into adulthood (NICHD Early Child Care Research Network, 1997; Sylva *et al*, 2003). A recent review of the international literature, undertaken on behalf of the National Audit Office in the UK (2003), showed that high-quality childcare for disadvantaged children in the first three years of life resulted in benefits in the areas of cognitive, language and social development. This review also concluded, however, that low-quality childcare produced either no benefits or had negative effects. In Ireland, a national review of policy, practice and research relating to quality in early childhood care and education was undertaken through the Centre for Early Childhood Development and Education (Duignan and Walsh, 2004). The review highlights the need for a coordinated policy framework, the use of a broad and flexible definition of quality, the engagement of all stakeholders, the provision of adequate pre-service and in-service training, and an adequate support infrastructure to assist implementation.

Measure

> **The number of children under 13 in various early childhood care and education arrangements, expressed as a proportion of all children in the same group. This can be subdivided into: (a) pre-school; (b) compulsory school; (c) centre-based care outside school hours; (d) crèche or day care; (e) professional childminder; and (f) family relative.**

Key findings

- In 2005, other than a parent/guardian, the main childcare arrangement for families with pre-school children was paid carer (12.1%) and unpaid relative (9.7%) for primary school children *(see Table 29 and Figure 14)*.
- In 2005, primary school children (78.5%) were more likely to be cared for by a parent/guardian than pre-school children (59.7%).
- 10.1% of families with pre-school children used a crèche/Montessori as their main type of childcare in 2005. This compares with only 1.3% of families with primary school children using this as their main type of childcare.

Table 29: Percentage of families and main type of childcare arrangement (2002 and 2005)

Main type of childcare	Pre-school children		Primary school children	
	2002	2005	2002	2005
Parent/guardian	62.1	59.7	78.0	78.5
Unpaid relative	10.5	11.5	9.2	9.7
Paid relative	4.6	4.5	3.2	2.6
Paid carer	12.0	12.1	7.5	6.5
Crèche/Montessori	9.3	10.1	1.4	1.3
Other	1.6	2.2	0.8	1.3
Total	100.0	100.0	100.0	100.0

Source: Quarterly National Household Survey, CSO

Figure 14: Main type of childcare arrangement for families (2005)

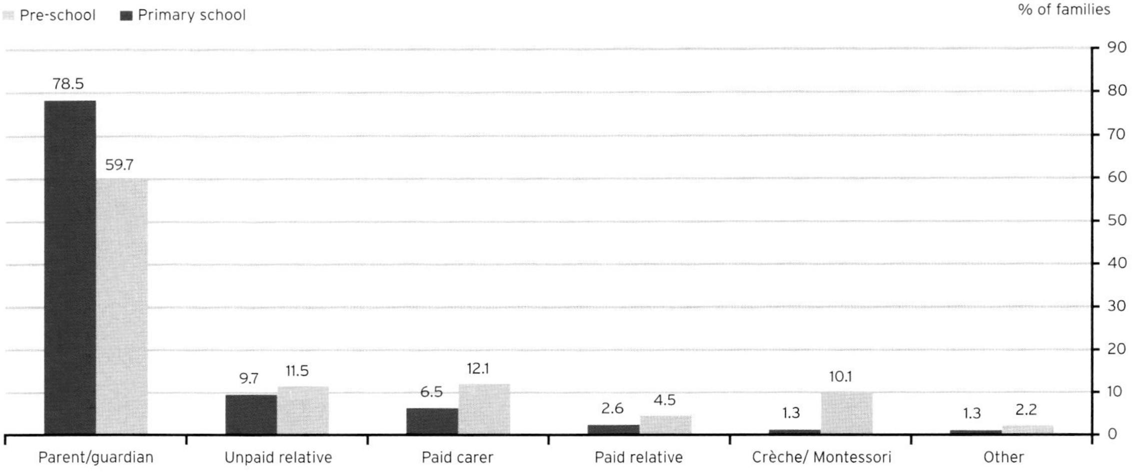

Source: Quarterly National Household Survey, CSO

Technical notes

Questions on childcare (including the main source of childcare, its cost and the hours involved) were included in a module attached to the Quarterly National Household Survey in Quarter 4 2002 and Quarter 1 2005. These questions were asked of all households in which there were primary school-going children or pre-school children.

Childcare was defined as types of childcare arrangements usually made by parents/guardians on a regular weekly basis during the working day (e.g. Monday to Friday, 7am-7pm, or similar, as applicable to the household).

Respondents were asked to indicate from the following categories the main type of childcare for their pre-school and primary school-going children:

Categories	Responses
Parent or guardian	Child minded at home by me/partner
Unpaid relative	Unpaid relative or family friend in your/his/her own home
Paid relative	Paid relative or family friend in your/his/her own home
Paid carer	Paid childminder in your/his/her home, or au-pair/nanny
Crèche or Montessori	Work-based crèche Naoínra Crèche or nursery Montessori school Playgroup, pre-school or sessional childcare
Other	Homework club, after-school activity-based facility Special needs facility, activity camps

References

CSO (2004) *Quarterly National Household Survey.* Dublin: Central Statistics Office.

Centre for Early Childhood Development and Education (2006) *Síolta: The National Quality Framework for Early Childhood Education.* Dublin: Centre for Early Childhood Development and Education.

Duignan, M. and Walsh, T. (2004) *Insights on Quality: A National Review of policy, practice and research relating to quality in early childhood care and education 1990-2004.* Dublin: Centre for Early Childhood Development and Education.

Government of Ireland (1996) *Child Care (Pre-School Services) Regulations.* Dublin: The Stationery Office.

Government of Ireland (1997) *Child Care (Pre-School Services) (Amendment) Regulations.* Dublin: The Stationery Office.

National Audit Office (2003) *Early Years: Progress in developing high quality childcare and early education accessible to all. Report by the Comptroller and Auditor-General.* London: HMSO.

NICHD Early Child Care Research Network (1997) 'The Effects of Infant Child Care on Infant-Mother Attachment Security: Results of the NICHD Study of Early Child Care', *Child Development,* No. 68, pp. 860-79.

OECD Directorate for Education (2004) *Early Childhood Education and Care Policy. Country Note for Ireland.* Paris: Organisation for Economic Cooperation and Development.

Sylva, K., Melhuish, E., Sammons, P., Siraj-Blatchford, I., Taggart, B. and Elliot, K. (2003) *The Effective Provision of Pre-School Education (EPPE) Project: Findings from the pre-school period.* London: Institute of Education, University of London.

PART 3: CHILDREN'S OUTCOMES

79

School attendance

Context

The statutory school-leaving age in Ireland is 15 years and children must remain in school until their 16th birthday or until completion of 3 years of post-primary education. In 2001, the National Education Welfare Board (NEWB) was set up as a national authority to implement the provisions of the Education (Welfare) Act (Government of Ireland, 2000), to promote school attendance and prevent school-leaving. Under this Act, parents must let the school know if their child is absent and the reason for the absence, and every school must notify the NEWB if a child is absent for more than 20 days in the school year (Weir, 2004; Ó Briain, 2006). An educational welfare officer will follow up on cases where there is concern about the child. Legally early school-leaving refers to non-participation in school before reaching the age of 16 or before completion of 3 years of post-primary education, whichever is later.

In addition, the Department of Education and Science has put in place a number of different initiatives, including the recent action plan for *Delivering Equality of Opportunity in Schools (DEIS) Programme* (Department of Education and Science, 2005a). This programme provides a standardised system for identifying and regularly reviewing levels of disadvantage, and a new integrated School Support Programme (SSP), which will bring together and build on the following existing schemes and programmes:
- Home School Community Liaison Scheme;
- School Completion Programme;
- Support Teachers Project;
- Early Start Pre-School Scheme;
- Giving Children an Even Break;
- Breaking the Cycle;
- Disadvantaged Area Scheme.

The DEIS initiative is designed to ensure that the most disadvantaged schools benefit from a comprehensive package of supports, while ensuring that others continue to get support in line with the level of disadvantage among their pupils. While there are benefits in individual interventions and programmes, a more integrated and joined-up response to the issue of educational inclusion is required. School attendance is also supported through the School Meals Programme and a number of schools now provide breakfast clubs.

Significance

There is a general view that early school-leaving can often be preceded by chronic truancy (National Economic and Social Forum, 2002). Educational policy in Ireland is geared towards increasing retention levels of young people at school to completion of the Leaving Certificate, usually at the age of 17-18 years. The most recent figures on retention rates of pupils in second-level schools show that 87.1% of people in Ireland aged 18-24 had attained at least a Leaving Certificate or equivalent qualification, or they had participated in education or training in the 4 weeks preceding the survey (Department of Education and Science, 2005b). This compares with the EU25 rate of 84.3%.

The causes of early school-leaving are complex. The National Economic and Social Forum (2002) has categorised them as follows:
■   the individual (e.g. learning difficulties, literacy and numeracy difficulties, self-esteem and confidence);
■   family (e.g. behavioural difficulties such as violence and drug abuse, attitudes to school and level of financial resources);
■   school (e.g. school ethos, discipline procedures and pupil selection);
■   community (e.g. infrastructure, including the availability of out-of school supports and locally based facilities).

There is substantial evidence of the relationships between educational under-achievement and poverty (Combat Poverty Agency, 2001). Consequences of early school-leaving include an increased likelihood of long-term unemployment, low-skilled and poorly paid employment, and an inability to access life changes, leading to social exclusion (Cullen, 2000). Layte *et al* (2006) found that decisions such as how long to stay in school are affected by 'not only economic circumstances, but also the kinds of cultural and social capital that allow parents and children to successfully negotiate the educational system'. They also found that those with lower education levels were more likely to be financially poor in adulthood.

The indicators of school attendance and transfer to second-level schooling are now examined.

School attendance

Measure

> **The number of children who are absent from school for 20 days or more in the school year, expressed as a proportion of all children.**

Key findings

- In the 2004-2005 school year, the overall average attendance for a student at primary school was 94.2% *(see Table 30)*. This translates to 11 days' absence on average for each student. This rate was higher for rural schools (94.9%) than for urban ones (92.8%).
- 10% of primary school students were absent for 20 days or more in the school year. The proportion of students with this level of absenteeism was, on average, lower in rural schools (7.8%) than in urban schools (14.9%).
- Almost one in five (19.4%) primary school students in the most disadvantaged schools missed 20 or more school days, compared to 6.2% of students in the least disadvantaged schools. An average of 15 days per student was missed in the most disadvantaged schools and an average of 10 days per student in the least disadvantaged schools.

Table 30: Attendance levels in primary schools, by school location and level of disadvantage (2004/2005)		
	Mean % annual attendance in school year	% of students missing 20 days or more in school year
Mean average	94.2	10.0
School location		
Urban	92.8	14.9
Rural	94.9	7.8
Level of disadvantage		
Least disadvantaged school	95.2	6.2
Most disadvantaged school	91.9	19.4

Source: National Educational Welfare Board

- The mean attendance level among students in post-primary schools was 91.6% in the 2004-2005 school year *(see Table 31)*. This translates to 14 days' absence on average for each student.
- 18.8% of post-primary school students were absent for 20 days or more in the school year. The proportion of students with this level of absenteeism was, on average, lowest in secondary schools (15.1%) and, on average, highest in vocational schools (24.9%).

■ More than one in three (34.8%) post-primary school students in the most disadvantaged schools missed 20 or more school days, compared to less than one in ten (9.2%) students in the least disadvantaged schools. On average, post-primary school students in the most disadvantaged schools missed 21 school days, while post-primary school students in the least disadvantaged schools missed 10 school days.

Table 31: Attendance levels in post-primary schools, by school type and level of disadvantage (2004/2005)		
	Mean % annual attendance in school year	% of students missing 20 days or more in school year
Mean average	91.6	18.8
School type		
Secondary	92.7	15.1
Vocational	89.6	24.9
Community and Comprehensive	91.5	20.7
Level of disadvantage		
Least disadvantaged school	94.2	9.2
Most disadvantaged school	86.9	34.8

Source: National Educational Welfare Board

Technical notes

Data in these tables are based on School Attendance Reports, which are prepared by individual schools at primary and post-primary level and submitted by schools to the National Educational Welfare Board (NEWB). For the 2004-2005 school year, 83.9% of primary schools and 76% of post-primary schools returned these reports to the NEWB.

The reports record the following information:
■ total enrolment for 2003/04;
■ sum of all individual student absences over the entire school year, up to and including the date the school closes;
■ number of students with 100% attendance;
■ number of students missing 20 days or more;
■ number of students expelled;
■ number of students suspended;
■ confirmation of availability of code of behaviour to parents and students;
■ confirmation of availability of admissions policy to parents and students.

Schools have been categorised into deciles of disadvantage on the basis of their overall points or rank in the national scheme of 'Giving Children an Even Break' and in the case of post-primary schools, into deciles of disadvantage on the basis of the indices used to rank schools for the '16:1' initiative.

PART 3: CHILDREN'S OUTCOMES

Transfer to second-level education

Measure

Children leaving national schools, by destination.

Key findings

■ Over the period 2001-2005, about 96% of children leaving national schools are known to have progressed to another form of schooling, either at first or second level *(see Table 32)*. About a further 2.5% were accounted for by emigration. Less than one-half of 1% of children leaving national schools were known not to have progressed to other schools, while the destination of just under a further 1% of these children was unknown. These final two categories accounted for about 800 children in 2005.

Table 32: Percentage of children leaving national schools, by destination (2001-2005)					
Destination	2001	2002	2003	2004	2005
Attending another school within the State	96.5	96.2	95.9	96.2	96.3
Emigrating	2.4	2.6	2.8	2.7	2.7
Not attending other school	0.4	0.4	0.4	0.3	0.3
Unknown	0.7	0.8	0.9	0.7	0.7
Total	100.0	100.0	100.0	100.0	100.0
Total no. of children	76,142	76,691	78,024	77,584	76,187

Source: Education Statistics, Department of Education and Science

■ Boys are more likely than girls to leave national school and not attend any other school. In the period 2001-2005, the proportion of boys in this group of school-leavers ranged from 67% in 2001 to 53% in 2005 *(see Figure 15)*.

Figure 15: National school-leavers not attending other school, by gender (2001-2005)

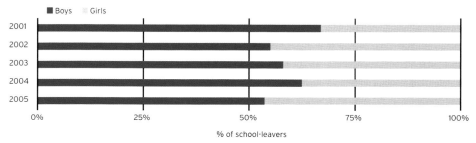

Source: Education Statistics, Department of Education and Science

Technical notes

Data in these tables refer to children leaving ordinary classes in national schools. Data on children leaving national schools in the State and their destination are collected by the Department of Education and Science via school-based returns and are published in its Annual Statistical Report.

The reference period for the data presented here runs from October to September. Data for the year 2003 refer to children leaving school between 1 October 2002 and 30 September 2003.

References

Combat Poverty Agency (2001) *Submission on Early School-leavers and Youth Unemployment to the National Economic and Social Forum.* Dublin: Combat Poverty Agency.

Cullen, B. (2000) *Evaluating Integrated Responses to Educational Disadvantage.* Dublin: Combat Poverty Agency.

Department of Education and Science (2005a) *Delivering Equality of Opportunity in Schools (DEIS): An Action Plan for Educational Inclusion.* Dublin: The Stationery Office.

Department of Education and Science (2005b) *Retention Rates of Pupils in Second-level Schools: 1996 Cohort.* Dublin: The Stationery Office.

Government of Ireland (2000) *Education (Welfare) Act.* Dublin: The Stationery Office.

Layte, R., Maître, B., Nolan, B. and Whelan, C.T. (2006) *Day In, Day Out – Understanding the Dynamics of Child Poverty.* Dublin: Combat Poverty Agency.

National Economic and Social Forum (2002) *Early School-leavers: Forum Report No. 24.* Dublin: The Stationery Office.

Ó Briain, E. (2006) *Analysis of school attendance data at primary and post-primary levels for 2004/2005.* Dublin: National Education Welfare Board.

Weir, S. (2004) *Analysis of school attendance data at primary and post-primary levels for 2003/2004.* Dublin: National Education Welfare Board.

Further information
- National Education and Welfare Board (www.newb.ie)

Achievement in Reading Literacy, Mathematics and Science

Context

Article 42 of the Irish Constitution provides that it is the duty of the State to ensure that children receive a certain minimum, moral, intellectual and social education, and this is in keeping with Article 28 and 29 of the United Nations Convention on the Rights of the Child (UN, 1989). The Education Act put the arrangements governing the running of schools at primary and post-primary level on a statutory footing and also included the right of every person in the State, including those who have a disability or who have other special educational needs, to an education (Government of Ireland, 1998). These provisions are further supported by the Education for Persons with Special Educational Needs Act (Government of Ireland, 2004) and the Equal Status Act (Government of Ireland, 2000a). The Education (Welfare) Act provides a statutory basis for school attendance and seeks to tackle the problems of absenteeism and early school-leaving through working with children and their families (Government of Ireland, 2000b).

Primary, secondary and third-level education is free at the point of delivery. Second-level education comprises secondary, vocational, community and comprehensive schools; children must be a minimum of 12 years of age to be eligible to attend. There are two national examinations of children's educational attainment – the Junior Certificate, which takes place after 3 years in post-primary schooling, and the Leaving Certificate, which takes place after a further 2-3 years depending on whether the transition year programme is undertaken. Special initiatives to tackle educational disadvantage have been undertaken and these are set out in the National Action Plan against Poverty and Social Exclusion 2003-2005 (Department of Social and Family Affairs, 2003), as well as in the latest Social Partnership Agreement (Department of the Taoiseach, 2006). Within this latter agreement, there is a commitment to:

- substantially reduce literacy/numeracy problems among children, particularly in schools serving disadvantaged communities, and in the adult population;
- encourage children to be active agents in their own learning and to engage in collaborative active learning.

These commitments will be supported by the rolling out of the measures set out under the *Delivering Equality of Opportunity in Schools (DEIS)* initiative for educational inclusion, increasing provision of services for those with special educational needs and for migrant children, as well as further developing mechanisms to combat early school-leaving and enhance attendance, educational progression, retention and achievement at primary and secondary level (Department of Education and Science, 2002 and 2005a).

Significance

Educational achievement is an important predictor of well-being and well-becoming for children. Despite this, literacy problems are widespread: it has been estimated that 5%-10% of children in English-speaking countries experience substantial literacy difficulties (Maughan and Carroll, 2006) and that such difficulties persist over time (Fletcher, 2005). Poorer levels of achievement among children from disadvantaged communities have been identified (Weir, 2001; Department of Education and Science, 2005b).

The evidence suggests that low levels of literacy have a number of impacts on people's lives. Literacy problems have been shown, for example, to be related to poorer health and lower levels of healthcare access (Sudore *et al,* 2006; Robinson and Wharrad, 2000), higher rates of unemployment and under-employment (Eivers *et al,* 2000; Gorby *et al,* 2005). In addition, both the drug-using population (Comiskey and Miller, 2000; Long *et al,* 2005) and the prison population (O'Mahony, 1997; Morgan and Kett, 2003) have been found to have higher levels of people with literacy problems than the general population.

Strong links have also been identified between literacy difficulties and anti-social behaviour (Trzesniewski *et al,* 2006). Literacy problems are strongly associated with psychiatric morbidity (Carroll *et al,* 2005) and, although some of these disorders appear to precede literacy problems (e.g. Attention Deficit Hyperactivity Disorder), the World Health Organization identifies a range of difficulties, including emotional and relationship problems, as features of reading problems (WHO, 1992; Maughan *et al,* 2003).

Reading literacy

Measure

> **The mean score for children aged 15 based on the OECD-PISA Combined Reading Literacy Scale.**

Key findings

- In 2003, Irish children aged 15 achieved a mean score of 515.5 on the OECD-PISA Combined Reading Literacy Scale *(see Table 33)*.

Differences by age, gender and social class
- Overall, girls in Ireland performed better at reading than boys, by achieving a mean score of 530.1 compared to 501.1.
- There was also a noticeable gradient by social class. The mean score for children from the lowest social class category was 484.3, while the mean score achieved by children from the highest social class category was 547.8.

Table 33: Mean score for children aged 15 based on OECD-PISA Combined Reading Literacy Scale, by gender, social class and area (2003)	Mean	SE
Overall	515.5	2.63
Gender		
Boys	501.1	3.26
Girls	530.1	3.71
Social class		
High SES	547.8	3.38
Medium SES	521.6	2.88
Low SES	484.3	3.85
Area		
Village, hamlet or rural area (fewer than 3,000 people)	500.1	5.62
Small town (3,000 to about 15,000 people)	518.0	5.03
Town (15,000 to about 100,000 people)	505.3	11.58
City (100,000 to about 1,000,000 people)	533.9	10.76
Large city (with over 1,000,000 people)	522.3	10.01

Source: PISA Survey

Differences by geographical area
- Children from city areas in Ireland achieved the highest mean score (533.9), while children from areas of population less than 3,000 people achieved the lowest (500.1).

International comparisons

■ From the 2003 PISA Survey, overall, children in Ireland achieved a mean score of 515 on the OECD-PISA Combined Reading Literacy Scale *(see Figure 16)*. This compared with the OECD mean score of 494.

■ The lowest mean score for this indicator for OECD countries participating in PISA was found among Mexican children (400) and the highest among Finnish children (543).

■ Irish children ranked 6th among the 29 participating OECD countries for which reliable achievement data were available.

Figure 16: Mean score for children aged 15 based on OECD-PISA Combined Reading Literacy Scale, by OECD country (2003)

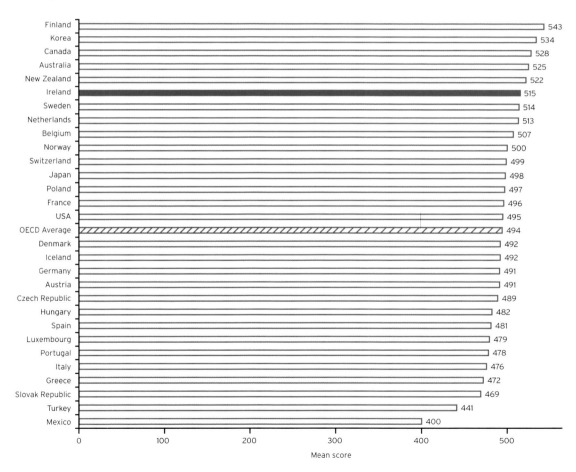

Source: PISA Survey

PART 3: CHILDREN'S OUTCOMES

Mathematics

Measure

> **The mean score for children aged 15 based on the OECD-PISA Combined Mathematics Literacy Scale.**

Key findings

- In 2003, Irish children aged 15 achieved a mean score of 502.8 on the OECD-PISA Combined Mathematics Literacy Scale *(see Table 34)*.

Differences by age, gender and social class

- Overall, boys in Ireland performed better at mathematics than girls, by achieving a mean score of 510.2 compared to 495.4.
- As with reading literacy, there was a significant gradient by social class. The mean score for children from the lowest social class category was 473.5, while the mean score achieved by children from the highest social class category was 535.7.

Table 34: Mean score for children aged 15 based on OECD-PISA Combined Mathematics Literacy Scale, by gender, social class and area (2003)

	Mean	SE
Overall	**502.8**	**2.45**
Gender		
Boys	510.2	3.01
Girls	495.4	3.39
Social class		
High SES	535.7	3.46
Medium SES	506.1	2.50
Low SES	473.5	3.42
Area		
Village, hamlet or rural area (fewer than 3,000 people)	490.7	4.85
Small town (3,000 to about 15,000 people)	508.4	4.37
Town (15,000 to about 100,000 people)	491.9	10.37
City (100,000 to about 1,000,000 people)	519.9	10.34
Large city (with over 1,000,000 people)	501.5	8.88

Source: PISA Survey

Differences by geographical area

- Children from city areas in Ireland achieved the highest mean score (519.9), while children from areas of population less than 3,000 people achieved the lowest (490.7).

International comparisons

■ From the 2003 PISA Survey, overall, children in Ireland achieved a mean score of 503 on the OECD-PISA Combined Mathematics Literacy Scale *(see Figure 17)*. This was similar to the OECD mean score of 500.

■ The lowest mean score for this indicator for OECD countries participating in PISA was found among Mexican children (385) and the highest among Finnish children (544).

■ Irish children ranked 17th among the 29 participating OECD countries in this study. Ireland's mean score was not significantly different from those countries ranked 14th-19th.

Figure 17: Mean score for children aged 15 based on OECD-PISA Combined Mathematics Literacy Scale, by OECD country (2003)

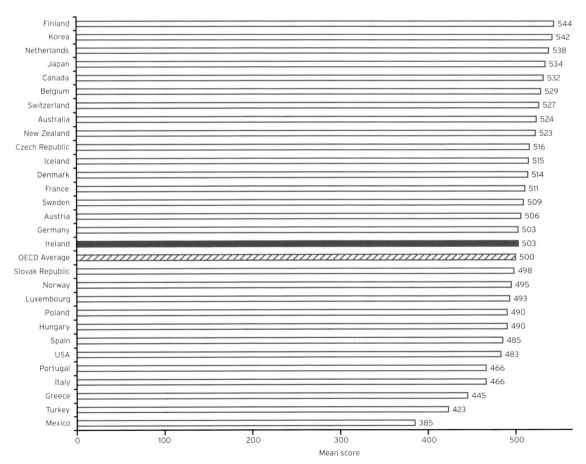

Source: PISA Survey

Science

Measure

> **The mean score for children aged 15 based on the OECD-PISA Combined Scientific Literacy Scale.**

Key findings

■ In 2003, Irish children aged 15 achieved a mean score of 505.4 on the OECD-PISA Combined Scientific Literacy Scale *(see Table 35)*.

Differences by age, gender and social class

■ There was little or no difference between boys and girls in Ireland, with boys achieving a mean score of 506.4 and girls 504.4.

■ As with reading and mathematics literacy, there was a significant gradient by social class. The mean score for children from the lowest social class category was 470.8, while the mean score achieved by children from the highest social class category was 542.5.

Table 35: Mean score for children aged 15 based on international scientific literacy scales, by gender, social class and area (2003)

	Mean	SE
Overall	**505.4**	**2.69**
Gender		
Boys	506.4	3.08
Girls	504.4	3.88
Social class		
High SES	542.5	3.49
Medium SES	509.6	2.68
Low SES	470.8	4.11
Area		
Village, hamlet or rural area (fewer than 3,000 people)	490.2	5.19
Small town (3,000 to about 15,000 people)	509.8	4.73
Town (15,000 to about 100,000 people)	495.0	11.41
City (100,000 to about 1,000,000 people)	522.1	10.40
Large city (with over 1,000,000 people)	508.6	9.44

Source: PISA Survey

Differences by geographical area

■ Children from city areas in Ireland achieved the highest mean score (522.1), while children from areas of population less than 3,000 people achieved the lowest (490.2).

International comparisons

- From the 2003 PISA Survey, overall, children in Ireland achieved a mean score of 505 on the OECD-PISA Combined Scientific Literacy Scale *(see Figure 18).* This compared with the OECD mean score of 500.
- The lowest mean score for this indicator for OECD countries participating in PISA was found among Mexican children (405) and the highest among Finnish and Japanese children (548).
- Irish children ranked 13th among the 29 participating OECD countries in this study.

Figure 18: Mean score for children aged 15 based on OECD-PISA Combined Scientific Literacy Scale, by OECD country (2003)

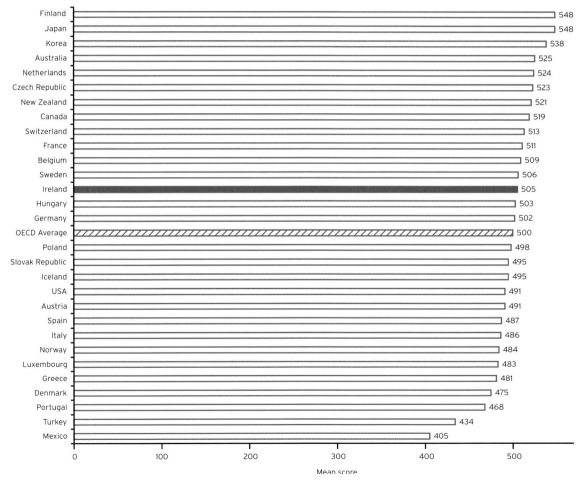

Mean score

Source: PISA Survey

Technical notes

In each assessment of 'literacy', the Programme for International Student Assessment (PISA) Survey includes the content or structure of knowledge, the processes that need to be performed and the situations in which skills and knowledge are applied.

PISA data are explicitly designed to enable the comparison of skills between students in various countries, to serve as benchmarks for the education system and assist in understanding the relative strengths and weaknesses within countries. Literacy and early school-leaving are intertwined in Irish policy: measures to tackle poor literacy levels encompass efforts to prevent early school-leaving and promote life long learning, including 'second-chance' education.

PISA assesses to what extent students near the end of compulsory education have acquired the knowledge and skills essential for full participation in society. Students' engagement with learning is crucial for the acquisition of proficiency and is also an important outcome of education. Students' engagement refers to students' active involvement in learning, their belief about their own ability to succeed in a subject, their motivation to learn a subject and their emotional relationship with a subject, as well as their choice of learning strategies for a subject.

PISA is based on the knowledge and skills considered important for students' future functioning within the education system and in society. However, PISA is not linked in any systematic way to the national curricula of participating countries. This may be a limitation in the case of mathematics in particular, where there is evidence of a mismatch between some aspects of the Junior Certificate syllabus in Ireland and PISA (Close and Oldham, 2005).

Percentage differences are presented for descriptive purposes only and may not reflect a statistically significant finding.

References

Carroll, J.M., Maughan, B., Goodman, R. and Meltzer H. (2005) 'Literacy Difficulties and Psychiatric Disorders: Evidence for Co-Morbidity', *Journal of Child Psychology and Psychiatry,* Vol. 46, No. 5, pp. 524-32.

Close, S. and Oldham, E.E. (2005) 'Junior Cycle Mathematics Examinations and the PISA Mathematics Framework', in *Proceedings of the First National Conference of Research in Mathematics Education,* S. Close, T. Dooley and D. Corcoran (eds.). Dublin: St. Patrick's College, pp. 174-92.

Comiskey, C.M. and Miller, R.T.H. (2000) *Young People, Drug Use and Early School-leaving. Report submitted to the Research and Development Committee, Department of Education and Science.* Dublin: Department of Education and Science.

Department of Education and Science (2002) *Summary of all initiatives funded by the Department to help alleviate educational disadvantage.* Dublin: The Stationery Office.

Department of Education and Science (2005a) *Delivering Equality of Opportunity in Schools (DEIS): An Action Plan for Educational Inclusion.* Dublin: The Stationery Office.

Department of Education and Science (2005b). *Literacy and Numeracy in Disadvantaged Schools: Challenges for Teachers and Learners. An Evaluation by the Inspectorate of the Department of Education and Science.* Dublin: The Stationery Office.

Department of Social and Family Affairs (2003) *National Action Plan against Poverty and Social Exclusion 2003-2005.* Dublin: The Stationery Office.

Department of the Taoiseach (2006) *Towards 2016: Ten-Year Framework Social Partnership Agreement 2006-2015.* Dublin: The Stationery Office.

Eivers, E., Ryan, E. and Brinkley, A. (2000) *Characteristics of Early School-leavers: Results of the Research Strand of the 8-15 year-old Early School-leavers Initiative.* Dublin: Education Research Centre.

Fletcher, J.M. (2005) 'Predicting Math Outcomes: Reading Predictors and Co-Morbidity', *Journal of Learning Disabilities,* Vol. 38, No. 4, pp. 308-12.

Gorby, S., McCoy, S. and Watson, D. (2005) 2004 Annual School-leavers' *Survey of 2002/2003 Leavers.* Dublin: Economic and Social Research Institute.

Government of Ireland (1998) *Education Act.* Dublin: The Stationery Office.

Government of Ireland (2000a) *Equal Status Act.* Dublin: The Stationery Office.

Government of Ireland (2000b) *Education (Welfare) Act.* Dublin: The Stationery Office.

Government of Ireland (2004) *Education for Persons with Special Educational Needs Act.* Dublin: The Stationery Office.

Long, J., Lynn, E. and Kelly, F. (2005) *Trends in Treated Problem Drug Use in Ireland: 1998 to 2002.* Occasional Paper No. 17. Dublin: Health Research Board.

Maughan, B. and Carroll, J. (2006) 'Literacy and Mental Disorders', *Current Opinions in Psychiatry,* Vol. 19, No. 4, pp. 350-54.

Maughan, B., Rowe, R., Loeber, R. and Stouthamer-Loeber, M. (2003) 'Reading Problems and Depressed Mood', *Journal of Abnormal Child Psychology,* Vol. 31, No. 2, pp. 219-29.

Morgan, M. and Kett, M. (2003) *The Prison Adult Literacy Survey: Results and Implications.* Dublin: The Prison Service.

O'Mahony, P. (1997) *Mountjoy Prisoners: A Sociological and Criminological Profile.* Dublin: The Stationery Office.

Robinson, J. and Wharrad, H. (2000) 'Invisible Nursing: Exploring Health Outcomes at a Global Level. Relationships between infant and under-5 mortality rates and the distribution of health professionals, GNP per capita, and female literacy', *Journal of Advanced Nursing,* Vol. 32, No. 1, pp. 28-40.

Sudore, R.L., Mehta, K.L., Simonsick, E.M., Harris, T.B., Newman, A.B., Satterfield, S., Rosano, C., Rooks, R.N., Rubin, S.M., Ayonayon, H.N. and Yaffe, K. (2006) 'Limited literacy in older people and disparities in health and healthcare access', *Journal of the American Geriatric Society,* Vol. 54, No. 5, pp. 770-76.

Trzesniewski, K.H., Moffitt, T.E., Caspi, A., Taylor, A. and Maughan, B. (2006) 'Revisiting the association between reading achievement and anti-social behaviour: New evidence of an environmental explanation from a twin study', *Child Development,* Vol. 77, No. 1, pp. 72-88.

UN (1989) *Convention on the Rights of the Child.* Geneva: United Nations Office of the High Commissioner for Human Rights. Available at www.ohchr.org

Weir, S. (2001) 'The reading achievements of primary school pupils from disadvantaged backgrounds', *The Irish Journal of Education,* No. 32, pp. 23-43.

WHO (1992) *The ICD-10 Classification of Mental and Behavioural Disorders. Clinical Descriptions and Diagnostic Guidelines.* Copenhagen: World Health Organization.

PART 3: CHILDREN'S OUTCOMES

95

HEALTH

Birth weight

Context

Birth weight is a major predictor of infant morbidity and mortality, and this is an important marker of population health. Concern about birth weight is generally focused on those infants who are born with a low birth weight. This has been defined by the World Health Organization as the percentage of total births that weigh less than 2,500 grams (WHO, 2004). The main causes of low birth weight are premature birth (birth before the end of the 37th week of pregnancy) and impaired/restricted intrauterine growth. Low birth weight thus defines a heterogeneous group of infants – some are born early, some are born growth-restricted and some are born both early and growth-restricted.

The National Action Plan against Poverty and Social Exclusion 2003-2005 identifies low birth weight as one of three core targets to reduce health inequalities in Ireland and recommends that the gap in low birth weight rates between children from the lowest and highest socio-economic groups should be reduced by 10% from the 2001 level by 2007 (Department of Social and Family Affairs, 2003).

Significance

Low birth weight is associated with a number of adverse health outcomes, including a higher risk of dying in the first few weeks of life. Other serious health problems, such as feeding problems, breathing difficulties, brain damage and infections, have also been found to be associated with low birth weight (Institute of Public Health in Ireland, 2005). Low birth weight is also associated with higher rates of neuro-developmental problems and disability, and although the mechanisms through which these occur are not well understood, longitudinal studies show that many of these effects last throughout childhood and into adulthood.

Infants born with low birth weight, for example, have been shown to have poorer academic performance (Richards *et al*, 2001) and increased frequency of behavioural problems (Kelly *et al*, 2001) compared with those born above the 2,500 gram level. In later life, those with low birth weight are at increased risk of coronary heart disease (Barker *et al*, 2001; Blane *et al*, 1996), higher levels of unemployment (Kristensen *et al*, 2004) and higher levels of premature mortality (Bartley *et al*, 1994). According to research by the Institute of Public Health in Ireland (2005) and Peacock *et al* (1995), infants born with low birth weight are more commonly born to:
- mothers who smoke;
- teenage mothers;
- mothers in lower socio-economic groups;
- mothers who engage in drug or alcohol abuse during pregnancy;
- mothers who are poor attendees at antenatal clinics.

Many other factors have also contributed to the overall rise in the incidence of pre-term birth. These factors include increasing rates of multiple births and greater use of assisted reproduction techniques.

Measure

> **The number of babies born weighing less than 2,500 grams, expressed as a proportion of all registered live and stillbirths.**

Key findings

■ In 2003, 77.8% (48,244) of all babies born were within the healthy birth weight category (2,500-4,000 grams), 16.8% were in the high birth weight category (4,000+ grams) and 5.4% were in the low birth weight category *(see Table 36)*. These percentages have been relatively stable over the years 1999-2003.

Table 36: Percentage of infants' birth weight groups, by gender (1999-2003)															
	1999			2000			2001			2002			2003		
	% Low	% Healthy	% High	% Low	% Healthy	% High	% Low	% Healthy	% High	% Low	% Healthy	% High	% Low	% Healthy	% High
Male	5.0	74.3	20.5	5.1	73.7	21.2	5.1	73.9	20.9	4.8	74.6	20.6	5.0	74.9	20.1
Female	5.6	81.1	13.3	5.3	80.9	13.8	5.9	80.9	13.2	5.7	81.1	13.1	5.8	81.0	13.3
Total	5.3	77.6	17.0	5.2	77.2	17.6	5.5	77.3	17.1	5.3	77.8	16.9	5.4	77.8	16.8

Source: National Perinatal Reporting System, Economic and Social Research Institute

Differences by gender and social class
■ The percentage of female births in the healthy birth weight category is consistently around 7% more than for male births for the period 1999-2003.
■ In 2003, the highest percentage (7.5%) of low birth weight babies were born to mothers in the unemployed socio-economic group *(see Figure 19)*. This was a consistent trend over the period 1999-2003.

Figure 19: Percentage of babies born weighing less than 2,500 grams (live and stillbirths), by occupation of mother (2003)

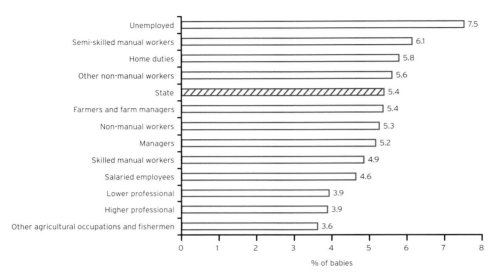

Source: National Perinatal Reporting System, Economic and Social Research Institute

Differences by geographical area

■ In 2003, 7% of babies born to mothers resident in counties Roscommon, Waterford and Longford weighed less then 2,500 grams, compared with less than 4.5% in counties Kildare, Tipperary NR and Leitrim *(see Figure 20).*

Figure 20: Percentage of babies born weighing less than 2,500 grams (live and stillbirths), by mother's county of residence (2003)

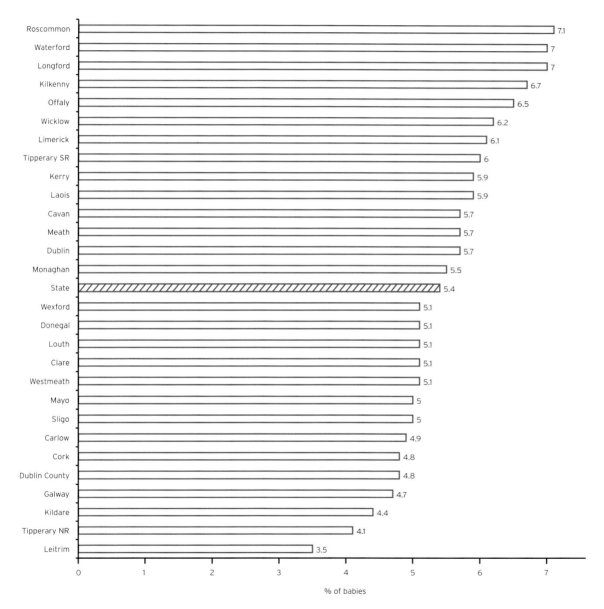

% of babies

Source: National Perinatal Reporting System, Economic and Social Research Institute

PART 3: CHILDREN'S OUTCOMES

101

International comparisons

- Calculating the percentage of babies born less than 2,500 grams based on live births only for the purpose of international comparisons, the percentage of Irish babies born weighing less than 2,500 grams was 5.1% *(see Figure 21)*. This compares with the EU average of 6.4%.

- Among the 17 EU countries for which data are available, the lowest percentage for this indicator was found among Finnish babies (4.1%) and the highest among Hungarian babies (8.7%). Irish babies ranked 5th.

Figure 21: Percentage of babies born weighing less than 2,500 grams (live births only), by country (2003)

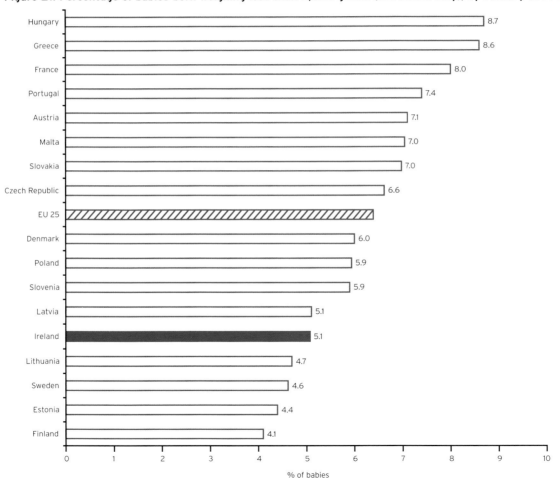

Source: National Perinatal Reporting System, Economic and Social Research Institute

Technical notes

The National Perinatal Reporting System (NPRS) dataset provides details of national statistics on perinatal events – live births and late foetal deaths (stillbirths). Information on every birth that occurs either in hospital or at home is returned to the NPRS. The information collected includes data on pregnancy outcomes, with particular reference to perinatal mortality and important aspects of perinatal care. The period to which the information applies is from 22 week's gestation to the first week of life. In addition, descriptive social and biological characteristics of mothers giving birth and their babies are recorded.

All births are registered and notified on a standard four-part form, which is completed where the birth takes place, either at the hospital or by the attending independent midwife. The first part of the form is sent to the Registrar of Births and subsequently to the Central Statistics Office. The second part goes to the Director of Community Care and Medical Officer of Health in the mother's area of residence. The NPRS dataset is compiled from the third part of the form. The fourth part is retained by the hospital or midwife.

The Economic and Social Research Institute (ESRI) is contracted by the Department of Health and Children to manage the NPRS system.

References

Barker, D.J.P., Forsén, T., Uutela, A., Osmond, C. and Eriksson J.G. (2001) 'Size at birth and resilience to effects of poor living conditions in adult life: Longitudinal Study', *British Medical Journal,* No. 323, pp. 1-5.

Bartley, M., Power, C., Blane, D., Davey-Smith, G. and Shipley, M. (1994) 'Birth weight and later socio-economic disadvantage: Evidence from the 1958 British Cohort Study', *British Medical Journal,* No. 309, pp. 1475-78.

Blane, D., Hart, C.L., Smith, G.D., Gillis, C.R., Hole, D.J. and Hawthorne, V.M. (1996) 'Association of cardiovascular disease risk factors with socio-economic position during childhood and during adulthood', *British Medical Journal,* No. 313, pp. 1434-38.

Department of Social and Family Affairs (2003) *National Action Plan against Poverty and Social Exclusion 2003-2005.* Dublin: The Stationery Office.

Institute of Public Health in Ireland (2005) *Inequalities in the Occurrence of Low Birth Weight Babies in Ireland: A Discussion Paper.* Dublin: Institute of Public Health in Ireland.

Kelly, Y.J., Nazroo, J.Y., McMunn, A., Boreham, R. and Marmot, M. (2001) 'Birth weight and behavioural problems in children: A modifiable effect?', *International Journal of Epidemiology,* Vol. 30, No. 1, pp. 88-94.

Kristensen, K., Bjerkedal, T. and Irgens, L.M. (2004) 'Birth weight and work participation in adulthood', *International Journal of Epidemiology,* Vol. 33, No. 4, pp. 849-56.

Peacock, J.L., Bland, J.M. and Anderson, H.R. (1995) 'Pre-term Delivery: Effects of socio-economic factors, psychological stress, smoking, alcohol and caffeine', *British Medical Journal,* No. 311, pp. 531-35.

Richards, M., Hardy, R., Kuh, D. and Wadsworth, M.E.S. (2001) 'Birth weight and cognitive function in the British 1946 birth cohort: Longitudinal Population-based Study', *British Medical Journal,* No. 322, pp. 199-203.

PART 3: CHILDREN'S OUTCOMES

103

WHO (2004) *Low Birth Weight in 2000: Global, Regional and Country Incidence. Estimates developed by UNICEF and WHO.* New York: Statistics and Monitoring, United Nations Children's Fund, and Geneva, Department of Reproductive Health and Research, World Health Organization.

Further information
- Economic and Social Research Institute (www.esri.ie)
- Ireland and Northern Ireland's Population Health Observatory (www.inispho.org)

Breastfeeding practice

Context

The first national Irish policy on breastfeeding was published in 1994 (Department of Health and Children, 1994). Since then, the protection, promotion and support of breastfeeding has been identified in many national policy documents as an important issue. A 5-year strategic action plan was published in 2005, with the stated mission of improving the nation's health by ensuring that breastfeeding is the norm for infants and young children in Ireland (Department of Health and Children, 2005). The strategic plan draws on the *Ottawa Charter for Health Promotion* (WHO, 1986) and identifies interrelated actions in the following areas:

- building public policy (by implementation of legislation and public policies that promote, support and protect breastfeeding);
- create supportive environments (by ensuring that Irish society recognises and facilitates breastfeeding as the optimal method of feeding infants and young children);
- strengthen community action (through enabling communities to support and promote breastfeeding in order to make it the normal and preferred choice for families in Ireland);
- develop personal skills (with a goal of ensuring that all families have the knowledge, skills and support to make and carry out informed infant feeding decisions, particularly those mothers least likely to breastfeed);
- reorientate health services (by ensuring the health sector takes responsibility for developing and implementing evidence-based breastfeeding policies and best practices).

The strategic action plan has four main targets: an improved system for collecting accurate data about breastfeeding in Ireland; increases in breastfeeding initiation and duration rates; 100% participation in the Baby Friendly Hospital Initiative; and the employment of breastfeeding coordinators with regional responsibility.

Significance

The 5-year strategic action plan described above provides an analysis of the scientific literature on breastfeeding and clearly demonstrates health, social and economic benefits from breastfeeding. Breastfed babies, for example, show better outcomes in neurological and cognitive development, and lower levels of infections, obesity and allergies than those who are not breastfed. There are also economic benefits associated with breastfeeding and, since there is a reduction in packaging and transport costs, there are also positive spin-offs for the environment (Department of Health and Children, 2005).

Systematic reviews of the scientific research have demonstrated that certain interventions can be effective in increasing the initiation and duration rates for breastfeeding. These interventions include health education, peer support, media campaigns and training of health

PART 3: CHILDREN'S OUTCOMES

105

personnel (Dyson *et al,* 2005; Fairbank *et al,* 2000). The benefits of breastfeeding for babies are very substantial, but despite a gradual increase in recent years, Ireland's breastfeeding rates remains the lowest in Europe.

Measure

> **The number of newborn babies who are (a) exclusively breastfed and (b) who are partially breastfed throughout the first 48 hours of life, expressed as a proportion of all newborn babies.**

Key findings

- The breastfeeding rate on discharge from hospital in 2003 was 44.5%. This includes 41% of mothers who were exclusively breastfeeding and a further 3.5% who were using a combination of bottle and breastfeeding *(see Table 37).*
- The percentage of infants who are exclusively breastfed has increased each year since 1999, from 35.9% in 1999 to 41.0% in 2003. Similarly, the percentage of infants who are both bottle and breastfed has also increased, from 0.8% in 1999 to 3.5% in 2003.
- The data show marked differences in the breastfeeding rates by mothers' age groups. Older mothers are more likely to breastfeed: in 2003, 47.9% of women aged over 45 years exclusively breastfed, compared with 19.5% of women aged 15-19.

Table 37: Percentage of infants breastfed (exclusive or combined), by mothers' age groups (1999-2003)

Years of age	1999 Exclusive %	1999 Combined %	2000 Exclusive %	2000 Combined %	2001 Exclusive %	2001 Combined %	2002 Exclusive %	2002 Combined %	2003 Exclusive %	2003 Combined %
<15	8.3	0.0	16.7	0.0	8.3	0.0	20.0	0.0	21.4	0.0
15-19	14.7	0.0	16.3	0.8	18.1	1.7	19.5	1.4	19.5	1.8
20-24	23.0	0.4	26.2	1.3	27.1	2.1	30.4	2.1	30.6	2.7
25-29	32.5	0.6	35.2	1.8	36.9	2.7	39.6	3.5	40.3	4.0
30-34	42.2	0.9	43.9	1.9	43.8	2.6	44.8	2.8	44.6	3.9
35-39	45.7	0.7	47.1	1.6	46.3	2.8	47.7	2.7	46.9	3.3
40-44	43.2	1.1	45.7	1.8	45.4	2.6	47.7	2.6	47.0	3.8
45 and over	33.8	0.9	37.3	0.0	44.3	1.3	44.1	2.9	47.9	9.9
Not stated	45.7	0.0	31.8	0.0	31.6	0.0	32.0	0.0	47.1	3.9
Total	35.9	0.8	38.2	1.6	38.8	2.5	40.9	2.8	41.0	3.5

Source: National Perinatal Reporting System, Economic and Social Research Institute

■ The data also show marked socio-economic differences *(see Figure 22)*. A larger percentage of mothers in higher socio-economic categories breastfeed their babies. For example, in 2003, 70.6% of women from higher professional groups either exclusively (65.7%) or partially (4.9%) breastfed their babies. This compares with 24.1% of women from semi-skilled manual worker groups, who either exclusively (22.1%) or partially (1.9%) breastfed their babies.

Figure 22: Percentage of infants breastfed (either exclusive or combined) throughout the first 48 hours of life, by mother's occupation (2003)

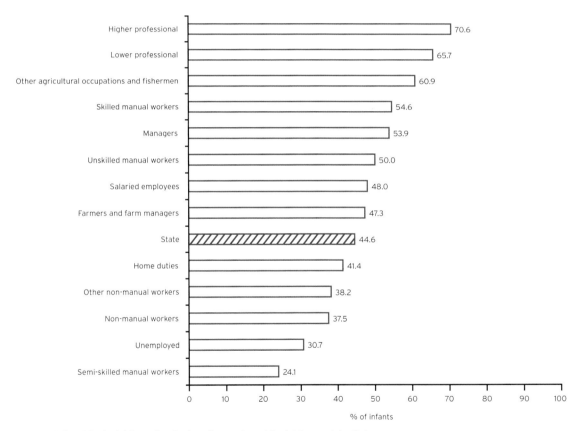

Source: National Perinatal Reporting System, Economic and Social Research Institute

■ Geographical differences are also apparent *(see Table 38)*. In 2003, the percentage of women exclusively breastfeeding their infants on discharge from hospital ranged from a low of 26.6% in Limerick to a high of 51.1% in Dublin County.

PART 3: CHILDREN'S OUTCOMES

Table 38: Mother's county of residence, by infant's type of feeding (2003)

County	Artificial		Breast		Combined		Not stated		Total
	No.	%	No.	%	No.	%	No.	%	No.
Carlow	529	62.8	300	35.6	12	1.4	1	0.1	842
Cavan	484	61.3	281	35.6	24	3.0	1	0.1	790
Clare	1,033	62.2	592	35.6	32	1.9	5	0.3	1,662
Cork	3,637	53.9	2,858	42.3	248	3.7	10	0.2	6,753
Donegal	1,327	66.9	541	27.3	115	5.8	2	0.1	1,985
Dublin	6,894	51.3	5,975	44.4	551	4.1	24	0.2	13,444
Dublin County	2,102	44.7	2,401	51.1	196	4.2	4	0.1	4,703
Galway	1,667	51.3	1,226	37.7	353	10.9	5	0.2	3,251
Kerry	934	55.1	719	42.4	43	2.5	0	0.0	1,696
Kildare	1,790	54.5	1,365	41.6	120	3.7	8	0.2	3,283
Kilkenny	616	54.5	509	45.0	3	0.3	2	0.2	1,130
Laois	546	55.3	427	43.3	14	1.4	0	0.0	987
Leitrim	186	54.6	150	44.0	5	1.5	0	0.0	341
Limerick	1,932	72.3	712	26.6	14	0.5	16	0.6	2,674
Longford	298	58.1	203	39.6	12	2.3	0	0.0	513
Louth	885	55.6	653	41.0	53	3.3	0	0.0	1,591
Mayo	904	57.0	606	38.2	74	4.7	3	0.2	1,587
Meath	1,304	49.9	1,221	46.7	85	3.3	5	0.2	2,615
Monaghan	390	58.5	242	36.3	35	5.3	0	0.0	667
Offaly	636	65.1	336	34.4	4	0.4	1	0.1	977
Roscommon	345	57.6	237	39.6	15	2.5	2	0.3	599
Sligo	490	63.3	261	33.7	22	2.8	1	0.1	774
Tipperary NR	525	69.1	231	30.4	3	0.4	1	0.1	760
Tipperary SR	800	64.6	434	35.1	3	0.2	1	0.1	1,238
Waterford	865	53.8	725	45.1	17	1.1	2	0.1	1,609
Westmeath	653	53.4	551	45.0	18	1.5	2	0.2	1,224
Wexford	1,262	63.0	685	34.2	54	2.7	1	0.1	2,002
Wicklow	1,017	53.3	823	43.2	61	3.2	6	0.3	1,907
Other	9	34.6	16	61.5	1	3.9	0	0.0	26
Not stated	0	0.0	1	50.0	0	0.0	1	50.0	2
Total	34,060	55.3	25,281	41.0	2,187	3.5	104	0.2	61,632

Source: National Perinatal Reporting System, Economic and Social Research Institute

Technical notes

Data on 'type of feeding' provide important information on breastfeeding rates in Ireland. Type of feeding is recorded as either (1) artificial, (2) breast or (3) combined. Hospitals are requested to record the type of feeding at discharge (at approximately 3-4 days) from hospital. Therefore, these rates do not capture feeding at 48 hours. The national breastfeeding rate is an indicator of the level of breastfed babies in Ireland.

References

Department of Health (1994) *A National Breastfeeding Policy for Ireland.* Dublin: The Stationery Office.

Department of Health and Children (2005) *Breastfeeding in Ireland: A Five-year Strategic Action Plan.* Dublin: The Stationery Office.

Dyson, L., McCormick, F. and Renfrew, M.J. (2006) *Interventions for promoting the initiation of breastfeeding.* The Cochrane Database of Systematic Reviews 2006, Issue 4, The Cochrane Collaboration. New York: John Wiley.

Fairbank, L., O'Meara, L., Renfrew, M.J., Woolridge, M., Sowden, A.J. and Lister-Sharp, D. (2000) 'A systematic review to evaluate the effectiveness of interventions to promote the initiation of breastfeeding', *Health Technology Assessment,* Vol. 4, No. 25, London: Department of Health. Available at: www.hta.ac.uk/project.asp?PjtId=1084

WHO (1986) *Ottawa Charter for Health Promotion.* Copenhagen: World Health Organization.

Further information
■ Health Promotion Unit, Department of Health and Children (www.healthpromotion.ie/breastfeeding)

PART 3: CHILDREN'S OUTCOMES

Chronic health conditions and hospitalisation

Context

The National Health Strategy sets out four principles around which health services in Ireland are to be organised – equality and fairness; a people-centred service; quality of care; and clear accountability (Department of Health and Children, 2001). Since the publication of the Strategy in 2001, there have been a number of changes in the organisation and structure of the primary, secondary and tertiary health services. Under the Health Act (Government of Ireland, 2004), the Health Service Executive (HSE) is responsible for providing health and personal social services for everyone living in the Republic of Ireland. The objective of the HSE is to use the resources available to it in the most beneficial, effective and efficient manner to improve, promote and protect the health and welfare of the public. In 2005, there were 101,978 people employed in the health services (Department of Health and Children, 2005).

Children may be hospitalised in specialist children's hospitals, on children's wards in general hospitals or in general wards in non-specialist hospitals. A recently published report sets out a blueprint for the development of a national tertiary health service for children (Department of Health and Children, 2006) and it was noted that the population of Ireland was such that only one world-class tertiary centre could be supported.

Within hospital services, it is recognised that play has an important function for children in hospital, particularly in helping to provide a sense of normality, reduce anxieties and act as an outlet for tension (Coyne *et al,* 2006; Children in Hospital Ireland, 2000). The National Play Policy (NCO, 2004) supports the development of play in hospital settings and makes a number of recommendations in this area, including:
- the development of recognised courses for hospital play in third-level institutions;
- the identification and promotion of the rehabilitative and therapeutic value of play;
- child-friendly public healthcare settings.

Significance

There is a general consensus that being in hospital can be a distressing and difficult situation for children and young people. Recent research, commissioned by the Office of the Minister for Children, identified a number of difficulties arising for children in hospital, including losing contact with friends and siblings, missing home and schooling, and losing freedom and privacy (Coyne *et al,* 2006). This study also found that children had varied experiences of being consulted about their condition and treatment, and that parents had a strong influence in this area.

Difficulties also arise for parents of hospitalised children. Fitzgerald (2004), in an examination of the costs of having a child in hospital, found that while the average cost was approximately €80 daily, parents came under financial strain when a child was in hospital more than once, when the child was a long-stay patient or when parents were on low incomes. Additional costs accrued from, for example, having meals away from home, travel costs, extra housekeeping and other extras (such as childcare, treats, laundry, phone calls). 60% of repeat hospitalisation led to financial strain and/or debt.

Measure

> **The 10 most frequent conditions resulting in hospitalisation among children and young people.**

Key findings

■ In 2004, 140,528 children and young people, aged 0-17, were discharged from hospitals across Ireland *(see Table 39)*. Of these discharges:
  -   20.8% were in the <1 year age group;
  -   28.8% were in the 1-4 age group;
  -   20.5% were in the 5-9 age group;
  -   16.6% were in the 10-14 age group;
  -   13.3% were in the 15-17 age group.

Table 39: Number of children discharged from hospital, by age group and gender (2004)			
Years of age	Boys	Girls	Total
<1	16,374	12,914	29,288
1-4	23,443	16,976	40,419
5-9	15,988	12,788	28,776
10-14	12,752	10,543	23,295
15-17	8,595	10,155	18,750
Total	77,152	63,376	140,528

Source: Hospital In-Patient Enquiry, Economic and Social Research Institute

■ 44.5% of discharges were accounted for by diseases of the respiratory (15.8%) and digestive systems (11.7%), injury and poisoning (10.9%), and certain infectious and parasitic diseases (6.1%) *(see Table 40)*.
■ With the exception of the 15-17 age group, boys are more likely to be discharged from hospital than girls.

PART 3: CHILDREN'S OUTCOMES

111

Table 40: Principal conditions resulting in hospitalisations of children, by age group and rate per 1,000 population (2004)

Conditions	<1 year		1-4 years		5-9 years		10-14 years		15-17 years		Total	
	No.	%	No.	%	No.	%	No.	%	No.	%	No.	%
Diseases of the respiratory system	5,100	17.4	8,989	22.2	4,153	14.4	2,196	9.4	1,779	9.5	22,217	15.8
Diseases of the digestive system	2,241	7.7	4,267	10.6	4,625	16.1	3,173	13.6	2,083	11.1	16,389	11.7
Injury, poisoning and certain other consequences of external causes	792	2.7	4,331	10.7	3,472	12.1	3,649	15.7	3,109	16.6	15,353	10.9
Certain infectious and parasitic diseases	2,532	8.6	3,341	8.3	1,260	4.4	912	3.9	574	3.1	8,619	6.1
Certain conditions originating in the perinatal period	7,467	25.5	16	0.0	3	0.0		0.0		0.0	7,486	5.3
Diseases of the genitourinary system	1,216	4.2	2,796	6.9	1,625	5.6	955	4.1	822	4.4	7,414	5.3
Congenital malformations, deformations and chromosomal abnormalities	2,574	8.8	2,407	6.0	1,130	3.9	717	3.1	263	1.4	7,091	5.0
Neoplasm	157	0.5	1,253	3.1	1,729	6.0	1,414	6.1	1,413	7.5	5,966	4.2
Diseases of the ear and mastoid process	235	0.8	2,170	5.4	1,870	6.5	901	3.9	374	2.0	5,550	3.9
Diseases of the skin and subcutaneous tissue	347	1.2	738	1.8	564	2.0	1,569	6.7	1,279	6.8	4,497	3.2
Diseases of musculoskeletal system and connective tissue	72	0.2	770	1.9	745	2.6	877	3.8	675	3.6	3,139	2.2
Diseases of blood and blood-forming organs and certain disorders involving the immune mechanism	167	0.6	888	2.2	910	3.2	624	2.7	344	1.8	2,933	2.1
Diseases of the nervous system	236	0.8	486	1.2	625	2.2	518	2.2	357	1.9	2,222	1.6
Endocrine, nutritional and metabolic diseases	294	1.0	400	1.0	398	1.4	522	2.2	268	1.4	1,882	1.3
Diseases of the eye and adnexa	162	0.6	645	1.6	464	1.6	283	1.2	226	1.2	1,780	1.3
Pregnancy, childbirth and the puerperium		0.0		0.0		0.0	12	0.1	1,530	8.2	1,542	1.1
Diseases of the circulatory system	157	0.5	126	0.3	121	0.4	225	1.0	223	1.2	852	0.6
Mental and behavioural disorders	31	0.1	150	0.4	82	0.3	222	1.0	229	1.2	714	0.5
All other conditions and reasons for admissions	5,508	18.8	6,646	16.4	5,000	17.4	4,526	19.4	3,202	17.1	24,882	17.7
Total	29,288	100.0	40,419	100.0	28,776	100.0	23,295	100.0	18,750	100.0	140,528	100.0

Source: Hospital In-Patient Enquiry, Economic and Social Research Institute

- The total number of hospitalisations of children aged 0-17 increased by 8,486 between 2000 and 2004 *(see Table 41)*.

Table 41: Hospitalisations of children, by age group (2000-2004)

Years of age	2000		2001		2002		2003		2004	
	No.	%	No.	%	No.	%	No.	%	No.	%
<1	26,093	19.8	25,693	19.3	26,887	20.4	26840	19.7	29,288	20.8
1-4	37,192	28.2	37,098	27.8	37,040	28.2	39382	29.0	40,419	28.8
5-9	25,031	19.0	26,644	20.0	25,417	19.3	26736	19.7	28,776	20.5
10-14	23,445	17.8	23,614	17.7	22,618	17.2	23803	17.5	23,295	16.6
15-17	20,281	15.4	20,391	15.3	19,560	14.9	19209	14.1	18,750	13.3
Total	132,042	100.0	133,440	100.0	131,522	100.0	135,970	100.0	140,528	100.0

Source: Hospital In-Patient Enquiry, Economic and Social Research Institute

- The principal cause of injuries among children in 2004 were accidental falls, which accounted for 37.3% of reported external causes *(see Table 42)*.
- Boys accounted for over 63.2% of all injuries and poisonings among children in 2004. While this was most evident for boys aged 10-17, this difference could be seen across all age groups.
- 65.2% of total hospitalisations of children for accidental poisonings were among the 1-4 age group.
- Over 70% of deliberately inflicted injuries (which include self-inflicted injuries and injuries deliberately inflicted by other people) occurred in the 15-17 age group in 2004. In general, this cause of hospitalisation was more common for girls than for boys.
- Road traffic accidents are a very significant cause of hospitalisation of children, with the exception of the <1 age group *(see Figure 23)*. In 2004, such accidents accounted for 1,822 hospitalisations *(see Table 43)*.

PART 3: CHILDREN'S OUTCOMES

Figure 23: Number of children hospitalised for road traffic accidents, by age group (2004)

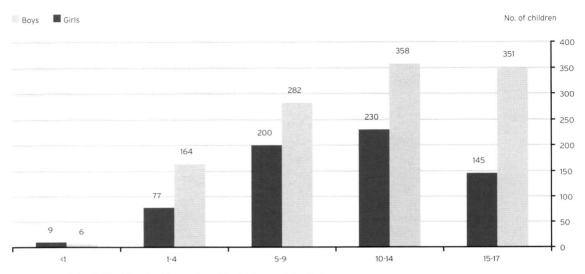

Source: Hospital In-Patient Enquiry, Economic and Social Research Institute

Table 42: External causes of injury and poisoning in children, by age group and gender (2004)																	
	<1 year			1-4 years			5-9 years			10-14 years			15-17 years			Total		
	Male	Female	Total	Male	Female	Total	Male	Female	Total	Male	Female	Total	Male	Female	Total	Male	Female	Total
Accidental falls	257	213	470	1,046	751	1,797	911	674	1,585	867	391	1,258	494	123	617	3,575	2,152	5,727
Accidents caused by objects*	46	21	67	574	419	993	510	237	747	730	208	938	598	89	687	2,458	974	3,432
Road traffic accidents	6	9	15	164	77	241	282	200	482	358	230	588	351	145	496	1,161	661	1,822
Deliberately inflicted injuries	10	2	12	6	6	12	13	6	19	60	98	158	241	281	522	330	393	723
Accidental poisonings	10	1	11	188	156	344	17	14	31	44	35	79	31	31	62	290	237	527
Accidents caused by submersion, suffocation and foreign bodies	18	4	22	102	88	190	61	48	109	29	13	42	19	4	23	229	157	386
Accidents caused by hot, caustic or corrosive substances and steam	24	23	47	110	68	178	13	6	19	7	3	10	3	2	5	157	102	259
Injury caused by animals or venomous animals and plants	0	1	1	41	27	68	26	34	60	25	14	39	12	9	21	104	85	189
Accidents caused by fire and flames	7	7	14	13	14	27	13	7	20	12	4	16	15	0	15	60	32	92
Complications of medical and surgical care	3	1	4	6	1	7	3	1	4	6	1	7	5	5	10	23	9	32
Other external causes	11	5	16	25	15	40	19	10	29	79	45	124	187	64	251	321	139	460
External cause not reported	56	57	113	246	188	434	203	164	367	239	151	390	258	142	400	1002	702	1704
Total	448	344	792	2,521	1,810	4,331	2,071	1,401	3,472	2,456	1,193	3,649	2,214	895	3,109	9,710	5,643	15,353

* Accidents caused by objects include striking against or being struck accidentally by objects or persons; caught accidentally in or between objects; accidents caused by machinery; and accidents caused by cutting/piercing objects.

Source: Hospital In-Patient Enquiry, Economic and Social Research Institute

PART 3: CHILDREN'S OUTCOMES

115

STATE OF THE NATION'S CHILDREN - IRELAND 2006

■ The number of hospitalisations for injuries and poisonings in children has decreased by 5.6% between 2000 and 2004.

■ There has been a decrease of 17.9% in hospitalisations due to road traffic accidents between 2000 and 2004.

■ Hospitalisation for accidental poisoning also shows a substantial decrease: the number of cases has decreased by 34.2% between 2000 and 2004.

Table 43: Hospitalisation number and percentage of children, by external cause (2000-2004)										
	2000		2001		2002		2003		2004	
	No.	%	No.	%	No.	%	No.	%	No.	%
Accidental falls	6,137	37.8	6,934	39.8	6,297	39.5	5,815	38.1	5,727	37.3
Accidents caused by objects*	3,254	20.1	3,455	19.8	3,367	21.1	3,259	21.4	3,432	22.4
Road traffic accidents	2,219	13.7	2,285	13.1	1,927	12.1	1,801	11.8	1,822	11.9
Deliberately inflicted injuries	927	5.7	948	5.4	823	5.2	779	5.1	723	4.7
Accidental poisonings	801	4.9	792	4.5	655	4.1	623	4.1	527	3.4
Accidents caused by submersion, suffocation and foreign bodies	446	2.7	429	2.5	432	2.7	445	2.9	386	2.5
Accidents caused by hot, caustic or corrosive substances and steam	307	1.9	324	1.9	256	1.6	263	1.7	259	1.7
Injury caused by animals or venomous animals and plants	179	1.1	198	1.1	174	1.1	157	1.0	189	1.2
Accidents caused by fire and flames	118	0.7	155	0.9	130	0.8	90	0.6	92	0.6
Complications of medical and surgical care	79	0.5	131	0.8	44	0.3	37	0.2	32	0.2
Other external causes	389	2.4	463	2.7	454	2.8	429	2.8	460	3.0
External cause not reported	1,369	8.4	1,315	7.5	1,373	8.6	1,549	10.2	1,704	11.1
Total	16,225	100.0	17,429	100.0	15,932	100.0	15,247	100.0	15,353	100.0

* Accidents caused by objects include striking against or being struck accidentally by objects or persons; caught accidentally in or between objects; accidents caused by machinery; and accidents caused by cutting/piercing objects.

Source: Hospital In-Patient Enquiry, Economic and Social Research Institute

Technical notes

The Hospital In-Patient Enquiry (HIPE) system is the source for the data supplied on the hospitalisation of children. The HIPE records data on in-patient and day case discharges from all publicly funded acute hospitals. The Economic and Social Research Institute (ESRI) is contracted by the Department of Health and Children to manage the HIPE system.

Coverage: HIPE data from 1995 onwards is estimated to be 95% complete. It covers 95% of all day case and in-patient discharges from publicly funded acute hospitals.

Coding: Diagnoses and procedures in HIPE are coded using the Clinical Modification of the 9th Revision of the International Classification of Diseases, known as ICD-9-CM. From 2005 onwards, HIPE has moved to the Australian modification of ICD-10 (ICD-10-AM). HIPE data record a principal diagnosis and up to 5 secondary diagnoses for data prior to 2002, and up to 9 secondary diagnoses from 2002 onwards. The data supplied are based on the principal diagnosis, with the exception of the external cause data. Where a patient has a principal diagnosis of injury or poisoning (ICD-9-CM 800-999), the external cause of the injury or poisoning should be recorded as an additional diagnosis. In some cases (approximately 10%), the cause of the injury or poisoning is not available to the coder and so is not recorded. The data supplied on external causes are based on the first recorded external cause in patients with a principal diagnosis of injury or poisoning.

Diagnoses: The diagnoses have been collated into main diagnosis chapters using the International Shortlist of Hospital Morbidity Tabulation. This shortlist has recently been accepted as the international standard by the EU and the World Health Organization. It was developed by an EU project led by the Irish Department of Health and Children, with the aim of improving the comparability of EU hospital discharge statistics.

It should be noted that ranking of principal conditions responsible for hospitalisation will depend on the level of detail provided by the shortlist. For present purposes, listing by high level chapters was felt to provide the most useful overview of broad clinical areas.

Data on the hospitalisation of children provide an important indication of the range of conditions affecting children which are serious enough to require hospital treatment. This data can also highlight differences between age groups and over time in population-based rates. Accidents are a very significant cause of serious illness in children and information on external causes of injury and poisoning, which is available in HIPE, can assist in identifying and targeting areas of high risk to children. Care must be taken, however, not to use hospitalisation rates as a proxy for incidence or prevalence of ill health in children. Rates are based on episodes of care such that an individual case will be counted separately in the statistics for each admission to hospital. In addition, hospital data will reflect changes in treatment protocols, as well as issues of access to care.

References

Children in Hospital Ireland (2000) *Update on Play Facilities Report.* Dublin: Children in Hospital Ireland.

Coyne, I., Hayes, E., Gallagher, P. and Regan, G. (2006) *Giving Children a Voice: An investigation of children's experiences of participation in consultation and decision-making within the Irish healthcare setting,* Office of the Minister for Children. Dublin: The Stationery Office.

Department of Health and Children (2001) *Quality and Fairness: A Health System for You.* Dublin: The Stationery Office.

Department of Health and Children (2005) *Numbers employed in the Public Health Service, December 2005.* Dublin: The Stationery Office.

Department of Health and Children (2006) *Report of the Joint Health Service Executive/ Department of Health and Children Task Group to advise on the optimum location of the new national paediatric hospital.* Dublin: The Stationery Office.

Fitzgerald, E. (2004) *Sick Children, Money Worries: The financial cost of a child in hospital.* Dublin: Children in Hospital Ireland.

Government of Ireland (2004) *Health Act.* Dublin: The Stationery Office.

NCO (2004) *Ready, Steady, Play! A National Play Policy,* National Children's Office. Dublin: The Stationery Office.

Disability

Context

The National Disability Authority (NDA) is an independent statutory agency established under the aegis of the Department of Justice, Equality and Law Reform by the National Disability Authority Act (Government of Ireland, 1999). It operates on behalf of the State to promote and help secure the rights of people with disabilities. It has published a number of guidelines and has a substantial database on all research undertaken on disability in Ireland. The NDA also helps to drive disability policy in Ireland, which has changed significantly in the last few years. Important publications in that regard include the *Report of the Commission on the Status of People with Disabilities* (Government of Ireland, 1996) and the more recent National Disability Strategy (Department of Justice, Equality and Law Reform, 2004).

The National Disability Strategy has four main components:
- the Disability Act (Government of Ireland, 2005a);
- the Comhairle (Amendment) Bill (Government of Ireland, 2004a), which provides for the establishment of a personal advocacy service;
- 6 outline sectoral plans published by 6 government departments, which set out actions to improve service provision and access to infrastructure by people with disability;
- a multi-annual investment programme for high-priority disability support services.

The Disability Act builds on existing legislation, including the Employment Equality Act (Government of Ireland, 1998), Equal Status Act (Government of Ireland, 2000), Equality Act (Government of Ireland, 2005b) and Education for Persons with Specific Educational Needs Act (Government of Ireland, 2004b). The Disability Act is a positive action measure designed to support the provision of disability-specific services to people with disabilities and to improve their access to mainstream public services. It provides a statutory basis for ensuring accessible public buildings and services.

Significance

The term 'disability' can mean different things to different people and the way in which it is defined and understood has implications for how people with disabilities are treated, the nature of service provision and the extent and type of legislation and policy that includes a disability focus (NDA, 2005). In Ireland, about 3% of children have a disability and, according to the 2002 Census, they represent less than 10% of people with disabilities. Boys are more likely to present with a disability than girls: in the 0-19 age group, about 16,000 boys were identified, compared with about 10,000 girls.

Disability is associated with social class. Data on children and young people show a higher incidence of disability where their parents report having unskilled occupations compared with those whose parents are working in skilled occupations or as managers. The extent to which services are required will depend on the type and nature of the disability in question. The prevalence of disability increases with age and this may be due to issues of acquired disability and also diagnosis.

The National Disability Survey, which is currently being undertaken by the Central Statistics Office, is based on the social model of disability and is coded to the WHO's International Classification of Functioning, Disability and Health.

Indicators reported on the following pages examine the number of children registered as having an intellectual disability and those having a physical or sensory disability.

Intellectual disability

Measure

> **The number of children under 18 years registered as having an intellectual disability, expressed as a proportion of all children. This can be subdivided by grade of disability: (a) mild; (b) moderate; (c) severe; and (d) profound.**

Key findings

- The number of children under 18 registered as having an intellectual disability has decreased from 7,960 in 2001 to 7,385 in 2005. This represents a decrease of 7.8% *(see Figure 24)*.

Figure 24: Number of children registered as having an intellectual disability (2001-2005)

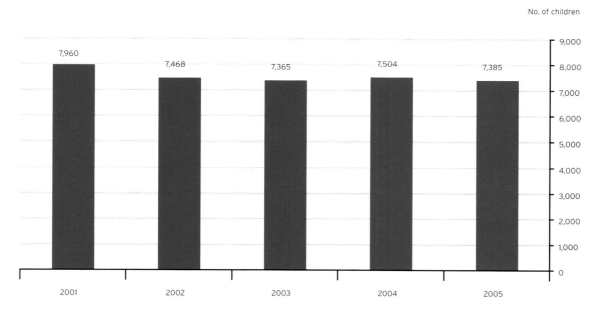

No. of children

Source: National Intellectual Disability Database, Health Research Board

- In 2005, 41% (3,013) of those registered on the National Intellectual Disability Database (NIDD) were identified as having a mild disability; 28% (2,098) as having a moderate disability; 11% (778) as having a severe disability; and 2% (151) as having a profound disability. The remaining 18% (1,345) were not verified *(see Figure 25)*.

PART 3: CHILDREN'S OUTCOMES

121

Figure 25: Number of children registered as having an intellectual disability, by severity of disability (2005)

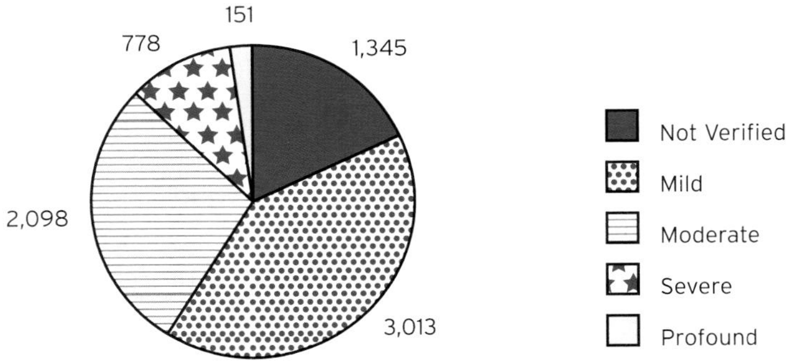

Source: National Intellectual Disability Database, Health Research Board

■ The number and rate of children registered as having an intellectual disability increases by age group *(see Table 44)*. In 2005, the rate (per 10,000) of children registered as having an intellectual disability was 37.9 per 10,000 children aged 0-4 and this increased to 103.6 per 10,000 children aged 15-17.

■ In 2005, 15.3% (1,127) of those registered on the NIDD were aged 0-4; 27.7% (2,049) were aged 5-9; 32.5% (2,400) were aged 10-14; and 24.5% (1,809) were aged 15-17.

Table 44: Number and rate (per 10,000) of children registered as having an intellectual disability, by age group (2005)

Years of age	Not verified	Mild	Moderate	Severe	Profound	No.	Rate
0-4	834	114	99	66	14	1,127	37.9
5-9	392	700	639	268	50	2,049	72.9
10-14	82	1178	812	270	58	2,400	87.4
15-17	37	1021	548	174	29	1,809	103.6
Total	1,345	3,013	2,098	778	151	7,385	71.8

Source: National Intellectual Disability Database, Health Research Board

■ In 2005, the rate (per 10,000) of children registered as having an intellectual disability varied according to gender, with 85.8 per 10,000 boys and just 57.2 per 10,000 girls registered as having an intellectual disability *(see Table 45)*.

■ Overall, 61.5% of children registered on the NIDD were boys. The only category of intellectual disability in which more girls than boys were registered was in the 'profound' category.

Table 45: Number and rate (per 10,000) of children registered as having an intellectual disability, by gender (2005)

	Not verified	Mild	Moderate	Severe	Profound	No.	Rate
Boys	817	1,875	1,294	466	71	4,523	85.8
Girls	528	1,138	804	312	80	2,862	57.2
Total	1,345	3,013	2,098	778	151	7,385	71.8

Source: National Intellectual Disability Database, Health Research Board

■ In 2005, 22.7% (1,675) of children registered as having an intellectual disability resided in Dublin, 10.6% (785) in Cork and 7.2% (531) in Galway *(see Table 46).*

County	2001	2002	2003	2004	2005	
Table 46: Number of children registered as having an intellectual disability, by county (2001-2005)						
	No.	No.	No.	No.	No.	%
Dublin	1,804	1,747	1,698	1,758	1,675	22.7
Cork	971	838	780	801	785	10.6
Galway	516	480	524	529	531	7.2
Limerick	424	366	362	360	334	4.5
Kerry	380	371	280	287	303	4.1
Kildare	256	253	278	292	285	3.9
Wexford	306	272	267	276	279	3.8
Wicklow	235	202	215	286	272	3.7
Donegal	291	284	284	254	261	3.5
Mayo	285	251	232	229	238	3.2
Meath	239	235	229	234	226	3.1
Louth	208	194	222	225	219	3.0
Tipperary SR	215	215	215	196	207	2.8
Clare	197	220	224	208	186	2.5
Waterford	219	213	193	179	177	2.4
Westmeath	124	118	135	152	161	2.2
Kilkenny	222	201	186	166	154	2.1
Carlow	126	134	136	142	143	1.9
Laois	132	113	135	138	139	1.9
Roscommon	131	126	125	137	144	1.9
Sligo	128	121	150	155	138	1.9
Offaly	129	127	113	109	125	1.7
Tipperary NR	150	131	115	119	112	1.5
Cavan	84	87	95	87	93	1.3
Monaghan	70	70	74	74	78	1.1
Leitrim	63	52	57	63	66	0.9
Longford	49	45	37	44	45	0.6
Other (incl. NI)	6	<5	<5	<5	9	0.1
State	**7,960**	**7,468**	**7,365**	**7,504**	**7,385**	**100.0**

Source: National Intellectual Disability Database, Health Research Board

Physical and sensory disability

Measure

> **The number of children under 18 years registered as having a physical or sensory disability, expressed as a proportion of all children.**

Key findings

- The number of children under 18 registered as having a physical and/or sensory disability has increased from 6,412 in 2004 to 7,039 in 2005 *(see Table 47)*. This increase may be due in part to increased coverage of the National Physical and Sensory Disability Database (NPSDD), which currently stands at an estimated 70%.
- In 2005, 71.7% of children under 18 registered as having a physical and/or sensory disability were boys and 28.3% were girls.
- In 2005, 10.7% of children under 18 registered as having a physical and/or sensory disability were 0-4 years; 39.9% were 5-9 years; 34.6% were 10-14 years; and 14.8% were 15-17 years.
- In 2005, 77.9% of children registered on the NPSDD were registered as having a physical disability.

Table 47: Number of children registered as having a physical or sensory disability, by age group and gender (2005)								
	Boys	Girls	0-4	5-9	10-14	15-17	Total No.	Total %
Physical	3,451	2,034	537	2,216	1,925	807	5,485	77.9
Hearing loss/Deafness	225	225	24	136	187	103	450	6.4
Visual	115	113	28	56	81	63	228	3.2
Physical and Hearing loss/Deafness	92	49	11	72	37	21	141	2.0
Physical and Visual	56	40	6	33	42	15	96	1.4
Hearing loss/Deafness and Visual	5	12	<5	6	8	<5	17	0.2
Physical, Hearing loss/Deafness and Visual	20	19	6	18	11	<5	39	<1.0
'Primary Speech and Language'	207	93	40	175	77	8	300	4.3
'Physical & Primary Speech and Language'	95	55	48	51	44	7	150	2.1
'Hearing & Primary Speech and Language'	26	17	18	16	6	<5	43	<1.0
'Visual & Primary Speech and Language'	<5	<5	<5	<5	<5	<5	<5	<1.0
'Physical & Hearing & Primary Speech and Language'	10	<5	<5	7	<5	<5	14	0.2
'Physical & Visual & Primary Speech and Language'	40	30	28	19	14	9	70	1.0
'Hearing & Visual & Primary Speech and Language'	<5	<5	<5	<5	<5	<5	<5	<1.0
'Physical & Hearing & Visual & Primary Speech and Language'	<5	<5	<5	<5	<5	<5	<5	<1.0
Refused	<5	<5	<5	<5	<5	<5	<5	<1.0
Total	4,343	2,696	754	2,808	2,435	1,042	7,039	100.0

Source: National Physical and Sensory Disability Database, Health Research Board

■ In 2005, 20.4% (1,438) of children registered as having a physical and/or sensory disability resided in Cork, 13.1% (921) in Dublin and 6.5% (460) in Galway *(see Table 48)*.

County	2004		2005	
	No.	%	No.	%
Carlow	81	1.3	78	1.1
Dublin Co. Borough	277	4.3	310	4.4
South Dublin	534	8.3	604	8.6
Fingal	<5	<1.0	<5	<1.0
Dun Laoghaire – Rathdown	<5	0.1	<5	0.1
Kildare	310	4.8	356	5.1
Kilkenny	226	3.5	214	3.0
Laois	141	2.2	152	2.2
Longford	71	1.1	70	1.0
Louth	206	3.2	196	2.8
Meath	236	3.7	229	3.3
Offaly	156	2.4	151	2.1
Westmeath	188	2.9	202	2.9
Wexford	218	3.4	204	2.9
Wicklow	23	0.4	26	0.4
Clare	190	3.0	232	3.3
Cork Co. Borough	359	5.6	436	6.2
Cork County	886	13.8	1,002	14.2
Kerry	268	4.2	325	4.6
Limerick Co. Borough (Limerick city)	83	1.3	92	1.3
Limerick County	193	3.0	199	2.8
Tipperary NR	87	1.4	104	1.5
Tipperary SR	130	2.0	127	1.8
Waterford Co. Borough (Waterford city)	79	1.2	70	1.0
Waterford County	100	1.6	96	1.4
Galway Co. Borough (Galway city)	79	1.2	99	1.4
Galway County	263	4.1	361	5.1
Leitrim	42	0.7	39	0.6
Mayo	371	5.8	418	5.9
Roscommon	109	1.7	126	1.8
Sligo	98	1.5	94	1.3
Cavan	79	1.2	101	1.4
Donegal	248	3.9	234	3.3
Monaghan	74	1.2	85	1.2
Total	6,412	100.0	7,039	100.0

Table 48: Number of children registered as having a physical or sensory disability, by county (2004-2005)

Source: National Physical and Sensory Disability Database, Health Research Board

PART 3: CHILDREN'S OUTCOMES

127

Technical notes

The **National Intellectual Disability Database (NIDD)** was established in 1995 to provide a comprehensive and accurate information base for decision-making in relation to the planning, funding and management of services for people with an intellectual disability. There is 100% coverage on this database of people accessing services.

The NIDD was established on the principle that minimum information with maximum accuracy was preferred; hence it incorporates only three basic elements of information: demographic details, current service provision and future service requirements. The objective is to obtain this information for every individual known to have an intellectual disability and assessed as being in receipt of, or in need of, an intellectual disability service. Information pertaining to diagnosis is specifically excluded since the database is not designed as a medical, epidemiological tool. The data held in any individual record represent the information available for that person at a specified point in time only. The record is updated whenever there are changes in the person's circumstances or during the annual review process in the spring of each year. The HSE is responsible for the administration of the NIDD and the Health Research Board (HRB), on behalf of the Department of Health and Children, manages the national dataset. The HRB oversees a system of ongoing validation, which aims to identify and correct gaps and inconsistencies in the data.

The **National Physical and Sensory Disability Database (NPSDD)** started in 2001 with the objective of gathering information on the specialised health and personal social service needs of people with a physical or sensory disability. The NPSDD monitors current service provision and future service requirements over a 5-year period. It will be used for planning service developments, prioritising service needs and assisting in resource allocation decisions at national, regional and local level. Currently, there is approximately 68% coverage on this database of people who access services.

Information is collected from people with a physical and/or sensory disability who are receiving, or who need, a specialised health or personal social service currently or within the next 5 years. Information is collected and recorded up until an individual's 66th birthday.

In general, where people with profound, severe or moderate intellectual disabilities who also have physical or sensory disabilities, they are more appropriately registered on the NIDD and consequently should not be included on the NPSDD. If it is felt that a case is not as clear-cut as this, it is recommended that a description of the case is recorded and made known to the Resource Officers at the NIDD.

References

Department of Justice, Equality and Law Reform (2004) *National Disability Strategy.* Dublin: The Stationery Office.

Government of Ireland (1996) *Report of the Commission on the Status of People with Disabilities.* Dublin: The Stationery Office.

Government of Ireland (1998) E*mployment Equality Act.* Dublin: The Stationery Office.

Government of Ireland (1999) *National Disability Authority Act.* Dublin: The Stationery Office.

Government of Ireland (2000) *Equal Status Act.* Dublin: The Stationery Office.

Government of Ireland (2004a) *Comhairle (Amendment) Bill.* Dublin: The Stationery Office.

Government of Ireland (2004b) *Education for Persons with Specific Educational Needs Act.* Dublin: The Stationery Office.

Government of Ireland (2005a) *Disability Act.* Dublin: The Stationery Office.

Government of Ireland (2005b) *Equality Act.* Dublin: The Stationery Office.

NDA (2005) *Measuring Health and Disability in Europe* (MHADIE). Dublin: National Disability Authority.

Further information

- Health Research Board (www.hrb.ie)
- National Disability Authority (www.nda.ie)
- Central Statistics Office (www.cso.ie/nds)

PART 3: CHILDREN'S OUTCOMES

Abuse and neglect

Context

Up to the mid-1990s, child abuse in Ireland tended to be defined in terms of omissions or assaults committed against children by their parents and within the family unit. However, during the past decade, a concern also emerged about the risk to children (including 'out of home' children living in official residential care settings) from people outside their families, including those in highly respected and authoritative positions in traditional institutions. Ireland has now come through a period of unprecedented inquiry in terms of child abuse, culminating in the recent publication of the *Report of the Ferns Inquiry* (Department of Health and Children, 2005). This document described the failure of those in positions of trust in one Diocese to take effective steps to defend and vindicate the rights of the children concerned.

The United Nations Convention on the Rights of the Child explicitly recognises children's rights to be protected from abuse, neglect and exploitation (UN, 1989). This Convention was ratified by Ireland in 1992. The main legislation governing the care and protection of children is the Child Care Act (Government of Ireland, 1991), which places a statutory duty on the HSE to promote the welfare of children who are not receiving adequate care and protection. In addition, it enables the immediate intervention of the HSE or An Garda Síochána in situations where children are in danger and also enables the Courts to place children who have been abused or who are at risk in the care of, or under the supervision of, the HSE.

Reporting of suspected child abuse in Ireland is not mandatory in the legal sense. All organisations, however, providing services to children are now obliged to develop and disseminate child-protection policies that are consistent with the *Children First: National Guidelines for the Protection and Welfare of Children* (Department of Health and Children, 1999). These guidelines were introduced to assist people in identifying and reporting child maltreatment, which is categorised into four different types: neglect, emotional abuse, physical abuse and sexual abuse.

Any suspected child maltreatment is reportable to An Garda Síochána. A Central Garda Vetting Unit was established in January 2002. Currently, this unit deals with more than 100,000 requests per annum. It is intended to extend vetting to a wide range of staff working with children in the near future. In addition, the joint Health Service Executive/Garda training in child protection is ongoing and a joint protocol has been developed to facilitate collaborative working between the two organisations.

The Protections for Persons Reporting Child Abuse Act (Government of Ireland, 1998a) provides immunity from civil liability to any person who reports child abuse 'reasonably and in good faith', as well as protection for employees who report child abuse. Further legislative protection is provided for in the Child Trafficking and Pornography Act (Government of Ireland, 1998b) and the Sex Offenders Act (Government of Ireland, 2001).

Significance

Abuse and neglect can have life-long consequences and there is consistent evidence that child maltreatment both undermines child well-being in childhood and increases vulnerability to a wide range of problems in later life (Hooper, 2002). For example, the effects of abuse on brain development (Teicher, 2000) and cognitive ability (Leach, 1999) are beginning to be recognised, and reported maltreatment has been found associated with reduced school attendance and performance (Sullivan and Knutson, 2000).

Other problems include mental health problems, low self-esteem and difficulties with interpersonal relationships, including parenting (Ferguson and McNamara, 1996; Bifulco and Moran, 1998). A recent Irish study reported that those with a history of two or more forms of childhood adversity (including physical, emotional and sexual abuse) were five times more likely to have depressed moods and more than three times more likely to report suicide ideation (Corcoran *et al,* 2006). Research suggests that physical abuse and neglect are more prevalent among lower socio-economic groups, while sexual and emotional abuse occurs fairly evenly across classes (Hooper, 2002). Furthermore, research in Ireland demonstrates that physical abuse and child sexual abuse receive a more assertive response than neglect (Buckley *et al,* 1997; Buckley, 2002). This is generally linked with the difficulty in labelling certain types of parenting as neglect because of their link with adversities such as addiction, domestic violence, mental illness and poverty. There is increasing awareness of the impact of domestic violence on children and the fact that living with domestic violence is now considered to be emotional abuse (Buckley *et al,* 2006).

Gilligan (1991 and 2000) suggests that both primary and secondary prevention need to take place in the area of child abuse, where primary prevention seeks to prevent the actual occurrence of problems and secondary prevention seeks to reduce their impact by early intervention. An evaluation of the Stay Safe Programme in the Irish context identified positive secondary preventive outcomes (MacIntyre and Carr 1999). Similarly, the evaluation by McKeown (2001) of Springboard, the Family Support Programme, demonstrates the positive impact of family support on parenting.

The indicators on the following pages examine the number of assessed and substantiated notifications of child abuse and neglect.

Child abuse and neglect assessments

Measure

> **The number of children assessed through the Child Protection Notification System, expressed as a proportion of all children.**

Key findings

- There were 6,188 children assessed by the former health board areas (now the HSE) for child welfare and protection concerns in 2004 *(see Table 49)*. This represents a rate of 61 per 10,000 children under the age of 18.
- Since 2000, there has been an inconsistent decrease in this number, from 8,269 cases to 6,188 cases.
- In 2004, the former Midland Health Board recorded the highest number of assessed cases (1,564), while the former North-Western Health Board recorded the lowest number (301).

Table 49: Number of child welfare and protection concerns assessed by the former health board areas (2000-2004)					
	2000	2001	2002	2003	2004
Midland Health Board	867	179	1,849	1,573	1,564
Eastern Regional Health Authority	1,565	1,574	1,891	1,624	1,301
South-Eastern Health Board	2,028	1,410	1,041	540	887
Southern Health Board	707	845	879	666	794
Western Health Board	807	748	777	631	540
Mid-Western Health Board	695	433	555	433	448
North-Eastern Health Board	1,277	409	1,037	556	353
North-Western Health Board	323	396	392	313	301
State	8,269	5,994	8,421	6,336	6,188
Rate per 10,000	81	59	83	62	61

Source: Childcare Interim Dataset, Department of Health and Children

Differences by type of concern

- In 2004, 34% (1,791) of children were assessed for neglect; 20% (1,081) for physical abuse; 28% (1,476) for sexual abuse; and 18% (942) for emotional abuse *(see Figure 26)*.
- Taken together, assessments for neglect and emotional abuse accounted for 52% (2,733) of all assessments undertaken in 2004.

Figure 26: Number of assessments according to the type of concern (2004)

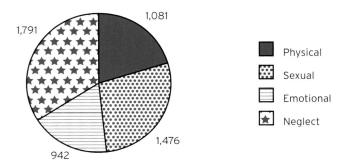

1,791
1,081
942
1,476

■ Physical
▦ Sexual
▤ Emotional
★ Neglect

Source: Childcare Interim Dataset, Department of Health and Children

PART 3: CHILDREN'S OUTCOMES

133

Substantiated child abuse and neglect

Measure

> **The number of children subject to substantiated notification,
> expressed as a proportion of all children.**

Key findings

- In 2004, there were 1,425 substantiated notifications to the Child Protection Notification System *(see Table 50)*. This represents a rate of 14 per 10,000 children under the age of 18 *(see Figure 27)*. In the national statistical system, substantiated cases are those in which an allegation of maltreatment or risk of maltreatment was supported following an investigation.
- Between 2000 and 2004, the number of substantiated notifications to the Child Protection Notification System has decreased, from 3,085 to 1,425.
- In 2004, the former Eastern Regional Health Authority recorded the highest number of substantiated notifications (407), while the former North-Western Health Board recorded the lowest number (10).

Table 50: Number of substantiated notifications to the Child Protection Notification System, by former health board area (2000-2004)

	2000	2001	2002	2003	2004
Eastern Regional Health Authority	633	550	633	417	407
Midland Health Board	186	67	272	448	287
Western Health Board	342	296	168	248	270
South-Eastern Health Board	909	342	179	368	173
North-Eastern Health Board	494	168	103	142	140
Mid-Western Health Board	305	254	217	185	98
Southern Health Board	173	155	44	84	40
North-Western Health Board	43	28	17	21	10
State	3,085	1,860	1,633	1,913	1,425
Rate per 10,000	30	18	16	19	14

Source: Childcare Interim Dataset, Department of Health and Children

Figure 27: Number of substantiated notifications to the Child Protection Notification System, rate per 10,000 children (2000-2004)

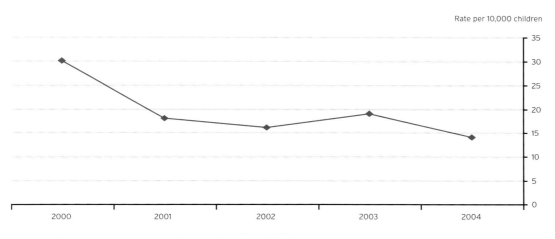

Source: Childcare Interim Dataset, Department of Health and Children

Differences by type of concern

- In 2004, of all substantiated notifications to the Child Protection Notification System, 15% (212) suffered sexual abuse; 19% (271) suffered physical abuse; 24% (335) suffered emotional abuse; and 42% (596) suffered neglect *(see Figure 28)*.

Figure 28: Number of substantiated concerns, by type of abuse and neglect (2004)

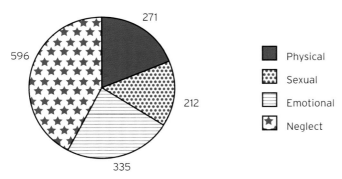

■ Physical
▦ Sexual
▤ Emotional
★ Neglect

Source: Childcare Interim Dataset, Department of Health and Children

- The number of substantiated cases of child abuse and neglect decreased from 3,085 in 2000 to 1,860 in 2001 *(see Table 51)*. Since that time, the number of substantiated cases has ranged between 1,425 (2004) and 1,913 (2003).

Table 51: Number of substantiated assessments to the Child Protection Notification System (2000-2004)					
	2000	**2001**	**2002**	**2003**	**2004**
Assessments	8,269	5,994	8,421	6,336	6,188
Substantiated	3,085	1,860	1,633	1,913	1,425

Source: Childcare Interim Dataset, Department of Health and Children

Technical notes

Some caution should be adopted when comparing across the former health board areas of the HSE because of differences in the way in which cases are recorded. Work is currently taking place on the development of consistent approaches across the HSE areas.

Both the number of assessed child welfare concerns and the number of substantiated reports of child abuse and neglect are important measures of the incidence of child abuse and neglect in Ireland. It should be noted, however, that these rates are affected by a number of factors other than the actual incidence of abuse and neglect, and some caution is thus required in drawing conclusions concerning the overall prevalence of abuse and neglect for the following reasons. First, some cases of abuse and neglect are never reported. Secondly, some incidents are reported more than once and several reports may relate to a single family. Thirdly, reports tend to increase for reasons unrelated to the actual prevalence of abuse and neglect, such as a highly publicised case or public awareness campaign. In addition, sufficient evidence may not be available to 'substantiate' the report and at times statistics reflect the different organisational arrangements for collecting data and the different definitions and thresholds that operate across regions.

References

Bifulco, A. and Moran, P. (1998) *Wednesday's Child: Research into women's experience of neglect and abuse in childhood, and adult depression.* London: Routledge Press.

Buckley, H. (1999) 'Child Protection', in *Child Poverty: Issues and Solutions.* Dublin: EAPN Ireland.

Buckley, H. (2002) *Child Protection: Innovations and Interventions.* Dublin: Institute of Public Administration.

Buckley, H., Skehill, C. and O'Sullivan, E. (1997) *Child Protection Practices in Ireland: A Case Study.* Dublin: Oak Tree Press.

Buckley, H., Whelan, S. and Holt, S. (2006) *Listen to Me! Children's Experience of Domestic Violence.* Dublin: Children's Research Centre, University of Dublin, Trinity College.

Corcoran, P., Gallagher, J., Keeley, H.S., Arensman, E. and Perry, I.J. (2006) 'Adverse Childhood Experiences and Lifetime Suicide Ideation: A cross-sectional study in a non-psychiatric hospital setting', *Irish Medical Journal,* Vol. 99, No. 2, pp. 42-45.

Department of Health and Children (1999) *Children First: National Guidelines for the Protection and Welfare of Children.* Dublin: The Stationery Office.

Department of Health and Children (2005) *Report of the Ferns Inquiry.* Dublin: The Stationery Office.

Ferguson, H. and McNamara, T. (eds.) (1996) *Protecting Irish Children: Investigation, Protection and Welfare.* Dublin: Institute of Public Administration.

Gilligan R. (1991) *Irish Childcare Services: Policy, Practice and Provision.* Dublin: Institute of Public Administration.

Gilligan, R. (2000) 'Family Support: Issues and Prospects', in *Family Support: Direction from Diversity,* J. Canavan, P. Dolan and J. Pinkerton (eds.). London: Jessica Kingsley.

Government of Ireland (1991) *Child Care Act.* Dublin: The Stationery Office.

Government of Ireland (1998a) *Protections for Persons Reporting Child Abuse Act.* Dublin: The Stationery Office.

Government of Ireland (1998b) *Child Trafficking and Pornography Act.* Dublin: The Stationery Office.

Government of Ireland (2001) *Sex Offenders Act.* Dublin: The Stationery Office.

Hooper, C.A. (2002) 'Maltreatment of Children', in *The Well-Being of Children in the UK,* J. Bradshaw (ed.). York: Save the Children, pp. 103-21.

Leach, P. (1999) 'The Physical Punishment of Children: Some input from recent research', *Journal of Child Centred Practice,* Vol. 7, No. 2, pp. 17-58.

MacIntyre, D. and Carr, A. (1999) 'Helping Children to the Other Side of Silence: A study of the impact of the Stay Safe Programme on Irish children's disclosures of sexual victimization', Child Abuse and Neglect, Vol. 23, No. 12, pp. 1327-40.

McKeown, K. (2001) *Promoting Family Well-being through Family Support Services,* Department of Health and Children. Dublin: The Stationery Office.

Sullivan, P.M. and Knutson, J.F. (2000) 'The Prevalence of Disabilities and Maltreatment among Runaway Youth', *Child Abuse and Neglect,* Vol. 24, pp. 1275-88.

Teicher, M.H. (2000) 'Wounds that time won't heal: The neurobiology of child abuse', *Cerebrum,* Vol. 4, No. 2, pp. 50-67.

UN (1989) *Convention on the Rights of the Child.* Geneva: United Nations Office of the High Commissioner for Human Rights. Available at www.ohchr.org

PART 3: CHILDREN'S OUTCOMES

SOCIAL, EMOTIONAL
AND BEHAVIOURAL OUTCOMES

PARTICIPATION IN DECISION-MAKING

Participation in making the school rules

Context

Article 12 of the United Nations Convention on the Rights of the Child notes that 'State Parties shall assure to the child who is capable of forming his or her own views the right to express those views freely in all matters affecting the child, the view of the child being given due weight in accordance with the age and maturity of the child' (UN, 1989).

The National Children's Strategy (Department of Health and Children, 2000) states that giving children a voice means:
■ encouraging children to express their views and demonstrating a willingness to take those views seriously;
■ setting out clearly for children the scope of such participation by them to avoid misunderstanding;
■ providing children with sufficient information and support to enable them to express informed views;
■ explaining the decisions taken, especially when the views of the child cannot be fully taken into account.

The Office of the Minister for Children (OMC) has responsibility for ensuring the implementation of Article 12 of the UN Convention and a number of initiatives to improve structures for children and young people to participate are being implemented, including:
■ Comhairle na nÓg;
■ Dáil na nÓg;
■ the Student Council Working Group;
■ guidelines on participation by children and young people;
■ establishment of an OMC Child and Youth Forum;
■ supporting the Young Social Innovators Exhibition;
■ supporting RTE *News2Day.*

The indicator reported here refers only to participation in making the school rules. Section 27 of the Education Act (Government of Ireland, 1998) established the right of students to be informed about their school's activities and also established the right to form and be supported in running student councils in both primary and post-primary schools. The purpose of Section 27 of the Education Act was to ensure that school boards would be responsible for helping students to become involved in the operation of the school. School boards were directed to facilitate the students to establish and maintain student councils. The boards draw up the rules governing the establishment of the student councils, but the students, following consultation with the boards, create the rules governing the meetings. In 2002, the Department of Education and Science published guidelines to provide practical guidance to students, teachers and school management in the establishment and operation of student councils (Department of Education and Science, 2002).

Significance

Student participation in school decision-making is important in its own right and also in preparing children and young people to participate fully in society. Effective student participation in school decision-making contributes to the improvement of school practices, the promotion of citizenship and the personal and social education and development of students (Csikszentmihalyi and Rathunde, 1992). Effective participation in decision-making creates opportunities for children and young people to increase their influence over what happens to them and around them (Education Review Office, 2003), and has immediate and long-term benefits for both students and schools.

For students, participation in decision-making at school can motivate students by showing them that their views are valued by school staff (Kohn, 1993); allow the voicing of a wide range of student views (Treseder and Crowley, 2001); allow more successful learning since students are involved in decisions about what and how to learn, in setting learning goals and in setting school rules (Alderson, 2002); provide an empowering experience and assist in building confidence and self-esteem (Doddington *et al,* 2000); and facilitate a wider recognition of increasing independence (Lansdown, 1995).

For schools, student participation in decision-making can lead to improved school policies and practices; support the successful development and implementation of school initiatives; strengthen democratic processes within the school; improve students' behaviour within, and contribution to, school and community environments (Rafferty, 1997); facilitate better relationships between students, teachers, parents and the wider community (Doddington *et al,* 2000); and improve understanding of and responsiveness to issues identified by students (Rafferty, 1997).

A recent study by Keogh and Whyte (2005), commissioned by the Office of the Minister for Children, investigated the barriers, enablers and supports to the development and operation of student councils in second-level schools. Findings showed some differences in the stakeholders' perspectives: while students understood student councils as having an active role in making the school a better place, managers understood them as a mechanism for facilitating communication between staff and students, and of assisting in the organisation of events.

PART 3: CHILDREN'S OUTCOMES

141

Measure

> ## The proportion of children aged 10-17
> ## who report students at their school participate in making the school rules.

Key findings

■ In 2002, 23.5% of children aged 10-17 reported that students in their school participate in making the school rules. This represents a decrease from the results in 1998, when 32.5% of children reported this *(see Table 52)*.

Differences by age, social class and gender
■ With the exception of 10-11 year-old children, boys report higher rates of participation in making the school rules than girls.
■ The percentage of children reporting that students in their school participate in making the school rules was higher among children from lower social classes.

Table 52: Percentage of children who report that students at their school participate in making the school rules, by age, social class and gender (1998 and 2002)						
	1998			2002		
	Boys	Girls	Total	Boys	Girls	Total
Total	34.0	31.0	32.5	25.0	22.4	23.5
Years of age						
10-11	38.2	40.6	39.5	33.7	38.0	36.0
12-14	35.4	33.0	34.2	27.9	23.9	25.6
15-17	29.3	20.1	24.7	15.5	13.9	14.6
Social class						
SC 1-2	30.5	27.3	28.8	23.4	20.3	21.5
SC 3-4	34.8	32.2	33.6	26.5	21.3	23.5
SC 5-6	36.5	32.2	34.2	26.8	26.9	26.8

Source: HBSC Survey

Differences by geographical area
■ In 2002, children in the former Midland Health Board area were most likely (29.6%) to report that students at their school participate in making the school rules, while children in the former South-Eastern Health Board area were least likely (20.9%) to report this *(see Table 53)*.

Table 53: Percentage of children aged 10-17 who report that students at their school participate in making the school rules, by former health board area (1998 and 2002)

	1998	2002
Midland Health Board	32.3	29.6
Western Health Board	37.1	25.7
North-Eastern Health Board	29.5	25.0
Eastern Regional Health Authority	34.9	23.0
Mid-Western Health Board	34.9	22.3
North-Western Health Board	32.3	22.3
Southern Health Board	31.1	21.7
South-Eastern Health Board	26.6	20.9
Mean average	32.5	23.5

Source: HBSC Survey

International comparisons

■ From the 2002 HBSC Survey, using the ages of 11, 13 and 15 only to draw international comparisons, 23.5% of Irish children reported that students at their school participate in making the school rules *(see Figure 29).* The HBSC average was 36.1%.

■ Among all 14 countries that used this HBSC item, the lowest percentage for this indicator was found among Belgian (Flemish) children (23.1%) and the highest among Estonian children (57.2%).

■ Overall, Irish children had the 2nd lowest reported level of participation in making the school rules (23.5%). Irish 11-year-old children were ranked 12th, Irish 13-year-old children were ranked 11th and Irish 15-year-old children were ranked 13th among the 14 countries that used this item.

Figure 29: Percentage of children who report that students at their school participate in making the school rules, by country (2002)

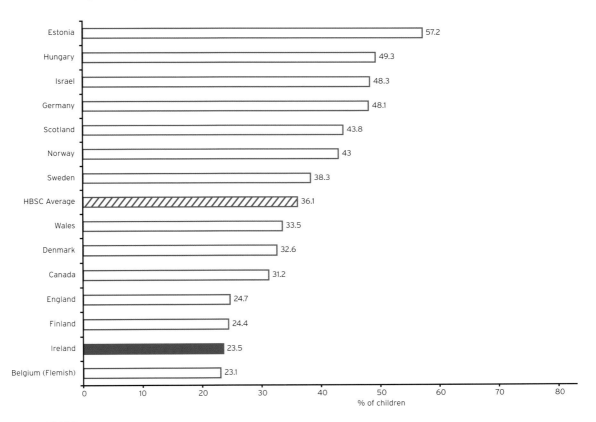

Source: HBSC Survey

Technical notes

The indicator presented here is one of an index and as such is less comprehensive than the full index. In addition, the HBSC uses a self-completion questionnaire that is prone to various biases, in particular for this indicator a social desirability bias.

Percentage differences are presented for descriptive purposes only and may not reflect a statistically significant finding.

References

Alderson, P. (2002) *Civil Rights in Schools.* London: National Children's Bureau and Barnardos.

Bond, L.A.E. and Compas, B.E.E. (1989) *Primary Prevention and Promotion in the Schools.* Newbury Park, CA: Sage.

Csikszentmihalyi, H. and Rathunde, K. (1992) 'The Measurement of Flow in Everyday Life: Toward a Theory of Emergent Motivation', *Nebraska Symposium on Motivation,* No. 40, pp. 57-97.

Department of Education and Science (2002) *Student Councils: A Voice for Students.* Dublin: The Stationery Office.

Department of Health and Children (2000) *The National Children's Strategy: Our Children – Their Lives.* Dublin: The Stationery Office.

Doddington, C., Flutter, J. and Ruddock, J. (2000) 'Taking their word for it: Can listening, and responding, to pupils' views give new directions for school improvement?', *Education,* Vol. 28, No. 3, pp. 46-51.

Education Review Office (2003). *Student Participation in School Decision-making. National Report.* Wellington, New Zealand: Education Review Office.

Government of Ireland (1998) *Education Act.* Dublin: The Stationery Office.

Keogh, F. and Whyte, J. (2005) *Second-level Student Councils in Ireland: A Study of Enablers, Barriers and Supports,* Office of the Minister for Children. Dublin: The Stationery Office.

Kohn, A. (1993) 'Choices for Children: Why and how to let students decide', *Phi Delta Kappan,* Vol. 75, No. 1, pp. 8-20.

Lansdown, G. (1995) *Taking Part: Children's participation in decision-making.* London: Institute for Public Policy Research.

Rafferty, S. (1997) *Giving Children a Voice – What Next? A study from one primary school.* Edinburgh: Scottish Council for Research in Education.

Treseder, P. and Crowley, A. (2001) *Taking the Initiative: Promoting young people's participation in decision-making in Wales.* London: Carnegie Young People Initiative.

UN (1989) *Convention on the Rights of the Child.* Geneva: United Nations Office of the High Commissioner for Human Rights. Available at www.ohchr.org

PART 3: CHILDREN'S OUTCOMES

145

Reading as a leisure activity

Context

Reading is considered a positive leisure activity. The *Consultation Document for a National Recreation Policy for Young People in Ireland* identified reading as an important recreational activity (NCO, 2005). The Department of the Environment, Heritage and Local Government has responsibility at central level for library services and provides grants for new public library developments. Publicly funded libraries aim to be fully accessible and to make themselves special places for children (An Comhairle Leabharlanna, 1998). They provide a range of specialised services for children, designed to encourage reading and access to both information and cultural activities, which may include story telling, competitions, exhibitions, school visits and children's book festivals. A range of other partners (including Children's Books Ireland, School Library Association, Reading Association of Ireland and Poetry Ireland) are also involved in supporting and promoting children's reading. In 2002, almost 300,000 children aged up to 14 were registered with a public library and facilities and services for children were rated by 89% of users as 'good' or 'very good' (Library Council, 2002).

Significance

Reading is often conceptualised as an academic skill, essential for full participation in society and economic and social development (Schinke *et al*, 2000). Eivers *et al* (2005) found that most 5th class pupils reported that they were able to read independently between the ages of 5 and 6. Children from lower socio-economic backgrounds, however, have been found to read less (Larson and Verma, 1999; De Roiste and Dineen, 2005) and reading has also been associated with parental education and job status (McHale *et al*, 2001). Girls tend to report more reading activity and reading for pleasure than boys (Posner and Vandell, 1999; De Roiste and Dineen, 2005). Although reading difficulties among children appear relatively persistent over time (Shaywitz *et al*, 1999; Svensson and Jacobson, 2006), examples of successful interventions are available (Shiel *et al*, 1998; Schinke *et al*, 2000).

De Roiste and Dineen (2005) reported that more than 50% of the 12-18 year-olds they surveyed read in their free time 'every' or 'most' days. Among primary school pupils, Eivers *et al* (2005) found that 58% of 1st class pupils reported borrowing books from a public library, while 88.7% reported reading books for fun on every or some days of the week. For 5th class pupils, 46.7% reported borrowing books from a public library a few times per month or more frequently, while 83.1% reported reading stories or novels at home a few times per month or more often.

Reading as a hobby bestows a range of benefits on children and adolescents, as well as adults. Reading is one method of socialisation for children and exposes them to the cultural and artistic facets of their communities. For example, reading appears to influence the ease with which a second or third language is learned (Van der Leij and Morfidi, 2006) and has been associated

146

with adult creativity (Simonton, 1994). Time spent reading is predictive of academic attainment and achievement (Cosgrove *et al*, 2005; Allen *et al*, 1992; McHale *et al*, 2001), although it has been suggested that those who believe themselves to be more academic or less sporting may spend their time reading rather than engage in other leisure activities (McHale *et al*, 2001).

Measure

> **The proportion of children aged 15 who report that reading is one of their favourite hobbies.**

Key findings

■ In 2000, 35.7% of children aged 15 reported that reading was one of their favourite hobbies *(see Table 54).*

Differences by age, social class and gender
■ The percentage of children who reported that reading was one of their favourite hobbies was higher among girls and among children from higher social classes:
   - 48.2% of girls reported this, compared to 22.9% of boys;
   - 40.7% of children from the highest social class category reported this, compared to 30.8% and 35.0% of children from the lowest and medium social class categories respectively *(see Table 54).*

Table 54: Percentage of children aged 15 who report that reading is one of their favourite hobbies, by gender, social class and area (2000)	
Total	35.7
Gender	
Boys	22.9
Girls	48.2
Social class	
High SES	40.7
Medium SES	35.0
Low SES	30.8
Area	
Village, hamlet or rural area (population <3,000)	34.2
Town (population 3,000 to about 15,000)	39.5
Large town/small city (population 15,000 to about 100,000)	37.5
Large city (population 100,000 to 1,000,000)	30.3
Close to Dublin city centre	32.9
Elsewhere in Dublin city	35.7

Source: PISA Survey

Differences by geographical area

■ Children living in large cities other than Dublin were least likely (30.3%) to report that reading was one of their favourite hobbies, while children living in towns were most likely (39.5%) to report this.

International comparisons

■ From the 2000 PISA Survey, 35.7% of Irish children reported that reading was one of their favourite hobbies *(see Figure 30)*. This was close to the OECD average of 35.4%.

■ Among all 27 countries that used this PISA item, the lowest percentage for this indicator was found among Norwegian children (24.1%) and the highest among Mexican children (61.6%). Irish children ranked 9th.

Figure 30: Percentage of children aged 15 who report that reading is one of their favourite hobbies, by country (2000)

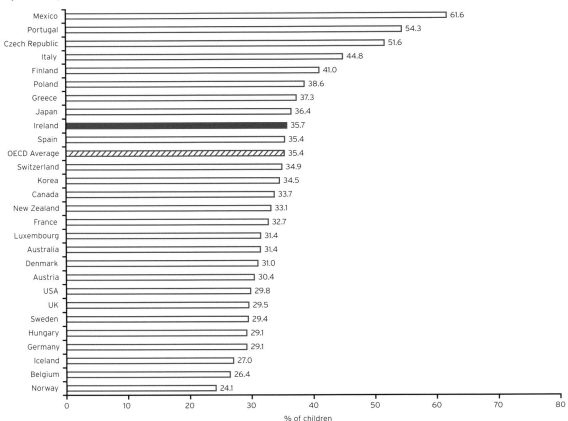

Source: PISA Survey

Technical notes

The data presented are based on self-report and may be subject to self-presentation bias. They were collected in 2000 as part of the PISA Survey and thus may not reflect the current picture of Irish children's reading.

Percentage differences are presented for descriptive purposes only and may not reflect a statistically significant finding.

References

Allen, L., Cipielewski, J. and Stanovich, K.E. (1992) 'Multiple Indicators of Children's Reading Habits and Attitudes: Construct Validity and Cognitive Correlates', *Journal of Educational Psychology,* No. 84, pp. 489-503.

An Comhairle Leabharlanna (1998) *Branching Out: A New Public Library Service,* Department of Environment and Local Government. Dublin: The Stationery Office.

Cosgrove, J., Shiel, G., Sofroniou, S., Zastrutski, S. and Shortt, F. (2005) *Education for Life: The Achievements of 15-year-olds in Ireland in the Second Cycle of PISA.* Dublin: Educational Research Centre.

De Roiste, A. and Dineen, J. (2005) *Young people's views about opportunities, barriers and supports to recreation and leisure,* National Children's Office. Dublin: The Stationery Office.

Eivers, E., Shiel, G., Perkins, R. and Cosgrove, J. (2005) *The 2004 National Assessment of English Reading.* Dublin: Educational Research Centre.

Larson, R. and Verma, S. (1999) 'How Children and Adolescents spend time across the world: Work, play and developmental opportunities', *Psychological Bulletin,* No. 126, pp. 701-36.

Library Council (2002) *Public Library Authority Statistics.* Dublin: The Library Council.

McHale, S.M., Crouter, A.C. and Tucker, C.J. (2001) 'Free-time Activities in Middle Childhood: Links with adjustment in early adolescence', *Child Development,* Vol. 72, No. 6, pp. 1764-78.

NCO (2005) *Consultation Document for a Recreation Policy for Young People in Ireland,* National Children's Office. Dublin: The Stationery Office.

Posner, J.K. and Vandell, D.L. (1999) 'After School Activities and the Development of Low-Income Children: A Longitudinal Study', *Developmental Psychology,* No. 35, pp. 868-79.

Schinke, S.P., Cole, K.C. and Poulin, S.R. (2000) 'Enhancing the Educational Achievement of At-Risk Youth', *Prevention Science,* Vol. 1, No. 1, pp. 51-60.

Shaywitz, S.E., Fletcher, J.M., Holahan, J.M., Shneider, A.E., Marchione, K.E., Stuebing, K.K., Francis, D.J., Pugh, K.R. and Shaywitz, B.A. (1999) 'Persistence of Dyslexia: The Connecticut Longitudinal Study of Adolescence', *Pediatrics,* Vol. 104, No. 6, pp. 1351-59.

Shiel, G., Morgan, M. and Larney, R. (1998). *Study of Remedial Education in Irish Primary Schools: Summary Report.* Dublin: The Stationery Office.

Simonton, D.K. (1994) *Greatness: Who makes history and why?* New York: Guilford Press.

Svensson, I. and Jacobson, C. (2006) 'How persistent are phonological difficulties? A Longitudinal Study of Reading Retarding Children', *Dyslexia,* Vol. 12, No. 1, pp. 3-20.

Van der Leij, A. and Morfidi, E. (2006) 'Core deficits and variable differences in Dutch poor readers learning English', *Journal of Learning Disability,* Vol. 39, No. 1, pp. 74-90.

PART 3: CHILDREN'S OUTCOMES

149

USE OF TOBACCO, ALCOHOL AND DRUGS

Tobacco use

Context

The National Health Promotion Strategy 2000-2005 aims 'to increase the percentage of the population who remain non-smokers, with a particular emphasis on narrowing the gap across social classes, and to protect non-smokers from passive smoke' (Department of Health and Children, 2000, p. 54).

A recent review of the National Health Promotion Strategy highlights a number of positive developments to prevent smoking initiation and to support smoking cessation (McKenna *et al,* 2004). These include: the establishment of a National Smokers' Quit Line; development of smoking cessation support services in all former health board areas; development of programmes at regional level, including work with local Youth Reach programmes and with young mothers' groups; anti-smoking advertisements; and the piloting of two 5-year projects aimed at delaying the onset of smoking among children.

Smoking in Ireland is both legally and socially sanctioned, and this is specifically the case for children. According to the Tobacco (Health Promotion and Protection) Act (Government of Ireland, 1988), it is illegal for any person to sell tobacco products to people under the age of 18. Those who do so and are caught are liable for a fine (now €3,000 maximum), conviction or both. The Public Health (Tobacco) Act (Government of Ireland, 2002) established a ban on tobacco advertising and sponsorship by the tobacco industry and also put in place provision for the establishment of a Tobacco Control Agency for regulating and controlling the sale of tobacco. Most recently, the Public Health Tobacco (Amendment) Act (Government of Ireland, 2004) introduced a ban on tobacco smoking in Irish workplaces, aimed at ensuring that working environments are smoke-free. A recent report by the Office of Tobacco Control showed a 97% compliance rate with the legislation (Office of Tobacco Control, 2005). This ban extends to public houses, restaurants and public facilities, covering all buildings where children may gather.

Significance

Tobacco is the leading cause of preventable death in the world (WHO, 2003), with 4.83 million premature deaths attributed to smoking in 2000 worldwide (Ezzati and Lopez, 2003). The main causes of death associated with smoking are cardiovascular diseases, chronic obstructive pulmonary diseases and lung cancer. Smoking also has short-term health effects on young people, including decreased lung function, decreased physical fitness, increased asthmatic problems and increased coughing, wheezing and shortness of breath (US Department of Health and Human Services, 1994). Although most smoking-related illnesses occur in middle-aged and elderly people, smoking behaviour is usually established in adolescence (Godeau *et al,* 2004; Pierce and Gilpin, 1996). Research shows that most adult smokers experienced smoking or were already addicted to nicotine before the age of 18 (Lamkin and Houston, 1998; Houston *et al,* 1998).

Since smoking-related health problems are a function of the duration (years of smoking) and the intensity of use (amount of cigarettes smoked) (US Department of Health and Human Services, 1994), monitoring smoking in adolescents is critically importance. Self-reported smoking status has been found to be a simple and inexpensive method to study smoking prevalence and is considered to be a reasonable indicator of actual smoking status, compared with biochemical validated smoking prevalence (Patrick *et al,* 1994; Newell *et al,* 1999). Fewer than half of all smokers successfully quit before the age of 60 (WHO, 1996). Half of all new male adolescent smokers will smoke for at least 16 years, while for females the estimate is at least 20 years (Pierce and Gilpin, 1996). Despite all the negative consequences of smoking, adolescents may see smoking as positive. The most prevalent functions of smoking are to control negative moods and depression (to relax, to concentrate, to reduce stress or boredom); to express control over the environment; to belong to a group or to have contact with a group; to control weight (especially in girls); and to adopt a certain image of maturity and self-reliance (Lambert *et al,* 2002).

Daily tobacco use

Measure

The proportion of children aged 10-17 who report smoking cigarettes every day.

Key findings

■ In 2002, 10.0% of children aged 10-17 reported smoking cigarettes every day *(see Table 55).*

Differences by age, social class and gender

■ The percentage of children who reported smoking every day was higher among older children and children from lower social classes:
  - 19.7% of 15-17 year-olds reported this, compared with less than 0.4% of 10-11 year-olds and 5.7% of 12-14 year-olds;
  - 10.4% of children from social class 5-6 reported this, compared with 9.5% of children from social class 3-4 and 7.2% of children from social class 1-2.

Table 55: Percentage of children who report smoking cigarettes every day, by age, social class and gender (1998 and 2002)

	1998			2002		
	Boys	Girls	Total	Boys	Girls	Total
Total	10.3	9.1	9.7	9.3	10.4	10.0
Years of age						
10-11	1.0	0.1	0.5	0.5	0.3	0.4
12-14	8.4	6.3	7.3	5.1	6.1	5.7
15-17	19.2	20.1	19.7	19.0	20.2	19.7
Social class						
SC 1-2	9.6	7.0	8.2	7.1	7.2	7.2
SC 3-4	10.6	8.3	9.4	7.7	10.7	9.5
SC 5-6	9.2	10.2	9.7	10.1	10.6	10.4

Source: HBSC Survey

Differences by geographical area

■ In 2002, reported levels of daily smoking among children were highest in the former South-Eastern Health Board area (14.6%) and lowest in the former North-Eastern Health Board area (6.6%) *(see Table 56).*
■ A very substantial decrease in the numbers of children who reported smoking every day took place in the former North-Eastern Health Board area between 1998 (13.1%) and 2002 (6.6%). This was also a slight decrease in the Eastern Regional Health Authority area.

Table 56: Percentage of children aged 10-17 who report smoking cigarettes every day, by former health board area (1998 and 2002)

	1998	2002
South-Eastern Health Board	10.2	14.6
Mid-Western Health Board	8.2	10.7
Eastern Regional Health Authority	10.4	9.9
North-Western Health Board	8.4	9.5
Southern Health Board	7.4	9.4
Midland Health Board	7.4	9.3
Western Health Board	9.8	9.2
North-Eastern Health Board	13.1	6.6
Mean average	9.7	10

Source: HBSC Survey

International comparisons

■ From the 2002 HBSC Survey, using the ages of 11, 13 and 15 only to draw international comparisons, 6.7% of Irish children reported smoking cigarettes every day *(see Figure 31)*. This compared with the HBSC average of 7.4%.

■ Among all 35 countries that used this HBSC item, the lowest percentage for this indicator was found among Macedonian children (4.0%) and the highest among children from Greenland (24.3%).

■ Overall, Irish children ranked 24th among all 35 countries participating in the survey. Irish 11-year-old children were ranked 26th, Irish 13-year-old children were ranked 25th and Irish 15-year-old children were ranked 26th.

Figure 31: Percentage of children who report smoking cigarettes every day, by country (2002)

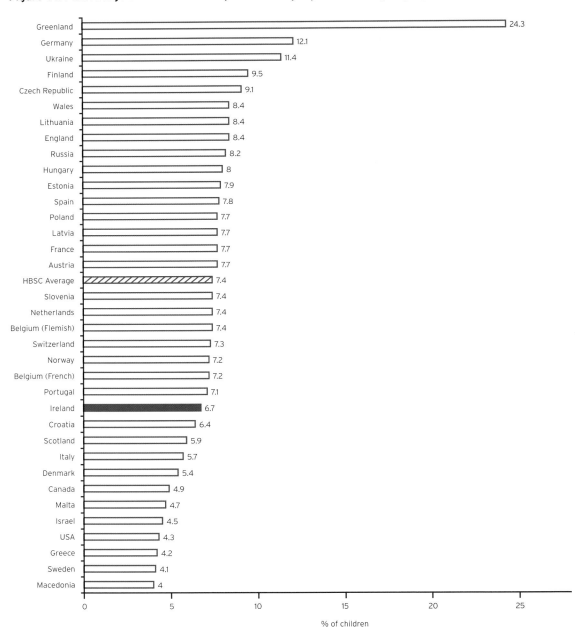

Country	% of children
Greenland	24.3
Germany	12.1
Ukraine	11.4
Finland	9.5
Czech Republic	9.1
Wales	8.4
Lithuania	8.4
England	8.4
Russia	8.2
Hungary	8
Estonia	7.9
Spain	7.8
Poland	7.7
Latvia	7.7
France	7.7
Austria	7.7
HBSC Average	7.4
Slovenia	7.4
Netherlands	7.4
Belgium (Flemish)	7.4
Switzerland	7.3
Norway	7.2
Belgium (French)	7.2
Portugal	7.1
Ireland	6.7
Croatia	6.4
Scotland	5.9
Italy	5.7
Denmark	5.4
Canada	4.9
Malta	4.7
Israel	4.5
USA	4.3
Greece	4.2
Sweden	4.1
Macedonia	4

% of children

154

Source: HBSC Survey

Weekly tobacco use

Measure

The proportion of children aged 10-17 who report smoking cigarettes every week.

Key findings

■ In 2002, 13.4% of children aged 10-17 reported smoking cigarettes every week *(see Table 57)*.

Differences by age, social class and gender

■ The percentage of children who reported smoking every week was higher among older children and children from lower social classes:
- 24.6% of 15-17 year-olds reported this, compared with 1.6% of 10-11 year-olds and 8.7% of 12-14 year-olds;
- 13.9% of children from social class 5-6 reported this, compared with 13.4% of children from social class 3-4 and 10.3% of children from social class 1-2.

Table 57: Percentage of children who report smoking cigarettes every week, by age, social class and gender (1998 and 2002)

	1998			2002		
	Boys	Girls	Total	Boys	Girls	Total
Total	14.6	14.3	14.5	12.7	13.9	13.4
Years of age						
10-11	2.5	1.6	2.0	2.1	1.2	1.6
12-14	13.1	11.4	12.2	8.3	9.1	8.7
15-17	24.5	28.2	26.3	23.6	25.2	24.6
Social class						
SC 1-2	14.1	12.3	13.1	10.8	9.9	10.3
SC 3-4	14.9	13.3	14.1	11.7	14.6	13.4
SC 5-6	13.4	15.2	14.4	13.1	14.6	13.9

Source: HBSC Survey

Differences by geographical area

■ In 2002, reported levels of weekly smoking among children were highest in the former South-Eastern Health Board area (20.2%) and lowest in the former North-Eastern Health Board area (9.8%) *(see Table 58)*.
■ The percentage of children who reported smoking every week in the former North-Eastern Health Board area almost halved between 1998 and 2002 – from 18.0% to 9.8%.

Table 58: Percentage of children aged 10-17 who report smoking cigarettes every week, by former health board area (1998 and 2002)

	1998	2002
South-Eastern Health Board	15.5	20.2
Mid-Western Health Board	11.7	13.9
Southern Health Board	12.2	13.6
Eastern Regional Health Authority	15.3	13.1
Western Health Board	15.2	12.1
North-Western Health Board	12.1	12.0
Midland Health Board	11.9	11.8
North-Eastern Health Board	18.0	9.8
Mean average	14.5	13.4

Source: HBSC Survey

International comparisons

■ From the 2002 HBSC Survey, using the ages of 11, 13 and 15 only to draw international comparisons, 9.4% of Irish children reported smoking cigarettes every week *(see Figure 32).* This compared with the HBSC average of 10.8%.

■ Among all 35 countries that used this HBSC item, the lowest percentage for this indicator was found among Macedonian children (5.7%) and the highest among children from Greenland (30.6%).

■ Overall, Irish children ranked 26th among all 35 countries participating in the survey.

Figure 32: Percentage of children who report smoking cigarettes every week, by country (2002)

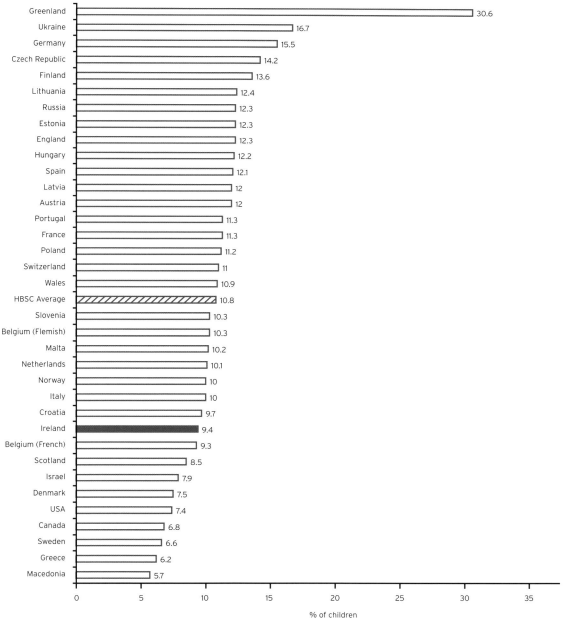

% of children

Source: HBSC Survey

Technical notes

The HBSC uses a self-completion questionnaire and as such may suffer from several biases. The factors influencing self-reports are the level of demand (perceived pressure to answer socially desirable), age (adolescents have higher rates of misreporting) and gender (men tend to report their smoking status less accurately than women) (Velicer *et al*, 1992; Newell *et al*, 1999). However, the level of demand in the HBSC Survey is low since the questionnaires are completed anonymously. Yet social desirability bias cannot be avoided and may result in an underestimation/overestimation of the real extent of smoking.

Percentage differences are presented for descriptive purposes only and may not reflect a statistically significant finding.

References

Department of Health and Children (2000) *National Health Promotion Strategy 2000-2005.* Dublin: The Stationery Office.

Ezzati, M. and Lopez, A.D. (2003) 'Estimates of global mortality attributable to smoking in 2000', *The Lancet,* No. 362, pp. 847-52.

Godeau, E., Rahav, G. and Hublet, A. (2004) 'Tobacco Smoking', in *Young People's Health in Context. Health Behaviour in School-aged Children (HBSC) Study: International Report from the 2001/02 Survey,* C. Currie, C. Roberts, R. Smith, W. Settertobulte, O. Samdal and V. Barnekow-Rasmussen (eds.). Copenhagen: WHO-Europe.

Government of Ireland (1988) *The Tobacco (Health Promotion and Protection) Act.* Dublin: The Stationery Office.

Government of Ireland (2002) *The Public Health (Tobacco) Act.* Dublin: The Stationery Office.

Government of Ireland (2004) *The Public Health Tobacco (Amendment) Act.* Dublin: The Stationery Office.

Houston, T.P., Kolbe, L.J. and Eriksen, M.P. (1998) 'Tobacco-use cessation in the 90s – Not 'Adults Only' anymore', *Preventive Medicine,* Vol. 27, No. 53, pp. A1-A2.

Lamkin, L. and Houston, T.P. (1998) 'Nicotine Dependency and Adolescents: Preventing and treating', *Primary Care,* Vol. 25, No. 1, pp. 123-35.

Lambert, M., Verduykt, P. and Van den Broucke, S. (2002) 'Summary on the Literature on Young People, Gender and Smoking', in *Gender Differences in Smoking in Young People,* M. Lambert, A. Hublet, P. Verduykt, L. Maes and S. Van den Broucke (eds.). Brussels: Flemish Institute for Health Promotion.

McKenna, V., Barry, M. and Friel, S. (2004) *Review of the National Health Promotion Strategy,* Department of Health and Children. Dublin: The Stationery Office.

Newell, S., Girgis, A. and Sanson-Fisher, R. (1999) 'The accuracy of self-reported health behaviours and risk factors relating to cancer and cardiovascular disease in the general population: A critical review', *American Journal of Preventive Medicine,* No. 17, pp. 211-29.

Office of Tobacco Control (2005) *Smoke-free Workplaces in Ireland: A One-year Review.* Kildare: Office of Tobacco Control.

Patrick, D.L., Cheadle, A., Thompson, D.C., Diehr, P., Koepsell, T. and Kinne, S. (1994) 'The validity of self-reported smoking: A review and meta-analysis', *American Journal of Public Health,* Vol. 84, No. 7, pp. 1086-93.

Pierce, J.P. and Gilpin, E. (1996) 'How long will today's new adolescent smokers be addicted to cigarettes?', *American Journal of Public Health,* Vol. 86, No. 2, pp. 253-56.

US Department of Health and Human Services (1994) *Preventing Tobacco Use among Young People: A Report of the Surgeon General.* Atlanta, GA: US Department of Health and Human Services, Public Health Service, Centers for Disease Control, Center for Health Promotion and Education, Office of Smoking and Health.

Velicer, W., Prochaska, J., Rossi, J. and Snow, M.G. (1992) 'Assessing Outcome in Smoking Cessation Studies', *Psychological Bulletin,* No. 111, pp. 23-41.

WHO (1996) *Trends in substance use and associated health problems,* WHO Fact Sheet No. 127. Geneva: World Health Organization.

WHO (2003) 'Neglected Global Epidemics: Three Growing Threats', in *World Health Report 2003: Shaping the Future.* Copenhagen: World Health Organization.

PART 3: CHILDREN'S OUTCOMES

Binge drinking

Context

Section 13 of the Intoxicating Liquor Act (Government of Ireland, 2003) restates the prohibition on the purchase or delivery of alcohol to a person under the age of 18 on licensed premises. The Act also places a general prohibition on persons under 18 years of age from bars or licensed premises, although this has been relaxed for premises where food is being served. In addition, the Act requires that all those aged between 18 and 20 carry an age document in a licensed premises and that alcohol consumption by a child in a private residence is conditional on parental consent.

Both the National Alcohol Policy for Ireland and the National Health Promotion Strategy identified a number of objectives in respect of sensible drinking (Department of Health and Children, 1996 and 2000). These included delaying the onset of alcohol consumption among children and adolescents, and decreasing the number of young people and adults who drink in excess on any one occasion. Ireland is also a signatory of the World Health Organization Declaration on Young People and Alcohol (WHO, 2001) and a number of the Declaration's elements have been embedded in Irish policy documents developed since that time.

The WHO Declaration aims to protect children and young people from the pressures to drink and reduce the harm done to them directly or indirectly by alcohol. It re-affirms the five principles of the European Charter on Alcohol, namely:
- All people have the right to a family, community and working life protected from accidents, violence and other negative consequences of alcohol consumption.
- All people have the right to valid impartial information and education, starting early in life, on the consequences of alcohol consumption on health, the family and society.
- All children and adolescents have the right to grow up in an environment protected from the negative consequences of alcohol consumption and, to the extent possible, from the promotion of alcoholic beverages.
- All people with hazardous or harmful alcohol consumption and members of their families have the right to accessible treatment and care.
- All people who do not wish to consume alcohol, or who cannot do so for health or other reasons, have the right to be safeguarded from pressures to drink and be supported in their non-drinking behaviour.

Based on a recommendation of the Commission for Liquor Licensing, a Strategic Task Force on Alcohol was established in 2002 and it reported in 2002 and again in 2004 (Department of Health and Children, 2002 and 2004). The Task Force has made approximately 100 recommendations on issues such as the regulation of alcohol availability, the promotion of alcohol products and the provision of information, education and treatment services. A review of the National Health Promotion Strategy shows that some progress has been made in this area (McKenna *et al,* 2004). Initiatives include the piloting of a General Practitioner Alcohol Awareness Programme, the development of a Responsible Serving of Alcohol Programme, the adoption of a College Alcohol Policy framework by third-level institutions and the completion of research on the impact of alcohol advertising on teenagers in Ireland. Further progress has been made with the commencement of the Irish Sports Council's Code of Ethics and Good Practice for Children's Sport (Irish Sports Council, 2000), which argues that children's sports should not be sponsored by the alcohol industry and that alcohol-free environments are most appropriate for underage events.

Key areas identified for future action include:
- the completion of the implementation of the recommendations of the Strategic Task Force on Alcohol;
- further expansion and evaluation of community mobilisation programmes;
- establishment of partnerships at regional level to develop initiatives to prevent alcohol misuse.

Significance

Alcohol is a major risk factor for social and physical harm, as well as disease. Although alcohol-related mortality peaks between 45 and 54 years of age, adolescence is the period of life in which lifestyle patterns are being adopted. Moreover, there is a link between the age of initiation to alcohol and the pattern of use (De Wit *et al*, 2000) and its abuse in adulthood where early initiation and frequent use lead to difficulties (Poikolainen *et al*, 2001; Duncan *et al*, 1997).

For a large number of adolescents, the use of alcohol (and other substances, such as tobacco and cannabis) may signify 'normal' psychological experimentation (Engles and Knibbe, 2000) as part of the 'adolescent culture' (Le Garrec, 2000). Problematic drinking behaviour, however, can impair adolescents' psychological development and result in significant behavioural problems (Godeau *et al,* 2001). (The 5-drink threshold, or 'binge drinking', is considered problematic alcohol intake.) Some recent changes in young people's drinking behaviour have been observed and these are considered to be problematic (Le Garrec, 2000), including:
- more alcohol is being consumed by young people;
- more girls drink and girls drink more alcohol;
- alcohol is being mixed with other substances;
- drunkenness is seen as an end in itself.

Data presented later in this report show that the most common reason for Irish young people being referred to the Garda Juvenile Diversion Programme are alcohol-related offences *(see p. 243).*

Measure

> **The proportion of children aged 15 who report to have had 5 or more alcoholic drinks in a row at least once in the last 30 days.**

Key findings

■ In 2003, 57% of children aged 15 reported to have had 5 or more alcoholic drinks in a row at least once in the last 30 days *(see Table 59)*. This represented an increase of 10% since 1995.

Differences by age, social class and gender

■ In 2003, the percentage of children aged 15 who reported to have had 5 or more alcoholic drinks in a row at least once in the last 30 days was similar for boys and girls.

■ The percentage of girls who reported this has increased significantly – from 42% in 1995 to 57% in 2003.

Table 59: Percentage of children aged 15 who report to have had 5 or more alcoholic drinks in a row at least once in the last 30 days, by gender and year

1995			1999			2003		
Boys	Girls	Total	Boys	Girls	Total	Boys	Girls	Total
52	42	47	57	56	57	57	57	57

Source: ESPAD Survey

■ 60% of those who indicated their parents had primary school education or less reported binge drinking, compared with 53% of those who indicated their parents had some college or university education *(see Table 60)*.

Table 60: Percentage of children aged 15 who report to have had 5 or more alcoholic drinks in a row at least once in the last 30 days, by parents' level of education (2003)

Parents' level of education	Boys	Girls	Total
Primary or less	61	60	60
Some secondary school	58	59	59
Completed secondary school	62	56	59
Some college or university	53	54	53
Completed college or university	56	55	56
Do not know or does not apply	52	57	54

Source: ESPAD Survey

International comparisons

- From the 2003 ESPAD Survey, among all 33 countries that used this ESPAD item, the lowest percentage for this indicator was found among Turkish children (15%) and the highest among children from Denmark (60%).

- Overall, Irish children reported the 3rd highest levels of binge drinking *(see Figure 33)*. Specifically, Irish boys reported the 4th highest and Irish girls the 2nd highest levels of binge drinking among all boys and girls.

Figure 33: Percentage of children who report to have had 5 or more alcoholic drinks in a row in the last 30 days, by country (2003)

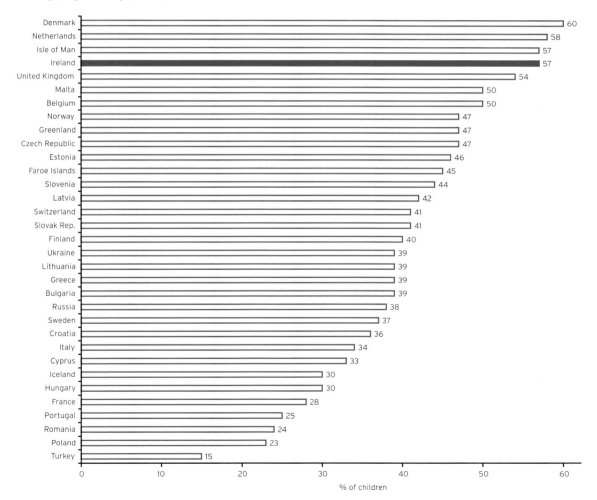

Source: ESPAD Survey

Technical notes

As with other survey data, figures reported here are based on self-reports from children in school classrooms and thus are subject to self-report and other bias. The factors influencing self-reports are the level of demand (perceived pressure to answer socially desirable), age (adolescents have higher rates of misreporting) and gender. However, the level of demand in the ESPAD Survey is low since the questionnaires are completed anonymously. Yet social desirability bias cannot be avoided and may result in an underestimation/overestimation of the real extent of drinking. In any case, this variable is specially recommended for 15-years-olds. The Irish ESPAD data are not amenable to presentation by region or locality.

Percentage differences are presented for descriptive purposes only and may not reflect a statistically significant finding.

References

De Wit, D.J., Adlaf, E.M., Offord, D.E. and Ogborne, A.C. (2000) 'Age at First Alcohol Use: A risk factor for the development of alcohol disorders', *American Journal of Psychiatry,* No. 157, pp. 745-50.

Department of Health and Children (1996) *National Alcohol Policy for Ireland.* Dublin: The Stationery Office.

Department of Health and Children (2000) *National Health Promotion Strategy 2000-2005.* Dublin: The Stationery Office.

Department of Health and Children (2002) *Strategic Task Force on Alcohol. Interim Report.* Dublin: The Stationery Office.

Department of Health and Children (2004) *Strategic Task Force on Alcohol. Second Report, September 2004.* Dublin: The Stationery Office.

Duncan, S.C., Alpert, A., Duncan, T.E. and Hops, H. (1997) 'Adolescent Alcohol Use Development and Young Adult Outcomes', *Drug and Alcohol Dependence,* Vol. 49, No. 1, pp. 39-48.

Engels, R.C. and Knibbe, R.A. (2000) 'Young People's Alcohol Consumption from a European Perspective: Risks and Benefits', *European Journal of Clinical Nutrition,* No. 54 (Supplement 1), S52-55.

Godeau, E., Ross, J., François, Y., Marshall, L., Maltby, J., Aszmann, A., Jensen, L., King, M., Nic Gabhainn, S., Rahav, G., Rasmussen, M., Terzidou, M. and Maka, Z. (2001) 'Focus Area Rationale: Risk Behaviour: Substance Use', in *Health Behaviour in School-aged Children: A World Health Organization Cross-national Study: Research Protocol for the 2001/02 Survey,* C. Currie, O. Samdal, W. Boyce and R. Smith (eds.). Edinburgh: Child and Adolescent Health Research Unit, University of Edinburgh.

Government of Ireland (2003) *Intoxicating Liquor Act.* Dublin: The Stationery Office.

Irish Sports Council (2000) *Code of Ethics and Good Practice for Children's Sport.* Dublin: Irish Sports Council.

Le Garrec, S. (2000) 'Le Sens de l'alcoolisation chez les Jeunes à Toulouse' ['Meaning of drinking among young people in Toulouse'], in *Actes du colloque les jeunes et l'alcool en Europe,* F. Navarro, E. Godeau and C. Vialas (eds.). Toulouse: Editions Universitaires du Sud.

McKenna, V., Barry, M. and Friel, S. (2004) *Review of the National Health Promotion Strategy, Department of Health and Children.* Dublin: The Stationery Office.

Poikolainen, K., Tuulio-Henriksson, A., Aalto-Setälä, T., Marttunen, M. and Lönnqvist, J. (2001) 'Predictors of Alcohol Intake and Heavy Drinking in Early Adulthood: A 5-year follow-up of 15-19 year-old Finnish adolescents', *Alcohol and Alcoholism,* Vol. 36, No. 1, pp. 85-88.

WHO (1995) *European Charter on Alcohol.* Copenhagen: World Health Organization.

WHO (2001) *Declaration on Young People and Alcohol.* Copenhagen: World Health Organization.

PART 3: CHILDREN'S OUTCOMES

Illicit drug use

Context

Possession of a controlled substance or illicit drug for supply is prohibited by the Misuse of Drugs Act (Government of Ireland, 1977) and the importation, exportation, production and supply of such a substance is prohibited by the Misuse of Drugs (Scheduled Substances) Regulations (Government of Ireland, 1993). The third National Drugs Strategy, *Building on Experience 2001-2008,* aims 'to significantly reduce the harm caused by the misuse of drugs through a concerted focus on supply reduction, prevention, treatment and research' (Department of Tourism, Sport and Recreation, 2001, p. 6).

It is envisaged that this aim will be met through a reduction in the supply of drugs, the prevention of drug use (including education and awareness), drug treatment (including rehabilitation and risk reduction) and research. The National Drugs Strategy is implemented via local and regional drugs task forces and monitored by the National Drugs Strategy Team. An interdepartmental group keeps the Cabinet Committee on Social Inclusion briefed in relation to the implementation of the National Drugs Strategy.

A review of the National Health Promotion Strategy identified a number of key developments, including the launch of a national drugs awareness campaign, the implementation of drugs awareness programmes, the development of substance misuse policies in schools and the establishment of regional drugs task forces (McKenna *et al*, 2004). The mid-term review of the National Drugs Strategy recommended that more action is required with schools in relation to prevention education and awareness (Department of Community, Rural and Gaeltacht Affairs, 2005). Specifically, it was noted that schools should be supported to develop drugs policies and to fully implement both Social, Personal and Health Education (SPHE) and the Substance Abuse Prevention (Education) Programme. In addition, a Young People's Facilities and Services Fund (YPFSF), administered by the Department of Community, Rural and Gaeltacht Affairs, has been in place since 1998. It has drawn substantial funding from the National Development Plan for projects and programmes that aim to divert at-risk youth into drug-free recreational and sporting activities.

The 2005 *Report of the Working Group on Treatment of Under-18 year-olds presenting to Treatment Services with Serious Drug Problems* set out a number of recommendations for drug prevention and treatment services for children and young people (Department of Health and Children, 2005). The report emphasised the need for a multidisciplinary approach and underlined the need for a service design that encourages and retains young people in treatment and rehabilitation services. The Working Group also recommended a four-tiered model of service delivery, which provides a realistic, flexible and adaptable framework.

Significance

Substance use is recognised as an important predictor of morbidity and mortality among adults and is viewed as a risk behaviour among adolescents. Substance use damages health in both the long and short term, and is an important indicator of well-being and social relations (Di Clemente *et al,* 1996). The factors contributing to the use of illicit drugs among young people have received much attention in the field of adolescent substance abuse. They include socio-demographic factors (e.g. age, gender, ethnicity and cultural background, parental socio-economic status, neighbourhood); personal factors (e.g. inadequate life skills, low self-esteem (McGee and Williams, 2000) and self-confidence, depression, stress, school failure); and behavioural factors (e.g. academic performance, lifestyle behaviours and risk-taking factors (Jessor *et al,* 1998)).

In addition, it is now widely acknowledged that social relations play an important role in adolescent risk behaviours, among them substance use. In this age group, smoking, drinking or using other drugs is rarely a solitary activity and can be seen, to a certain extent, as part of 'adolescent culture'. Problems associated with substance use cover a broad spectrum that include significant health consequences, social and family disruption, and economic issues (Godeau *et al,* 2001).

Measure

> **The proportion of children aged 15 who report having used any illicit drugs in their lifetime.**

Key findings

- In 2003, 40% of children aged 15 reported to have used an illicit drug in their lifetime *(see Table 61).* This represented an increase of 3% since 1995.

Differences by age, social class and gender
- In 2003, the percentage of children who reported to have used an illicit drug in their lifetime was similar for boys (41%) and girls (40%).
- The percentage of girls who reported to have used an illicit drug in their lifetime has increased significantly – from 32% in 1995 to 40% in 2003.

PART 3: CHILDREN'S OUTCOMES

167

Table 61: Percentage of children aged 15 who report having used an illicit drug in their lifetime, by gender

1995			1999			2003		
Boys	Girls	Total	Boys	Girls	Total	Boys	Girls	Total
42	32	37	35	29	32	41	40	40

Source: ESPAD Survey

- The pattern according to parental level of education was inconsistent *(see Table 62)*: 37% of those who indicated their parents had some secondary school education reported having used an illicit drug in their lifetime, compared with 43% who indicated their parents had some college or university education.

Table 62: Percentage of children aged 15 who report having used an illicit drug in their lifetime, by parents' level of education (2003)

Parents' level of education	Boys	Girls	Total
Primary or less	42	41	42
Some secondary school	37	37	37
Completed secondary school	41	42	41
Some college or university	43	43	43
Completed college or university	38	39	39
Do not know or does not apply	40	38	39

Source: ESPAD Survey

International comparisons

- From the 2003 ESPAD Survey, overall, 40% of Irish children aged 15 reported to have used an illicit drug in their lifetime *(see Figure 34).* This compared with the ESPAD average of 22%.
- Among all 36 countries that used this ESPAD item, the lowest percentage for this indicator was found among Romanian children (3%) and the highest among children from the Czech Republic (44%).
- Overall, Irish children reported the 3rd highest levels of lifetime illicit drug use (together with the Isle of Man). Specifically, Irish boys reported the 6th highest and Irish girls the highest levels of lifetime illicit drug use among all boys and girls.

Figure 34: Percentage of children aged 15 who report having used any illicit drugs in their lifetime, by country (2003)

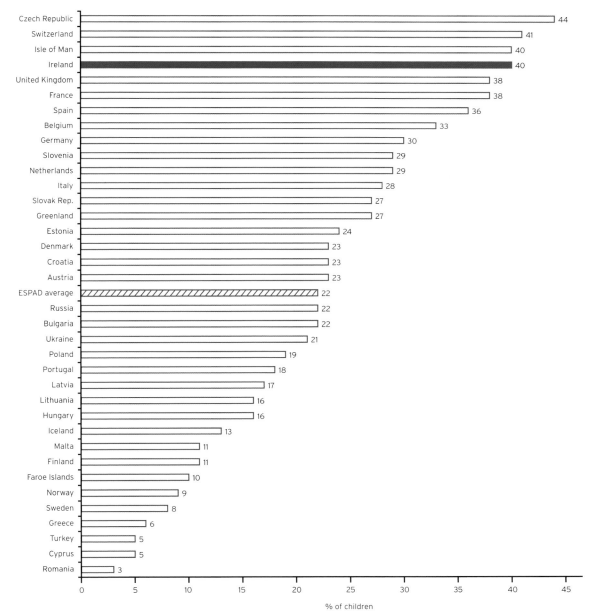

% of children

Source: ESPAD Survey

Illicit drug use other than marijuana

- From the 2003 ESPAD Survey, 9% of Irish children aged 15 reported to have used an illicit drug other than marijuana in their lifetime *(see Figure 35).* This compared with the ESPAD average of 6%.
- Among all 36 countries that used this ESPAD item, the lowest percentage for this indicator was found among children from the Ukraine, Romania, Greece and the Faroe Islands (2%), and the highest among children from the Czech Republic (11%).
- Among all 36 countries that took part in this survey, Irish 15-year-olds ranked in joint 3rd place in their reported use of an illicit drug other than marijuana.

Figure 35: Percentage of children aged 15 who report having used any illicit drug other than marijuana in their lifetime, by country (2003)

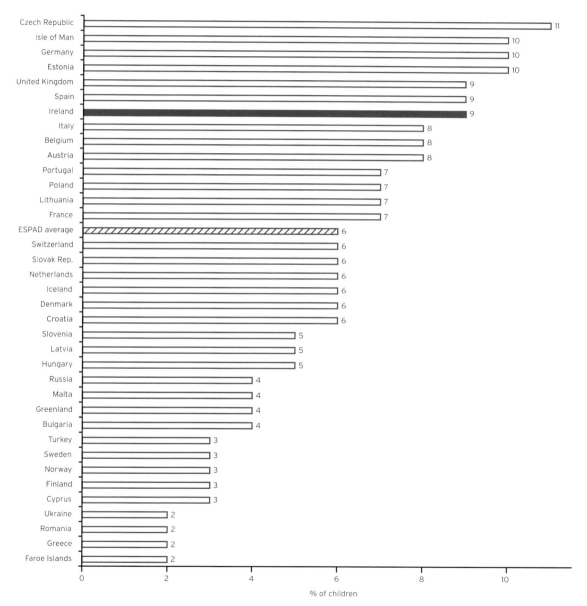

% of children

Source: ESPAD Survey

PART 3: CHILDREN'S OUTCOMES

Technical notes

As with other survey data, those reported here are based on self-reports from children in school classrooms and thus are subject to self-report and other bias. The factors influencing self-reports are the level of demand (perceived pressure to answer socially desirable), age (adolescents have higher rates of misreporting) and gender. However, the level of demand in the ESPAD Survey is low since the questionnaires are completed anonymously. Yet social desirability bias cannot be avoided and may result in an underestimation/overestimation of the real extent of illicit substance use. The Irish ESPAD data are also not amenable to presentation by region or locality.

Percentage differences are presented for descriptive purposes only and may not reflect a statistically significant finding.

References

Department of Community, Rural and Gaeltacht Affairs (2005) *Mid-Term Review of the National Drugs Strategy.* Dublin: The Stationery Office.

Department of Health and Children (2005) *Report of the Working Group on Treatment of Under-18 year-olds presenting to Treatment Services with Serious Drug Problems.* Dublin: The Stationery Office.

Department of Tourism, Sport and Recreation (2001) *The National Drugs Strategy: Building on Experience 2001-2008.* Dublin: The Stationery Office.

Di Clemente, R.J., Hansen, W.B. and Ponton, P.E. (1996) *Handbook of Adolescent Health Risk Behaviour: Issues in Clinical Child Psychology.* New York: Plenum.

Godeau, E., Ross, J., François, Y., Marshall, L., Maltby, J., Aszmann, A., Jensen, L., King, M., Nic Gabhainn, S., Rahav, G., Rasmussen, M., Terzidou, M. and Maka, Z. (2001) 'Focus Area Rationale: Risk Behaviour: Substance Use', in *Health Behaviour in School-aged Children: A World Health Organization Cross-national Study: Research Protocol for the 2001/02 Survey,* C. Currie, O. Samdal, W. Boyce and R. Smith (eds.). Edinburgh: Child and Adolescent Health Research Unit, University of Edinburgh.

Government of Ireland (1977) *Misuse of Drugs Act.* Dublin: The Stationery Office.

Government of Ireland (1993) *Misuse of Drugs (Scheduled Substances) Regulations.* Dublin: The Stationery Office.

Jessor, R., Turblin, M.S. and Costa, F.M. (1998) 'Protective Factors in Adolescent Health Behaviour', *Journal of Personality Psychology,* Vol. 75, No. 3, pp. 788-800.

McGee, R. and Williams, S. (2000) 'Does low self-esteem predict health compromising behaviours among adolescents?', *Journal of Adolescence,* Vol. 23, No. 5, pp. 569-82.

McKenna, V., Barry, M. and Friel, S. (2004) *Review of the National Health Promotion Strategy,* Department of Health and Children. Dublin: The Stationery Office.

SEXUAL HEALTH AND BEHAVIOUR

Teenage pregnancy

Context

The age of consent to sexual activity in Ireland is currently under review and it is expected that some changes to the current legislation may take place in the near future. The minimum age at which a person can marry is 18 years and the legal age of consent for heterosexual intercourse is 17 years for girls and 15 years for boys. One of the aims of the National Health Promotion Strategy 2000-2005 is 'to promote sexual health and safer sexual practices amongst the population' (Department of Health and Children, 2000, p. 61).

The Crisis Pregnancy Agency, established in October 2001, published its Strategy to address the issue of *Crisis Pregnancy 2004-2006* in 2003. Its aims were:
- to reduce the number of crisis pregnancies by the provision of education, advice and contraceptive services;
- to reduce the number of women with crisis pregnancies who opt for abortion by offering services and supports that make other options more attractive;
- to provide counselling and medical services after crisis pregnancy.

This Strategy draws attention to the research finding that, despite often presenting social and/ or educational challenges for the teenagers' parents and others, teenage pregnancies are not always considered a crisis by the teenagers themselves. In 2001, the report called *Get Connected* recommended that a sexual health strategy be developed in each former health board area (Best Health for Children, 2001). The National Action Plan against Poverty and Social Exclusion 2003-2005 includes commitments to reduce the number of teenage pregnancies (Department of Social and Family Affairs, 2003).

Significance

There is a strong link between teenage pregnancy and deprivation. Research in the UK has found that teenage pregnancy is associated with increased risk of poor social, economic and health outcomes for both mother and child (NHS Centre for Reviews and Dissemination, 1997). Specific outcomes have been identified, including babies with a low birth weight; high infant mortality; high child mortality; high hospital admissions for children; high rates of post-natal depression; and low take-up of breastfeeding (Social Exclusion Unit, 1999). A comparative international analysis, compiled by the United Nations, found that, on average, in all countries teenage mothers are twice as likely to be living in poverty compared to other teenagers (UN, 2001). Evidence from the UK suggests that this disadvantage persists into adulthood (Kemp *et al,* 2004).

Findings from qualitative research, commissioned by the Crisis Pregnancy Agency, indicate that for those adolescents who are sexually active, the average age for initiation of sexual activity is less than 16 years of age (Mayock and Byrne, 2004). In this study of the sexual attitudes, beliefs and behaviours of early school-leavers, it was found that the average age of first sex was 13.5 years (12.9 years for young men and 14.5 years for young women). Their findings also showed that, while 78% of the young people in the study had received some form of sex education while attending either primary or secondary school, there was general consensus that school-based sex education was inadequate, too biological and did not address broader emotional, moral or social issues.

Measure

> **The number of births to girls aged 10-17 and in total, expressed as a proportion of all girls in the same age group.**

Key findings

- The number of babies born in Ireland in 2000 was 54,789 *(see Table 63).* This has increased in each year since then, to reach 61,684 in 2004. In contrast, the number of babies born to girls aged 10-17 has decreased – from 777 in 2000 to 654 in 2004 *(see Figure 36).*

Table 63: Number and rate (per 100,000) of births among girls aged 10-17 (2000-2004)

Years of age	2000		2001		2002		2003		2004	
	No.	Rate	No.	Rate	No.	Rate	No.	Rate	No.	Rate
10-17	777	325	801	343	779	339	753	333	654	295
18 and over	54,012	3,239	57,053	3,355	59,724	3,430	60,776	3,422	61,030	3,370
Total - all ages	54,789	2,874	57,854	2,991	60,503	3,070	61,529	3,074	61,684	3,035

Source: Vital Statistics and Census Population Estimates, CSO

Figure 36: Number of births to girls aged 10-17 (2000-2004)

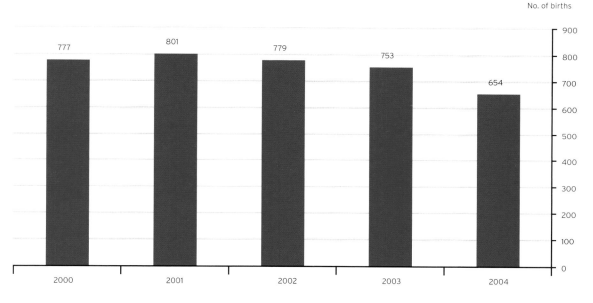

Source: Vital Statistics and Census Population Estimates, CSO

- In 2004, the number of births to girls aged 10-17 represents 1.1% of the births to females of all age groups *(see Table 64).*
- Births to girls aged 10-17 as a percentage of all births has shown a consistent decrease between 2000 (1.4%) and 2004 (1.1%).

Table 64: Births to girls aged 10-17 as a percentage of all births (2000-2004)	
2000	1.4
2001	1.4
2002	1.3
2003	1.2
2004	1.1

Source: Vital Statistics and Census Population Estimates, CSO

- There were, on average, fewer than 10 babies born to girls in the 10-14 age group between 2000-2004.
- Just over 37% of births in 2004 to girls aged 10-17 occurred in Dublin *(see Table 65).*

Table 65: Number and proportion of births to mothers aged 10-17, by county (2004)			
County	No. of births to 10-17 year-olds	No. of births to all ages	Births to 10-17 year-olds as % of total births
Westmeath	19	1,235	1.5
Donegal	29	1,897	1.5
Wexford	28	2,040	1.4
Dublin	243	17,739	1.4
Limerick	33	2,600	1.3
Kildare	41	3,318	1.2
Monaghan	8	670	1.2
Waterford	18	1,666	1.1
Roscommon	7	676	1.0
Carlow	8	788	1.0
Tipperary	21	2,082	1.0
Louth	16	1,697	0.9
Cork	60	6,873	0.9
Kerry	13	1,807	0.7
Clare	12	1,677	0.7
Kilkenny	8	1,120	0.7
Mayo	11	1,561	0.7
Offaly	7	994	0.7
Wicklow	14	1,993	0.7
Meath	17	2,682	0.6
Galway	19	3,114	0.6
Other counties	22	3,455	0.6
Total	654	61,684	1.1

Source: Vital Statistics, CSO

Technical notes

Figures relate to registered live births and exclude stillborn babies. Population estimates are based on the defacto population present on Census night in any area. This includes visitors present on Census night as well as those in residence, while usual residents temporarily absent from the area are excluded from the Census count.

References

Best Health for Children (2001) *Get Connected.* Dublin: Best Health for Children.

Crisis Pregnancy Agency (2003) *Strategy to address the issue of Crisis Pregnancy 2004-2006.* Dublin: Crisis Pregnancy Agency.

Department of Health (2000) *National Health Promotion Strategy 2000-2005.* Dublin: The Stationery Office.

Department of Social and Family Affairs (2003) *National Action Plan against Poverty and Social Exclusion 2003-2005.* Dublin: The Stationery Office.

Kemp, P., Bradshaw, J., Dornan, P., Finch, N. and Mayhew, E. (2004) *Routes out of poverty: A research review.* York: Joseph Rowntree Foundation.

Mayock, P. and Byrne, T. (2004) *A Study of Sexual Health Issues, Attitudes and Behaviours: The views of early school-leavers,* Report No. 8. Dublin: Crisis Pregnancy Agency.

NHS Centre for Reviews and Dissemination (1997) 'Preventing and reducing the adverse effects of unintended teenage pregnancies', *Effective Health Care,* Vol. 3, No. 1, pp. 1-12.

Social Exclusion Unit (1999) *Teenage Pregnancy Report.* London: Social Exclusion Task Force.

Tabberer, S. (2002) 'Teenage Pregnancy and Teenage Motherhood', in *The Well-Being of Children in the UK,* J. Bradshaw (ed.). York: Save the Children, pp. 187-97.

UN (2001) *The Outcomes of Teenage Motherhood in Europe,* Innocenti Working Papers 86. Florence: United Nations Children's Fund.

PART 3: CHILDREN'S OUTCOMES

Self-esteem

Context

Self-esteem and self-perception are inextricably linked to mental health. Ireland is party to international commitments to provide mental health services for children. The National Health Promotion Strategy 2000-2005 notes that mental health is as important as physical health to overall well-being (Department of Health and Children, 2000). In addition, the Strategy links positive mental health to a reduction in suicide and includes as a strategic aim to promote positive mental health as well as to reduce the percentage of the population experiencing poor mental health.

The capacity-building and personal development elements of the Social, Personal and Health Education (SPHE) curriculum represent important mental health promotion opportunities for school-aged children (Department of Education and Science, 2001). The preventative component of this nationwide intervention, now compulsory in all schools, is endorsed in *Developing an Adolescent-friendly Health Service* and supports for the extension of lifeskills and SPHE-type approaches in out-of-school settings are also widespread (Best Health for Children, 2000). Provisions in the Education Act (Government of Ireland, 1998) place an obligation on schools to promote the social and personal development of students and to provide health education for them.

The aims of the SPHE programme are:
- to enable students to develop skills for self-fulfilment and living in communities;
- to promote self-esteem and self-confidence;
- to enable students to develop a framework for responsible decision-making;
- to provide opportunities for reflection and discussion;
- to promote physical, mental and emotional health and well-being.

Significance

Females report lower levels of self-esteem than males (Bagley *et al,* 1997; Houlihan *et al,* 1994) and it has been noted that self-esteem decreases with age (Alasker and Olweus, 1992; Bagley *et al,* 1997). It has been suggested that most Irish young people have healthy, if modest, perceptions of their self-esteem. Mullan and Nic Gabhainn (2003), for example, reported that among Irish children, self-esteem was significantly higher in males than in females, and also higher in the age group 10-12 compared with the age group 13-17.

The role of self-esteem in well-being has been conceptualised primarily as a protective factor against high risk behaviour or as a desired end in itself. Evidence for the protective role has

178

varied over time. Low self-esteem has been identified as a significant predictor of a range of negative outcomes, including depression, relationship difficulties, anti-social behaviour, substance use and suicidal behaviour (DuBois and Tevendale, 1999; Emler, 2001). However, these relationships have been challenged and some investigations reveal more ambiguous patterns (Newmark-Sztainer *et al*, 1997; West and Sweeting, 1997; Goodson *et al*, 2006). Nevertheless, positive self-perception and self-esteem are important in their own right and are associated with overall health and well-being (Harter, 1999; Crocker and Park, 2004; DuBois and Flay, 2004), as well as positive social, psychological and occupational outcomes during adulthood (DuBois and Tevendale, 1999). Furthermore, DuBois and Flay (2004) argue that the strongest evidence for the role of self-esteem is found in evaluations of specific interventions, where enhanced self-esteem leads to increased role functioning and performance, for example, in mentoring programmes (Rhodes, 2002).

Measure

> **The proportion of children aged 8-17 who report feeling happy with the way they are.**

Key findings

- Children aged 8-11 (51.1%) are twice as likely to report always feeling happy with the way they are than children aged 12-17 (25.5%) (*see Table 66*).
- 53.5% of boys aged 8-11 and 37.0% of boys aged 12-17 report that they are always happy with the way they are, compared with 48.9% and 18.6% of girls respectively.
- There are few differences between children from high, medium or low affluence families (*see Table 67*).

Table 66: Percentages of children who report feeling happy with the way they are, by gender and age group						
	8-11 year-olds			12-17 year-olds		
	Boys	Girls	Total	Boys	Girls	Total
Never/Seldom	7.0	6.1	6.5	7.7	18.8	14.6
Quite often	10.5	15.0	12.8	19.4	30.4	26.3
Very often	29.1	30.0	29.5	36.1	32.2	33.6
Always	53.5	48.9	51.1	37.0	18.6	25.5

Source: KIDSCREEN

PART 3: CHILDREN'S OUTCOMES

179

Table 67: Percentages of children who report feeling happy with the way they are, by family affluence and age group

	8-11 year-olds			12-17 year-olds		
	Low affluence	Middle affluence	High affluence	Low affluence	Middle affluence	High affluence
Never/Seldom	7.8	6.6	5.4	17.1	15.7	11.7
Quite often	10.9	13.0	12.7	31.0	25.2	26.0
Very often	29.7	30.2	27.3	27.9	32.7	36.7
Always	51.6	50.3	54.5	24.0	26.4	24.9

Source: KIDSCREEN

- Irish children aged 8-11 were ranked 5th for their mean self-perception score out of the 11 countries that took part in the KIDSCREEN study *(see Figure 37)*.
- Older children, aged 12-18, had a lower mean score, indicating more negative self-perception, and ranked 12th out of the 13 countries that took part in the KIDSCREEN study for that age group *(see Figure 38)*.

Figure 37: Mean self-perception scores for children aged 8-11 (a higher score indicates a more positive self-perception)

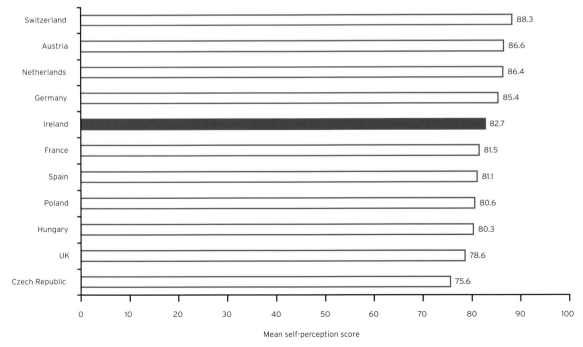

Source: KIDSCREEN

Figure 38: Mean self-perception scores for children aged 12-18 (a higher score indicates a more positive self-perception)

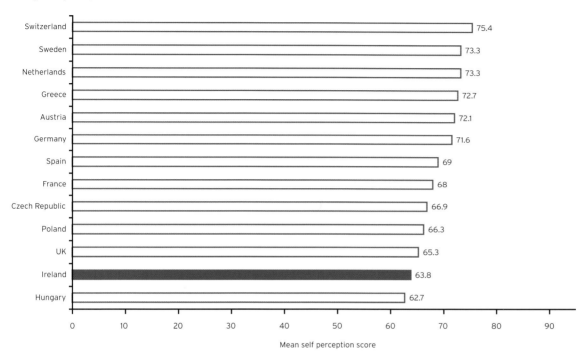

Country	Mean self perception score
Switzerland	75.4
Sweden	73.3
Netherlands	73.3
Greece	72.7
Austria	72.1
Germany	71.6
Spain	69
France	68
Czech Republic	66.9
Poland	66.3
UK	65.3
Ireland	63.8
Hungary	62.7

Source: KIDSCREEN

Technical notes

These data are drawn from the Irish KIDSCREEN database, which does not include data on parental social class or socio-economic status. Thus in Table 67 the data are presented by family affluence. In addition, data are not identifiable by region, country or province, nor are internationally comparative data currently available. In common with the other self-report items included here, this item may be susceptible to self-report or social desirability bias.

Percentage differences are presented for descriptive purposes only and may not reflect a statistically significant finding.

References

Alasker, F.D. and Olweus, D. (1992) 'Stability of global self-evaluations in early adolescence: A Cohort Longitudinal Study', *Journal of Research on Adolescence,* No. 2, pp. 123-45.

Bagley, C., Bolitho, F. and Bertrand, L. (1997) 'Norms and Construct Validity of the Rosenberg Self-Esteem Scale in Canadian High School Populations: Implications for counselling', *Canadian Journal of Counselling,* No. 31, pp. 82-92.

Best Health for Children (2000) *Get connected: Developing an Adolescent-friendly Health Service.* Dublin: Best Health for Children.

Crocker, J. and Park, L.E. (2004) 'The costly pursuit of self-esteem', *Psychological Bulletin,* No. 130, pp. 392-414.

Department of Education and Science (2001) *Social, Personal and Health Education: Guidelines for Teachers.* Dublin: The Stationery Office.

Department of Health and Children (2000) *National Health Promotion Strategy 2000-2005.* Dublin: The Stationery Office.

DuBois, D.L. and Flay, B.R. (2004) 'The healthy pursuit of self-esteem: Comment on and alternative to the Croker and Park Formulation', *Psychological Bulletin,* Vol. 130, No. 3, pp. 415-20.

DuBois, D.L. and Tevendale, H.D. (1999) 'Self-esteem in childhood and adolescence: Vaccine or epiphenomenon?', *Applied and Preventive Psychology,* No. 8, pp. 103-17.

Emler, N. (2001) *Self-esteem: The costs and consequences of low self-worth.* York: Joseph Rowntree Foundation.

Goodson, P., Buhi, E.R. and Dunsmore, S.C. (2006) 'Self-esteem and adolescent sexual behaviours, attitudes and intentions: A systematic review', *Journal of Adolescent Health,* Vol. 38, No. 3, pp. 310-19.

Government of Ireland (1998) *Education Act.* Dublin: The Stationery Office.

Harter, S. (1999) *The Construction of the Self: A developmental perspective.* New York: Guilford Press.

Houlihan, B., Fitzgerald, M. and O'Regan, M. (1994) 'Self-esteem, depression and hostility in Irish adolescents', *Journal of Adolescence,* No. 17, pp. 565-77.

Mullan, E. and Nic Gabhainn, S. (2003) 'Self-esteem and health risk behaviour: Is there a link?', *Irish Journal of Psychology,* Vol. 23, No. 1-2, pp. 27-36.

Neumark-Sztainer, D., Story, M., French, S. and Resnick, M. (1997) 'Psycho-social correlates of health compromising behaviours among adolescents', *Health Education Research*, No. 12, pp. 37-52.

Rhodes, J.E. (2002) *Stand by me: The risks and rewards of mentoring today's youth.* Cambridge, MA: Harvard University Press.

West, P. and Sweeting, H. (1997) ' "Lost Souls" and "Rebels": A challenge to the assumption that low self-esteem and unhealthy lifestyles are related', *Health Education,* No. 97, pp. 161-67.

Further information

■ KIDSCREEN/DISABKIDS Programme (www.kidscreen.diehauptstadt.de)

Self-reported happiness

Context

Ireland's commitment to the aims of the United Nations Convention on the Rights of the Child is evidenced by the significant policy and legislative developments that have taken place in recent years. The National Children's Strategy provides a coherent policy statement that reflects the aspirations and concerns of children themselves, as well as those who care for them, and within this recognises that good quality formal and informal supports for services are critical to children's well-being and well-becoming (Department of Health and Children, 2000). The Strategy sets out a vision of:

> 'An Ireland where children are respected as young citizens with a valued contribution to make and a voice of their own; where all children are cherished and supported by family and the wider society; where they enjoy a fulfilling childhood and realise their potential.'

Ireland's Second Report to the United Nations Committee on the Rights of the Child identifies significant developments across a number of areas of children's lives, including civil rights and freedoms, family environment and alternative care, basic health and welfare, education, leisure and cultural activities, and special protection measures (NCO, 2005). While recognising that these developments need to be continued and in some cases, improved, it is clear that considerable progress is being made in supporting all aspects of children's lives.

Significance

Adolescence is a period of greatly enhanced awareness of, and attention to, physical status and well-being. This period is traditionally viewed as a time of optimal health, with low levels of morbidity and chronic disease (Sells and Blum, 1996). Nevertheless, suicide, depression and other mental health conditions, as well as other adolescent-focus risks, threaten this notion of prevailing good health for adolescents (Scheidt *et al,* 2000).

The World Health Organization's definition of health includes physical, mental and social well-being as major components of health, suggesting that a thorough understanding of adolescent health should incorporate these components. The need to emphasise well-being is further strengthened by WHO reports showing that mental health problems increase their share of the overall disease burden, with specific attention given to youth since mid-adolescence is the typical onset age for a range of mental disorders (WHO, 2000). Well-being is multifaceted, according to several authors (Diener, 1984; Huebner, 1991; Wilkinson and Walford, 1998). Absence of distress is a major component, but equally important is the presence of positive affective states, such as happiness and excitement. Monitoring and documenting trends and cross-national differences in the psychological, social and physical well-being of young people may serve as a first important step in addressing the need for public health services adapted to the rising burden of mental health problems (Torsheim *et al*, 2001).

Measure

The proportion of children aged 10-17 who report being happy with their lives at present.

Key findings

■ In 2002, 89.5% of children aged 10-17 reported being happy with their lives at present *(see Table 68)*. This was similar to findings from 1998 (88.6%).

Differences by age, social class and gender
■ The percentage of children who reported being happy with their lives at present was higher among boys and younger children:
  - 91.2% of boys reported this, compared with 88.3% of girls;
  - 94.8% of 10-11 year-olds reported this, compared with 86.5% of 15-17 year-olds;
  - 10-11 year-old girls were most likely (96.0%) to report this, while 15-17 year-old girls were least likely (84.5%).

Table 68: Percentage of children who report being happy with their lives at present, by age, social class and gender (1998 and 2002)						
	1998			2002		
	Boys	Girls	Total	Boys	Girls	Total
Total	90.7	86.6	88.6	91.2	88.3	89.5
Years of age						
10-11	92.8	93.7	93.3	93.3	96.0	94.8
12-14	92.2	87.1	89.6	91.6	88.9	90.1
15-17	86.9	81.1	84.0	89.6	84.5	86.5
Social class						
SC 1-2	89.9	85.1	87.3	93.1	90.2	91.4
SC 3-4	89.7	88.8	89.3	92.4	88.4	90.1
SC 5-6	92.9	87.1	89.8	90.8	89.2	89.9

Source: HBSC Survey

Differences by geographical area

■ Children in the former Mid-Western Health Board area were more likely (91.4%) to report being happy with their lives at present, while children in the former South-Eastern Health Board area were least likely (87.9%) to report this *(see Table 69)*.

Table 69: Percentage of children aged 10-17 who report being happy with their lives at present, by former health board area (1998 and 2002)		
	1998	2002
Mid-Western Health Board	86.7	91.4
Western Health Board	88.7	91.3
North-Western Health Board	89.7	90.3
Midland Health Board	90.2	89.7
North-Eastern Health Board	87.5	89.4
Eastern Regional Health Authority	88.1	89.1
Southern Health Board	89.7	88.9
South-Eastern Health Board	88.6	87.9
Mean average	88.6	89.5

Source: HBSC Survey

Technical notes

This indicator is based on self-report and as such is susceptible to differences in interpretation. Children's perception of the word 'happy' is different to that of adults; it is also different between genders and is vulnerable to short-term stress (O'Higgins, 2002).

Percentage differences are presented for descriptive purposes only and may not reflect a statistically significant finding.

References

Department of Health and Children (2000) *The National Children's Strategy: Our Children – Their Lives.* Dublin: The Stationery Office.

Diener, E. (1984) 'Subjective Well-Being', *Psychological Bulletin*, No. 95, pp. 542-75.

Huebner, E.S. (1991) 'Initial Development of the Student's Life Satisfaction Scale', *School Psychology International,* No. 12, pp. 231-40.

NCO (2005) *Ireland's Second Report to the UN Committee on the Rights of the Child,* National Children's Office. Dublin: The Stationery Office.

O'Higgins, S. (2002) *'Through the Looking Glass': Young people's perceptions of the words 'Health' and 'Happy'* (unpublished MA Thesis). Galway: Department of Health Promotion, National University of Ireland.

Scheidt, P., Overpeck, M.D., Wyatt, W. and Aszmann, A. (2000) 'Adolescents' general health and well-being', in *Health and Health Behaviour among Young People,* C. Currie, K. Hurrelman, W. Settertobulte, R. Smith and J. Todd (eds.). Copenhagen: WHO-Europe.

Sells, W.C. and Blum, R.W. (1996) 'Morbidity and mortality among US adolescents: An overview of data and trends', *American Journal of Public Health,* Vol. 86, No. 4, pp. 513-19.

Torsheim, T., Samdal, O., Danielson, M., Dür, W., Hetland, J., Kostarova Unkovska, L. and Välimaa, R. (2001) 'Focus Area Rationale: Positive Health', in *Health Behaviour in School-aged Children: A World Health Organization Cross-national Study: Research Protocol for the 2001/02 Survey,* C. Currie, O. Samdal, W. Boyce and R. Smith (eds.). Edinburgh: Child and Adolescent Health Research Unit, University of Edinburgh.

UN (1989) *Convention on the Rights of the Child.* Geneva: United Nations Office of the High Commissioner for Human Rights. Available at www.ohchr.org

Wilkinson, R.B. and Walford, W. (1998) 'The measurement of adolescent psychological health: One or two dimensions?', *Journal of Youth and Adolescence,* No. 27, pp. 443-55.

WHO (2000) 'Cross-national comparisons of the prevalence and correlates of mental disorders', *Bulletin of the World Health Organization,* Vol. 78, No. 4, pp. 413-26.

Youth suicide

Context

Suicide was decriminalised in Ireland in 1993 and since that time, efforts to achieve a coordinated approach to prevention have been developed. Most recently, these efforts have resulted in the publication of *Reach Out: National Strategy for Action on Suicide Prevention 2005-2014* (HSE, 2005). This 10-year strategy builds on the work of the National Task Force on Suicide (1998) and takes account of the many strategic and operational initiatives developed by voluntary, statutory and community groups and individuals.

The vision of the Strategy is of a society where life is valued across all age groups, where the young learn from, and are strengthened by, the experiences of others and where the needs of those who are going through a difficult time are met in a caring way, so that:
■ the mental health and well-being of the whole population is valued;
■ mental illness is more widely recognised and understood, and those experiencing difficulties are offered the most effective and timely support possible;
■ the abuse of alcohol and other drugs is reduced considerably;
■ everyone who has engaged in deliberate self-harm is offered the most effective and timely support possible;
■ those affected by a suicide death or deliberate self-harm receive the most caring and helpful response possible.

Significance

There is an increasing recognition that suicide and deliberate self-harm represent a significant and growing problem in many Western countries (WHO, 2005). The National Suicide Research Foundation (2004) conducted a study with 3,830 teenagers, aged 15-17 years, in one area of Ireland as part of an ongoing international collaborative research project, the Child and Adolescent Self-harm in Europe (CASE) Study. The Irish study found that while overall, Irish adolescents have good mental health and report high levels of general well-being, 6.7% were identified as having a 'probable depression' and 9.2% a 'probable emotional disorder'. Self-harm was also common and 12.2% reported a lifetime history of deliberate self-harm.

Measure

The number of suicides among children aged 10-17, expressed as a proportion of all children in the same age group.

Key findings

■ In 2004, youth suicide among children aged 10-17 accounted for 18 out of a total of 457 suicides in the State *(see Table 70)*.

■ The suicide mortality rate among 10-17 year-olds was higher for boys than for girls. In 2004, the suicide mortality rate for boys aged 10-17 was 6 per 100,000 boys in this age group, which was over three times the rate for girls in the same age group (1.8).

Table 70: Number and rate (per 100,000) of suicides among persons aged 10-17 (2000-2004)										
	2000		2001		2002		2003		2004	
	No.	Rate	No.	Rate	No.	Rate	No.	Rate	No.	Rate
Boys	21	8.3	13	5.3	10	4.1	17	7.2	14	6.0
Girls	4	1.7	3	1.3	5	2.2	4	1.8	4	1.8
Total - 10-17 years	25	5.1	16	3.3	15	3.2	21	4.5	18	4.0
Total - all ages	486	12.8	519	13.5	478	12.2	497	12.5	457	11.3

Source: Vital Statistics, CSO

■ Overall, in 2004, youth suicide accounted for 22% of the total deaths in the 10-17 age group *(see Table 71)*. By gender, youth suicide accounted for 23.7% of all deaths for boys aged 15-17 and for 17.4% of all deaths for girls aged 15-17.

Table 71: Suicides as percentage of total deaths, by gender (2000-2004)					
	2000	2001	2002	2003	2004
Boys	24.7	16.3	13.2	26.6	23.7
Girls	6.9	7.3	10.4	14.3	17.4
Total	17.5	13.2	12.1	22.8	22.0

Source: Vital Statistics, CSO

Technical notes

Causes of deaths since 1979 have been classified using the 9th Revision of the International Classification of Diseases, Injuries and Causes of Death, as recommended by the World Health Organization.

The population figures used in the calculation of suicide rates per 100,000 people are based on the defacto population present on Census night in any area. This includes visitors present on Census night as well as those in residence, while usual residents temporarily absent from the area are excluded from the Census count.

References

HSE (2005) *Reach Out: National Strategy for Action on Suicide Prevention 2005-2014.* Dublin: Health Service Executive.

National Suicide Research Foundation (2004) *Young People's Mental Health: A Report from the Lifestyle and Coping Survey.* Cork: National Suicide Research Foundation and Department of Epidemiology and Public Health, University College Cork.

National Task Force on Suicide (1998) *Report of the National Task Force on Suicide,* Department of Health and Children. Dublin: The Stationery Office.

WHO (2005) *The European Health Report 2005. Public health action for healthier children and populations.* Copenhagen: World Health Organization.

Further information

- National Suicide Review Group (www.nsrg.ie)

Physical activity

Context

There are three main areas around which structured physical activity for children and young people can take place – the physical education curriculum in schools, extra-curricular sports played in schools and sports played outside the school (Fahey *et al*, 2005). Each of these areas is supported by Government policy and a number of different Government departments are involved. *Ready, Steady, Play! A National Play Policy*, published in 2004, provides a framework for building on existing provision and for the creation of new public play opportunities for children up to the age of 12 years (NCO, 2004). The Office of the Minister for Children, in consultation with major stakeholders, including young people themselves, is currently working on the development of a National Recreation Policy for children in the 12-18 age group.

Physical activity is an important focus within these policies. The Cardiovascular Health Strategy highlighted the importance of physical activity and provided the impetus for the development of a national infrastructure to support physical activity among adults and children (Department of Health and Children, 1999). This included the appointment of Physical Activity Coordinators in all former health board areas to work closely with local sports partnerships and voluntary organisations. Initiatives under this Strategy include the development of a physical activity pyramid for young people, the launch of a number of physical activity campaigns and the implementation of physical activity programmes in primary schools.

One of the aims of the National Health Promotion Strategy 2000-2005 is 'to increase participation in regular, moderate, physical activity' (Department of Health and Children, 2000). To accomplish this, the Strategy recommends working in partnership with relevant bodies to facilitate access and participation in regular physical activity, and identifying models of good practice that encourage young people (especially young girls) to participate in regular physical activity. The Irish Sports Council (which operates as an agency under the aegis of the Department of Arts, Sport and Tourism) has a mandate, arising from the Irish Sports Council Act (Government of Ireland, 1999), to develop strategies for increasing participation in recreational sport.

Significance

There is general agreement that regular participation in physical activities contributes to improved quality of life, both physical and psychological (De Roiste and Dineen, 2005; US Department of Health and Human Services, 1996; Sallis and Owen, 1999; Sallis *et al*, 2000). The contribution of physical activity to health includes, among others, reducing the risk of cardiovascular disease, cancer of the colon, non-insulin-dependent diabetes mellitus and osteoporosis (US Department of Health and Human Services, 1996; Sallis and Owen, 1999; Sallis *et al*, 2000; Welk *et al*, 2000). An increase in physical activity is also often associated with an increase in fitness, which in turn can influence the quality of sleep (Shapiro *et al*, 1984).

Involvement in physical activity is also associated with strong social support, such as encouragement from parents, siblings and peers. Data from one international survey suggests that those who make friends easily and spend time with friends after school are more likely to undertake physical activity (Hickman *et al*, 2000). However, it should also be noted that the likelihood of musculoskeletal injuries increases with physical activity levels (Baker *et al*, 1992; Williams *et al*, 1998; Patel and Nelson, 2000). Physical activity is particularly important among adolescents because participation at that time has been shown to be an important predictor of future levels of physical activity (Biddle, 1994).

Findings from a national study, commissioned by the Office of the Minister for Children, found that almost 9 out of 10 young people play at least one sport, either competitively or recreationally (De Roiste and Dineen, 2005). Soccer, Gaelic football and hurling are by far the most popular sports for boys and young men. For girls and young women, the most popular sports are basketball, Gaelic football and swimming. Participation in sport declines with age: 96% of 12-year-olds are involved in at least one sport, compared to 77% of 18-year-olds. Findings from another study, however, highlight the fact that students in second-level schools receive, on average, 69 minutes of PE per week, which is less than the recommended 2 hours (Fahey *et al*, 2005).

PART 3: CHILDREN'S OUTCOMES

Measure

> **The proportion of children aged 10-17 who report being physically active for at least 60 minutes per day on at least 2 days per week.**

Key findings

- In 2002, 87.4% of children aged 10-17 reported being physically active for at least 60 minutes per day on 2 days or more per week *(see Table 72)*.

Differences by age, social class and gender

- The percentage of children who reported being physically active for at least 60 minutes per day on 2 days or more per week was higher among boys, younger children and children from higher social classes:
  - 91.1% of boys reported this, compared with 84.7% of girls;
  - 89.7% of 10-11 year-olds reported this, compared with 84.1% of 15-17 year-olds;
  - 89.7% of children from social class 1-2 reported this, compared to 86.3% of children from social class 5-6.

Table 72: Percentage of children who report to be physically active for at least 60 minutes per day on 2 days per week, by age, social class and gender (2002)			
	Boys	Girls	Total
Total	91.1	84.7	87.4
Years of age			
10-11	92.0	87.8	89.7
12-14	91.8	87.6	89.4
15-17	89.8	80.2	84.1
Social class			
SC 1-2	93.7	87.1	89.7
SC 3-4	91.9	84.6	87.7
SC 5-6	89.9	83.4	86.3

Source: HBSC Survey

Differences by geographical area

- 89.4% of all children in the former Eastern Regional Health Authority reported that they are active for at least 60 minutes per day on 2 or more days per week, compared with 83.7% of children in the former North-Western Health Board area *(see Table 73)*.

Table 73: Percentage of children aged 10-17 who report to be physically active for at least 60 minutes per day on 2 days per week, by former health board area (2002)

Eastern Regional Health Authority	89.4
Midland Health Board	88.5
Western Health Board	88.5
North-Eastern Health Board	87.6
Southern Health Board	86.4
Mid-Western Health Board	85.8
South-Eastern Health Board	85.1
North-Western Health Board	83.7
Mean average	**87.4**

Source: HBSC Survey

International comparisons

- From the 2002 HBSC Survey, using the ages of 11, 13 and 15 only to draw international comparisons, 89.7% of Irish children reported being physically active for at least 60 minutes per day on 2 or more days per week *(see Figure 39).* This compared with the HBSC average of 86.8%.

- Among all 34 countries that used this HBSC item, the lowest percentage for this indicator was found among children from Malta (75.4%) and the highest among children from Scotland (92.3%).

- Overall, Irish children ranked 9th among all 35 countries participating in the survey. Irish 11-year-old children were ranked 3rd, Irish 13-year-old children were ranked 10th and Irish 15-year-old children were ranked 16th.

PART 3: CHILDREN'S OUTCOMES

Figure 39: Percentage of children who report being physically active for at least 60 minutes per day on 2 days per week, by country (2002)

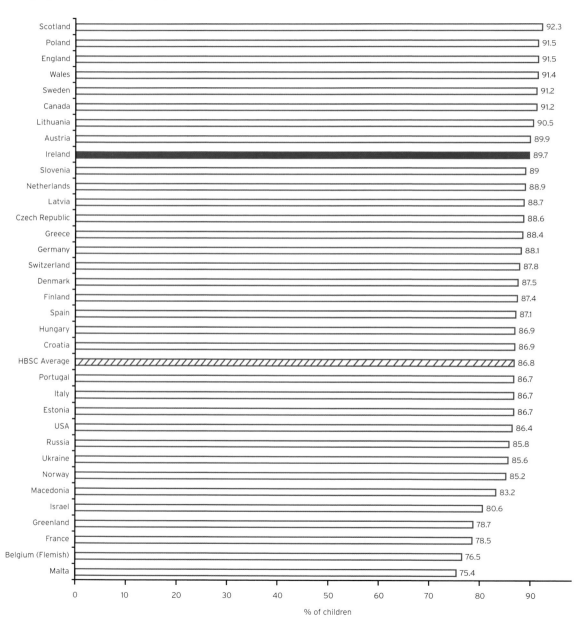

Country	%
Scotland	92.3
Poland	91.5
England	91.5
Wales	91.4
Sweden	91.2
Canada	91.2
Lithuania	90.5
Austria	89.9
Ireland	89.7
Slovenia	89
Netherlands	88.9
Latvia	88.7
Czech Republic	88.6
Greece	88.4
Germany	88.1
Switzerland	87.8
Denmark	87.5
Finland	87.4
Spain	87.1
Hungary	86.9
Croatia	86.9
HBSC Average	86.8
Portugal	86.7
Italy	86.7
Estonia	86.7
USA	86.4
Russia	85.8
Ukraine	85.6
Norway	85.2
Macedonia	83.2
Israel	80.6
Greenland	78.7
France	78.5
Belgium (Flemish)	76.5
Malta	75.4

% of children

Source: HBSC Survey

Measure

> **The proportion of children aged 10-17 who report being physically active for at least 60 minutes per day on more than 4 days per week.**

Key findings

- In 2002, 47.4% of children aged 10-17 reported being physically active for at least 60 minutes per day on 4 or more days per week *(see Table 74).*

Differences by age, social class and gender

- The percentage of children who reported being physically active for at least 60 minutes per day on 4 or more days per week was higher among boys, younger children and children from higher social classes:
  - 57.5% of boys reported this, compared with 39.9% of girls;
  - 59.8% of 10-11 year-olds reported this, compared with 37.7% of 15-17 year-olds;
  - some 48% of children from social classes 1-4 reported this, compared to 46% of children from social class 5-6.

Table 74: Percentage of children who report to be physically active for at least 60 minutes per day on more than 4 days per week, by age, social class and gender (2002)

	Boys	Girls	Total
Total	57.5	39.9	47.4
Years of age			
10-11	65.9	54.7	59.8
12-14	60.4	43.7	51.1
15-17	49.7	29.6	37.7
Social class			
SC 1-2	58.0	42.3	48.6
SC 3-4	59.5	39.3	48.0
SC 5-6	55.2	38.4	46.1

Source: HBSC Survey

Differences by geographical area

- Fewer children in the former South-Eastern Health Board area report that they are active for at least 60 minutes per day on 4 or more days per week (42.7%) *(see Table 75).* The highest percentage was in the former Eastern Regional Health Authority (51.4%).

PART 3: CHILDREN'S OUTCOMES

195

Table 75: Percentage of children aged 10-17 who report to be physically active for at least 60 minutes per day on more than 4 days per week, by former health board area (2002)	
Eastern Regional Health Authority	51.4
Mid-Western Health Board	50.3
Southern Health Board	49.6
Western Health Board	49.2
North-Eastern Health Board	46.5
Midland Health Board	45.2
North-Western Health Board	42.9
South-Eastern Health Board	42.7
Mean average	**47.4**

Source: HBSC Survey

International comparisons

■ From the 2002 HBSC Survey, using the ages of 11, 13 and 15 only to draw international comparisons, 50.7% of Irish children reported to be physically active for at least 60 minutes per day on 4 days or more per week *(see Figure 40)*. This compared with the HBSC average of 36.7%.

■ Among all 34 countries that used this HBSC item, the lowest percentage for this indicator was found among children from France (21.5%) and the highest among children from the USA (53.3%).

■ Overall, Irish children ranked 2nd. Irish 11-year-old children were ranked 1st, Irish 13-year-old children were ranked 1st and Irish 15-year-old children were ranked 6th.

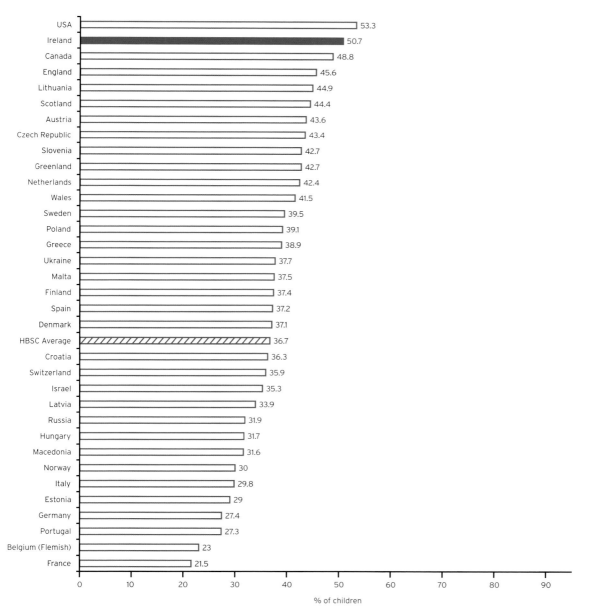

Figure 40: Percentage of children who report being physically active for at least 60 minutes per day on more than 4 days per week, by country (2002)

Country	% of children
USA	53.3
Ireland	50.7
Canada	48.8
England	45.6
Lithuania	44.9
Scotland	44.4
Austria	43.6
Czech Republic	43.4
Slovenia	42.7
Greenland	42.7
Netherlands	42.4
Wales	41.5
Sweden	39.5
Poland	39.1
Greece	38.9
Ukraine	37.7
Malta	37.5
Finland	37.4
Spain	37.2
Denmark	37.1
HBSC Average	36.7
Croatia	36.3
Switzerland	35.9
Israel	35.3
Latvia	33.9
Russia	31.9
Hungary	31.7
Macedonia	31.6
Norway	30
Italy	29.8
Estonia	29
Germany	27.4
Portugal	27.3
Belgium (Flemish)	23
France	21.5

% of children

Source: HBSC Survey

Technical notes

This indicator looks at moderate to intense activity, including activity undertaken during school hours, in a 'normal' or 'typical' week. This indicator was developed to provide a reasonable method for assessing participation in overall physical activity and for assessing achievement of current guidelines and was validated to meet the requirements, the 60-minute Moderate-to-Vigorous Physical Activity (MVPA) screening measure (Prochaska *et al*, 2001). The indicator has been part of the international HBSC since 2001.

The HBSC uses a self-completion questionnaire and as such is based on self-report. Most validation studies on self-reported physical activity in young people have demonstrated moderate correlations at best between self-report measures of activity and objective criteria (Sallis, 1991). Where studies have assessed absolute validity of self-report measures using heart rate monitors or accelerometers, there has been evidence of substantial over-reporting of physical activity, although reports for the number of days with at least 60 minutes of moderate activity are more accurate (Welk *et al*, 2000).

Percentage differences are presented for descriptive purposes only and may not reflect a statistically significant finding.

References

Baker, S.P., O'Neill, B., Ginsburg, M.J. and Li, G. (1992). *The Injury Fact Book* (2nd edition). New York: Oxford University Press.

Biddle, S. (1994) 'What helps and hinders people becoming more physically active?', in *Moving on International Perspectives promoting Physical Activity,* A. Killoran, P. Fentem and C. Caspersen (eds.). London: Health Education Authority.

Biddle, S., Sallis, J. and Cavill, N. (1998) 'Policy framework for young people and health-enhancing physical activity', in *Young and Active? Young people and health-enhancing physical activity: Evidence and implications,* S. Biddle, J. Sallis and N. Cavill (eds.). London: Health Education Authority.

De Roiste, A. and Dineen, J. (2005) *Young people's views about opportunities, barriers and supports to recreation and leisure,* National Children's Office. Dublin: The Stationery Office.

Department of Health and Children (1999) *Cardiovascular Health Strategy – Building healthier hearts.* Dublin: The Stationery Office.

Department of Health and Children (2000). *National Health Promotion Strategy 2000-2005.* Dublin: The Stationery Office.

Due, P., Hickman, M., Komkov, A., Gaspar de Matos, M., Mandoza, R., Roberts, C., Todd, J., Tynjälä, J. and Woynarowska, B. (2001) 'Focus Area Rationale: Physical Activity', in *Health Behaviour in School-aged Children: A World Health Organization Cross-national Study: Research Protocol for the 2001/02 Survey,* C. Currie, O. Samdal, W. Boyce and R. Smith (eds.). Edinburgh: Child and Adolescent Health Research Unit, University of Edinburgh.

Fahey, T., Delaney, L. and Gannon, B. (2005) *School Children and Sport in Ireland.* Dublin: Economic and Social Research Institute.

Government of Ireland (1999) *Irish Sports Council Act.* Dublin: The Stationery Office.

Hickman, M., Roberts, C. and Matos, M. (2000) 'Exercise and leisure time activities', in *Health and Health Behaviour among Young People,* C. Currie, K. Hurrelmann, W. Settertolute, R. Smith and J. Todd (eds.). Copenhagen: WHO-Europe.

NCO (2004) *Ready, Steady, Play! A National Play Policy,* National Children's Office. Dublin: The Stationery Office.

Patel, D.R. and Nelson, T.L. (2000) 'Sports injuries in adolescents', *Medical Clinics of North America,* Vol. 84, No. 4, pp. 983-1007.

Prochaska, J.J., Sallis, J.F. and Long, B. (2001) 'A physical activity screening measure for use with adolescents in primary care', *Archives of Paediatrics and Adolescent Medicine,* No. 155, pp. 554-59.

Sallis, J.F. (1991). 'Self-report measures of children's physical activity', *Journal of School Health,* No. 61, pp. 215-19.

Sallis, J.F. and Owen, N. (1999) *Physical activity and behavioural medicine.* Thousand Oaks: Sage.

Sallis, J.F., Prochaska, J.J and Taylor, W.C. (2000) 'A review of correlates of physical activity of children and adolescents', *Medicine & Science in Sports & Exercise,* Vol. 32, No. 5, pp. 963-75.

Shapiro, C.M., Warren, P.M., Trinder, J., Paxton, S.J., Oswald, I., Flenley, D.C. and Catterall, J.R. (1984) 'Fitness facilitates sleep', *European Journal of Applied Physiology,* No. 53, pp. 1-4.

US Department of Health and Human Services (1996) *Physical Activity and Health: A Report of the Surgeon General.* Atlanta, GA: US Department of Health and Human Services, Centers for Disease Control and Prevention, and National Center for Chronic Disease Prevention and Health Promotion.

Welk, G.J., Corbin, C.B. and Dale, D. (2000) 'Measurement issues in the assessment of physical activity in children', *Research Quarterly for Exercise and Sport,* Vol. 71, No. 2, pp. 59-73.

Williams, J.M., Wright, P., Currie, C.E. and Beattie, T.F. (1998) 'Sports-related injuries in Scottish adolescents aged 11-15', *British Journal of Sports Medicine,* Vol. 32, No. 4, pp. 291-96.

PART 3: CHILDREN'S OUTCOMES

199

Eating habits

Context

The strategic aim of the National Health Promotion Strategy 2000-2005 in relation to eating well is 'to increase the percentage of the population who consume the recommended daily servings of food and maintain a healthy weight' (Department of Health and Children, 2000). It also includes the objective to promote healthy eating habits and healthy body image among school-going children and young people. More recently, the *Report of the National Task Force on Obesity* notes a probable decreased risk of overweight and obesity associated with home and school environments that support healthy food choices for children and a possible increased risk associated with high proportions of food prepared outside the home (Department of Health and Children, 2005).

The 2003 Food and Nutrition Guidelines for Primary Schools highlight the importance for children of eating breakfast on a daily basis (Department of Health and Children, 2003). The guidelines recommend that schools set up breakfast clubs to promote healthy breakfasts. The 2005 *Report of the National Task Force on Obesity* reinforces these guidelines. A new National Nutritional Policy will be published in 2006. Initiatives identified in a recent review of the National Health Promotion Strategy include the implementation of the 'Health food made easy' Community Programme (which is based on peer-led healthy eating interventions for the socially disadvantaged); the provision of nutrition training to teachers, community workers, Youth Reach workers and other service providers; and the appointment of additional community dieticians (McKenna *et al*, 2004). In addition, the School Meals Programme, which operates under the auspices of the Department of Social and Family Affairs, provides funding to assist in meeting the costs of groups operating innovative school meals projects.

Significance

Proper food intake can prevent immediate health problems, such as iron deficiency anaemia, obesity, eating disorders and dental caries. It may also prevent long-term health problems, such as coronary heart disease, cancer and stroke (Center for Disease Control and Prevention, 1997). Eating habits acquired and shaped during childhood and adolescence have been tracked into adulthood (Kelder *et al*, 1994; Lien *et al*, 2001; Post *et al*, 2001), where the association between diet and health is well established (Willett, 1994).

Part of having a healthy diet is having a regular breakfast (Keski-Rahkonen *et al*, 2004) since breakfast contributes to the quality and quantity of a person's daily dietary intake (Pollitt, 1995). Breakfast is considered to be an important factor in a healthy lifestyle (Keski-Rahkonen *et al*, 2004) and has been used as an indicator of food poverty. Skipping breakfast has been linked to inadequate dietary intake (Sampson *et al*, 1995; Nicklas *et al*, 1993), which, in turn, prevents

200

children from taking full advantage of the learning opportunities provided in schools. This habit was also found to interfere with cognition and learning (Benton and Parker, 1998; Wesnes *et al*, 2003). Psycho-social changes encountered during adolescence (e.g. risk-taking, search for self-identity), together with busy schedules, may affect eating patterns and food choices (Story *et al*, 2002; Sigman-Grant, 2002) and this may put children at increased risk for unhealthy eating habits and/or weight-related eating disorders, resulting in poor nutritional health. Skipping breakfast has also been linked with smoking (Hoglund *et al*, 1998), alcohol and drug use (Isralowitz and Trostler, 1996), sedentary lifestyles (Baumert *et al*, 1998) and obesity (Wolfe *et al*, 1994). In addition, people who skip breakfast appear more likely to consume snacks higher in fat and lower in fibre during the remainder of the day (Resnicow, 1991).

Measure

> **The proportion of children aged 10-17 who report eating breakfast on 5 or more days per week.**

Key findings

■ In 2002, 77.3% of children aged 10-17 reported eating breakfast on 5 or more days per week *(see Table 76).*

Differences by age, social class and gender
■ The percentage of children who reported eating breakfast on 5 or more days per week was higher among boys and younger children:
   - 81.4% of boys reported this, compared with 74.3% of girls;
   - 87.4% of 10-11 year-olds reported this, compared with 70.9% of 15-17 year-olds.

Table 76: Percentage of children who report to eat breakfast 5 or more days per week, by age, social class and gender (2002)			
	Boys	Girls	Total
Total	81.4	74.3	77.3
Years of age			
10-11	87.3	87.4	87.4
12-14	82.4	76.1	78.9
15-17	77.5	66.4	70.9
Social class			
SC 1-2	84.6	79.9	81.5
SC 3-4	79.8	71.8	75.3
SC 5-6	82.8	73.5	77.7

Source: HBSC Survey

PART 3: CHILDREN'S OUTCOMES

Differences by geographical area

■ Children in the former North-Eastern Health Board area were most likely (84.3%) to report eating breakfast on 5 or more days per week, while children in the former South-Eastern Health Board area were least likely (74.6%) to report this *(see Table 77)*.

Table 77: Percentage of children aged 10-17 who report to eat breakfast on 5 or more days per week, by former health board area (2002)	
North-Eastern Health Board	84.3
North-Western Health Board	81.6
Mid-Western Health Board	80.4
Midland Health Board	78.3
Western Health Board	76.9
Eastern Regional Health Authority	75.9
Southern Health Board	75.2
South-Eastern Health Board	74.6
Mean average	77.3

Source: HBSC Survey

International comparisons

■ From the 2002 HBSC Survey, using the ages of 11, 13 and 15 only to draw international comparisons, 80.1% of Irish children reported eating breakfast on 5 or more days per week *(see Figure 41)*. This compared with the HBSC average of 75.7%.

■ Among all 32 countries that used this HBSC item, the lowest percentage for this indicator was found among Slovenian children (52.7%) and the highest among children from Portugal (86.2%).

■ Overall, Irish children ranked 14th. Irish 11-year-old children were ranked 8th, Irish 13-year-old children were ranked 14th and Irish 15-year-old children were ranked 16th.

Figure 41: Percentage of children who report to eat breakfast on 5 or more days per week, by country (2002)

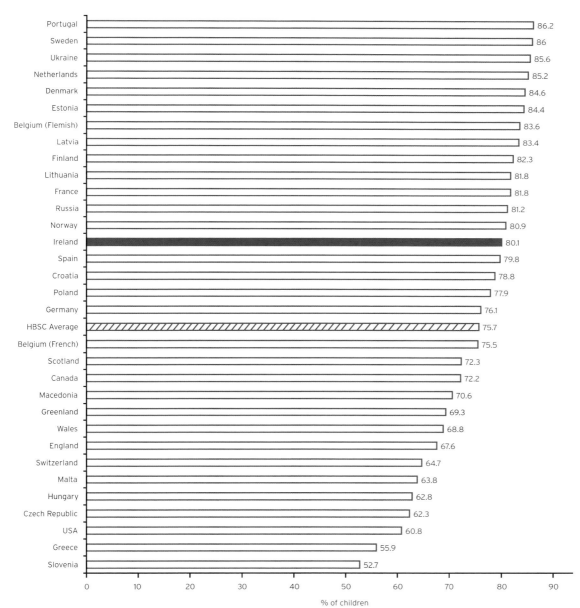

Country	%
Portugal	86.2
Sweden	86
Ukraine	85.6
Netherlands	85.2
Denmark	84.6
Estonia	84.4
Belgium (Flemish)	83.6
Latvia	83.4
Finland	82.3
Lithuania	81.8
France	81.8
Russia	81.2
Norway	80.9
Ireland	80.1
Spain	79.8
Croatia	78.8
Poland	77.9
Germany	76.1
HBSC Average	75.7
Belgium (French)	75.5
Scotland	72.3
Canada	72.2
Macedonia	70.6
Greenland	69.3
Wales	68.8
England	67.6
Switzerland	64.7
Malta	63.8
Hungary	62.8
Czech Republic	62.3
USA	60.8
Greece	55.9
Slovenia	52.7

% of children

Source: HBSC Survey

PART 3: CHILDREN'S OUTCOMES

203

Technical notes

This indicator is based on self-report and as such is susceptible to differences in interpretation. Although the item was not in Ireland, the findings from pilot studies in Scotland and Belgium (Flanders) showed that the interpretation of breakfast was clear. An additional possible bias is that of recall, as students are asked to report retrospectively on their behaviour.

Percentage differences are presented for descriptive purposes only and may not reflect a statistically significant finding.

References

Baumert, P.W. Jr., Henderson J.M. and Thompson N.J. (1998) 'Health risk behaviours of adolescent participants in organised sports', *Journal of Adolescence Health,* Vol. 22, No. 6, pp. 460-65.

Benton, D. and Parker P.Y. (1998) 'Breakfast, blood glucose and cognition', *American Journal of Clinical Nutrition,* Vol. 67, No. 4, pp. 772S-778S.

Center for Disease Control and Prevention (1997) 'Guidelines for school health programs to promote lifelong healthy eating', *Journal of School Health,* No. 67, pp. 9-26.

Department of Health and Children (2000) *National Health Promotion Strategy 2000-2005.* Dublin: The Stationery Office.

Department of Health and Children (2003) *Food and Nutrition Guidelines for Primary Schools.* Dublin: The Stationery Office.

Department of Health and Children (2005) *Obesity – The Policy Challenges. The Report of the National Task Force on Obesity.* Dublin: The Stationery Office.

Hoglund, D., Samuelson, G. and Mark, A. (1998) 'Food habits in Swedish adolescents in relation to socio-economic conditions', *European Journal of Clinical Nutrition,* Vol. 52, No. 11, pp. 784-89.

Isralowitz, R.E. and Trostler, N. (1996) 'Substance use: Towards an understanding of its relation to nutrition-related attitudes and behaviour among Israeli high-school youth', *Journal of Adolescence Health,* Vol. 19, No. 3, pp. 184-89.

Kelder, S.H., Perry, C.L., Klepp, K.I. and Lytle, L.A. (1994) 'Longitudinal tracking of adolescent smoking, physical activity and food choice behaviours', *American Journal of Public Health,* Vol. 84, No. 7, pp. 1121-26.

Keski-Rahkonen, A., Viken, R.J., Kaprio, J., Rissanen, A. and Rose, R.J. (2004) 'Genetic and environmental factors in breakfast eating patterns', *Behaviour Genetics,* Vol. 34, No. 5, pp. 503-14.

Lien, N., Lytle, L.A. and Klepp K.I. (2001) 'Stability in consumption of fruit, vegetables and sugary foods in a cohort from age 14 to age 21', *Preventive Medicine,* Vol. 33, No. 3, pp. 217-26.

McKenna, V., Barry, M. and Friel, S. (2004) *Review of the National Health Promotion Strategy,* Department of Health and Children. Dublin: The Stationery Office.

Nicklas, T.A., Bao, W., Webber, L.S. and Berenson, G.S. (1993) 'Breakfast consumption affects adequacy of total daily intake in children', *Journal of the American Dietetic Association,* Vol. 93, No. 8, pp. 886-91.

Pollitt, E. (1995) 'Does breakfast make a difference in school?', *Journal of the American Dietetic Association,* Vol. 95, No. 10, pp. 1134-39.

Post, B., De Vente, W., Kemper, H.C. and Twisk, J.W. (2001) 'Longitudinal trends in and tracking of energy and nutrient intake over 20 years in a Dutch cohort of men and women between 13 and 33 years of age: The Amsterdam growth and health longitudinal study', *British Journal of Nutrition,* Vol. 85, No. 3, pp. 375-85.

Resnicow, K. (1991) 'The relationship between breakfast habits and plasma cholesterol levels in school children', *Journal of School Health,* No. 61, pp. 81-85.

Sampson, A.E., Dixit, S., Meyers, A.F. and Houser R. Jr. (1995) 'The nutritional impact of breakfast consumption on the diets of inner-city African-American elementary school children', *Journal of the National Medical Association,* Vol. 87, No. 3, pp. 195-202.

Sigman-Grant, M. (2002) 'Strategies for counselling adolescents', *Journal of the American Dietetic Association,* Vol. 102 (Supplement 3), S32-39.

Story, M., Neumark-Sztainer, D. and French, S.A. (2002) 'Individual and environmental influences on adolescent eating behaviours', *Journal of the American Dietetic Association,* Vol. 102, No. 3, S40-51.

Wesnes, K.A., Pincock, C., Richardson, D., Helm, G. and Hails, S. (2003) 'Breakfast reduces declines in attention and memory over the morning in school children', *Appetite*, No. 41, pp. 329-31.

Willett, W.C. (1994). 'Diet and Health: What should we eat?', *Science,* Vol. 264, No. 5158, pp. 532-37.

Wolfe, W.S., Campbell, C.C., Frongillo, E.A. Jr., Haas, J.D. and Melnik, T.A. (1994) 'Overweight school children in New York State: Prevalence and characteristics', *American Journal of Public Health,* Vol. 84, No. 5, pp. 807-13.

PART 3: CHILDREN'S OUTCOMES

Homeless children

Context

According to the Housing Act (Government of Ireland, 1988), a person shall be regarded as being homeless if 'there is no accommodation available which, in the opinion of the Authority, he, together with any other person who normally resides with him or might be reasonably expected to reside with him, can reasonably occupy or remain in occupation of, or he is living in a hospital, county home, night shelter or other such institution and is so living because he has no accommodation of the kind referred to in paragraph (a) and he is, in the opinion of the Authority, unable to provide accommodation from his own resources'.

The Child Care Act (Government of Ireland, 1991) provides the legislative basis for addressing the needs of homeless young people in Ireland by making the Health Service Executive (HSE) responsible for those under the age of 18. A strategic commitment has been given by the Irish Government to improving the lives of children and young people who are homeless and this framework is set out in the Youth Homelessness Strategy (Department of Health and Children, 2001). It is reiterated in the most recent national Social Partnership Agreement (Department of the Taoiseach, 2006). The goal of the Youth Homelessness Strategy is 'to reduce and if possible eliminate youth homelessness through preventative strategies and where a child becomes homeless to ensure that he/she benefits from a comprehensive range of services aimed at re-integrating him/her into his/her community as quickly as possible'.

There is no single, universally accepted definition of 'homelessness'. Definitions can range across a continuum, from those who sleep rough on the streets to those who are in inadequate accommodation or are at risk of becoming homeless. Within the Youth Homelessness Strategy, young homeless people are defined as 'those who are sleeping on the streets or in other places not intended for night-time accommodation or not providing safe protection from the elements or those whose usual night-time residence is a public or private shelter, emergency lodging, B&B or such, providing protection from the elements but lacking the other characteristics of a home and/or intended for only a short stay' (Department of Health and Children, 2001, p. 11).

Periodic assessments of the numbers of homeless young people have been undertaken in three counties in Ireland (Dublin, Kildare and Wicklow) since 1999. The findings from these assessments have shown a consistent decrease in numbers, from a high of 210 in 1999 to 62 in 2005 (Homeless Agency, 2006). The only national data available in respect of homeless young people are those from the HSE and for that reason, along with the legal obligation placed on the HSE to care for these children, the data presented here relate to 'those children known to the Health Service Executive'.

Since 2001, a number of significant developments have taken place. Approximately €12 million has been allocated by the Department of Health and Children to the HSE for the development of youth homelessness services; 195 new whole-time equivalent posts have been filled across the 10 former health board areas; 11 new residential units have opened nationally; and over 422 new or extended services have been developed around the country (NCO, 2005).

Significance

Homelessness among children and young people is one of the most significant forms of social exclusion and many children are already disadvantaged before they become homeless. Reasons why children and young people presented as homeless to the former health board areas in 2004 included:
■ abuse (including emotional, physical and sexual abuse, and neglect);
■ difficulties with the child (including emotional/behavioural problems, abuse of drugs/alcohol, involvement in crime, pregnancy, mental health problems and physical illness/disability);
■ family (including family members abusing drugs/alcohol, domestic violence, parent unable to cope because of financial/housing problems).

The Irish as well as the international research literature, however, has consistently demonstrated that a history of State care is a characteristic common to homeless children and young people (Keane and Crowley, 1990; Mayock and Vekić, 2006; Perris, 1999; Kelleher *et al*, 2000).

A number of studies have demonstrated a range of both short- and long-term physical difficulties experienced by people who are homeless. These include chest infections, dental health problems (Costello and Howley, 1999) and hepatitis C (Hickey and Downey, 2003). Substantial mental health problems have also been identified: one Irish study estimated that at least one-third of all homeless people in Ireland have mental health problems (McKeown, 1999). Although the complexity of the relationship between drug and alcohol use and being homeless is not fully understood, there is a general agreement that drug and alcohol use are both very prevalent among that population (Smith *et al*, 2001; Crawley and Daly, 2004). Young people who are homeless are vulnerable to victimisation of all types, including robbery and sexual harassment, and also more likely to report having a history of offending (Mayock and Vekić, 2006).

PART 3: CHILDREN'S OUTCOMES

207

Measure

The number of homeless children, expressed as a proportion of all children.

Key findings

- The total number of young people who appeared to the former health boards to be homeless in 2004 was 495 *(see Table 78)*.
- The former Eastern Regional Health Authority had the highest number of young people who appeared to be homeless (213) and this accounted for almost 43% of the total.
- The overall rate of youth homelessness in 2004 was 45.8 per 100,000. This figure has varied over the last five years, from 41.6 per 100,000 (2001) and 53.9 per 100,000 (2000).
- The data suggest a strong urban bias in respect of the number of children 'out of home' each year. The highest numbers of children known to the former health boards to be out of home are, in general, in the former Eastern and Southern Health Boards areas, with the lowest number in the former North-Western Health Board area *(see also Figure 42)*.

Table 78: Number of homeless children, by former health board area (2000-2004)	2000	2001	2002	2003	2004
Eastern Regional Health Authority	268	186	242	207	213
Midland Health Board	9	12	33	17	18
Mid-Western Health Board	60	60	34	33	43
North-Eastern Health Board	19	36	18	20	15
North-Western Health Board	6	11	1	2	5
South-Eastern Health Board	110	57	77	61	23
Southern Health Board	79	55	102	102	132
Western Health Board	37	34	27	34	46
State	588	451	534	476	495
Rate per 100,000	53.9	41.6	49.6	44.2	45.8

Source: Childcare Interim Dataset, Department of Health and Children

Figure 42: Number of homeless children, by former health board area (2000 and 2004)

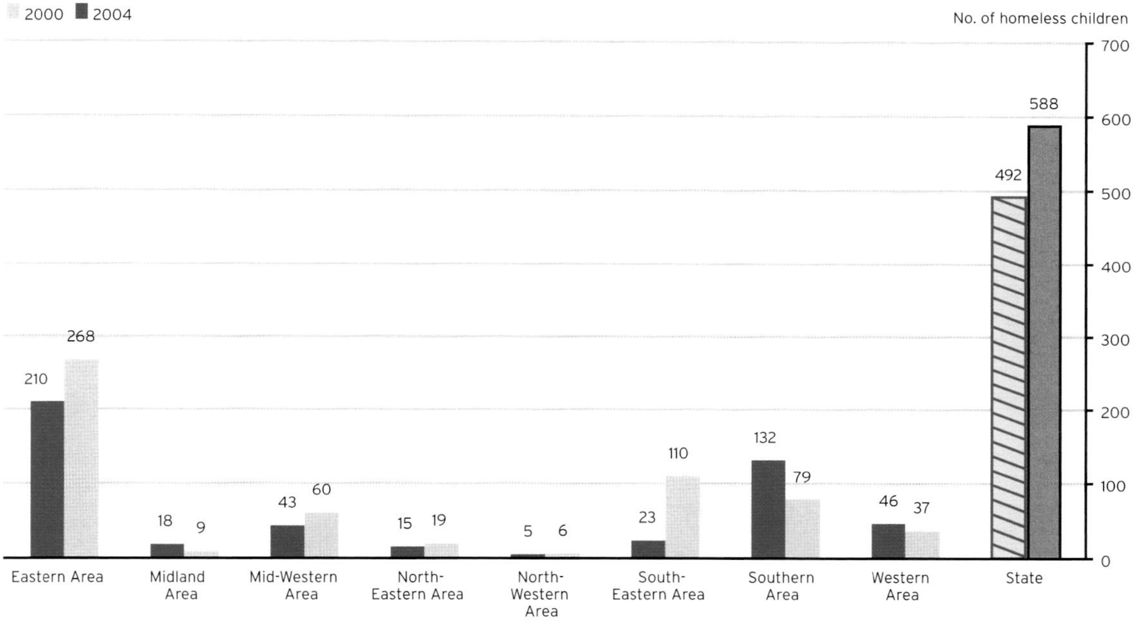

Source: Childcare Interim Dataset, Department of Health and Children

Differences by gender

■ In 2004, more girls (254) than boys (241) appeared to the former health boards to be homeless *(see Table 79).*

Table 79: Number and rate (per 100,000) of homeless children, by gender and former health board area (2004)			
	Boys	Girls	Total
Eastern Regional Health Authority	115	98	213
Midland Health Board	9	9	18
Mid-Western Health Board	18	25	43
North-Eastern Health Board	3	12	15
North-Western Health Board	3	2	5
South-Eastern Health Board	8	15	23
Southern Health Board	64	68	132
Western Health Board	21	25	46
State	241	254	495

Source: Childcare Interim Dataset, Department of Health and Children

Differences by age

■ The number of young people aged less than 12 years who appeared to the former health boards to be homeless decreased between 2000 and 2004 – from 61 to 21 respectively *(see Table 80)*.

■ Between 2001 and 2002, the rate per 100,000 for the 17-18 age group increased from 117.7 per 100,000 to 279.3 per 100,000. This rate was 256.7 per 100,000 in 2004.

■ In 2004, 63% of young people considered to be homeless by the former health boards were aged 17-18. Of the remaining children, 24% were aged 15-16; 9% were aged 12-14; and 4% were aged less than 12 years.

Table 80: Number and rate (per 100,000) of homeless children, by age group (2000-2004)										
Years of age	2000		2001		2002		2003		2004	
	No.	Rate	No.	Rate	No.	Rate	No.	Rate	No.	Rate
<12	61	9.4	46	7.1	21	3.2	14	2.1	21	3.1
12-14	124	68.1	67	37.9	33	19.1	35	20.4	44	25.7
15-16	225	177.1	177	142.7	128	104.4	128	106.1	117	100.2
17-18	178	131.1	154	117.7	352	279.3	299	241.6	313	256.7
0-18 years	588	53.9	444	41.0	534	49.6	476	44.2	495	45.8

Source: Childcare Interim Dataset, Department of Health and Children

Technical notes

The data used here are collated by the Health Service Executive (HSE) and therefore include only those children and young people who are known to the HSE. Data are also collected through the local authorities, but only on a 3-yearly basis and thus the same level of detail is not available. An indicator is also available on the number of children on housing waiting lists *(see p.227)*. A survey undertaken by Williams and Gorby (2002) showed high levels of under-reporting to both the HSE and the local authorities.

References

Costello, L. and Howley, D. (1999) *Under Dublin's Neon: A Report on Street Drinkers in Dublin City*. Dublin: Centrecare.

Crawley, M. and Daly, M. (2004) *Heroin – The Mental Roof Over Your Head: Links between Homelessness and Drug Use*. Dublin: National Advisory Committee on Drugs.

Department of Health and Children (2001) *Youth Homelessness Strategy*. Dublin: The Stationery Office.

Department of the Taoiseach (2006) *Towards 2016: Ten-Year Framework Social Partnership Agreement 2006-2015*. Dublin: The Stationery Office.

Government of Ireland (1988) *Housing Act*. Dublin: The Stationery Office.

Government of Ireland (1991) *Child Care Act*. Dublin: The Stationery Office.

Hickey, C. and Downey, D. (2003) *Hungry for Change: Social Exclusion, Food Poverty and Homelessness in Dublin: A Pilot Research Study.* Dublin: Focus Ireland.

Homeless Agency (2006) *Counted in 2005.* Dublin: The Homeless Agency.

Keane, C. and Crowley, G. (1990) *On My Own: Report on Youth Homelessness in Limerick City.* Limerick: Mid-Western Health Board and Limerick Social Service Centre.

Kelleher, P., Kelleher, C. and Corbett, M. (2000) *Left out on their own: Young people leaving care in Ireland.* Dublin: Focus Ireland.

Mayock, P. and Vekić, K. (2006) *Understanding Youth Homelessness: Key Findings from the First Phase of a Longitudinal Cohort Study,* Office of the Minister for Children. Dublin: The Stationery Office.

McKeown, K. (1999) *Mentally Ill and Homeless in Ireland.* Dublin: Disability Federation of Ireland.

NCO (2005) *Ireland's Second Report to the UN Committee on the Rights of the Child,* National Children's Office. Dublin: The Stationery Office.

Perris, A. (1999) *Youth Homelessness in Clondalkin: A Community Perspective.* Dublin: Clondalkin Area Partnership.

Smith, M., McGee, H., Shannon, W. and Holohan, T. (2001) *One Hundred Homeless Women: Health status and health service use of homeless women and their children in Dublin.* Dublin: Royal College of Surgeons in Ireland and the Eastern Regional Health Authority.

Williams, J. and Gorby, S. (2002) *Counted in 2002: The report of the assessment of homelessness in Dublin.* Dublin: ESRI and Homeless Agency.

PART 3: CHILDREN'S OUTCOMES

PART 4:
FORMAL AND
INFORMAL SUPPORTS

'Essential supports and services are provided for children through the primary, social networks of family, extended family and community, known as the informal supports, and through the formal support services provided by the voluntary sector, commercial sector, the State and its agencies.'

(National Children's Strategy 2000, p. 25)

PUBLIC EXPENDITURE ON EDUCATION FOR CHILDREN AND YOUNG PEOPLE

Context

A key objective of the National Action Plan against Poverty and Social Exclusion 2003-2005 is 'to build a fair and inclusive society and ensure that people have the resources and opportunities to live a life with dignity and have access to the quality public services that underpin life chances and experiences' (Department of Social and Family Affairs, 2003).

Against a background of rapid economic growth, Ireland has been able to make considerable progress in addressing this objective, particularly in relation to the key priority areas of health, education and social welfare, where the level of resources invested has been significantly increased (Department of Finance, 2005; Lawlor and McCarthy, 2003). The recently published Social Partnership Agreement has presented a new framework to address key social challenges that the individual faces at each stage of the life cycle (Department of the Taoiseach, 2006). Within this, the framework takes explicit account of the importance of supporting children and the following long-term goals have been identified:

- Every child should grow up in a family with access to sufficient resources, supports and services, to nurture and care for the child, and foster the child's development and full and equal participation in society.
- Every family should be able to access childcare services that are appropriate to the circumstances and needs of their children.
- Every child should leave primary school literate and numerate.
- Every student should complete a senior cycle or equivalent programme (including ICT) appropriate to their capacity and interests.
- Every child should have access to world-class health, personal social services and suitable accommodation.
- Every child should have access to quality play, sport, recreational and cultural activities to enrich their experience of childhood.
- Every child and young person will have access to appropriate participation in local and national decision-making.

These commitments have been made against a backdrop of increased levels of public expenditure across a number of different areas. In the last decade, gross current expenditure has more than doubled, from €19,504 million in 1996 to €48,215 million in 2006 (Department of Finance, 2006).

214

This indicator is focused on public expenditure on education and data relating to both Gross Domestic Product (GDP) and Gross National Income (GNI) are presented. GDP refers to the central aggregate of National Accounts and represents the total value added in the production of goods and services in the country; GNI is the sum of GDP and net factor income, which is 'the difference between investment income (interest, profits, etc) and labour income earned abroad by Irish resident persons and companies (inflows) and similar incomes earned in Ireland by non-residents (outflows)' (CSO, 2006). The situation in Ireland is exceptional among EU Member States, with Luxembourg the only other country where the difference between GDP and GNI is more than 10% of GDP. This gap reflects the importance of foreign direct investment to the Irish economy. In the Irish context, therefore, the percentage of public expenditure on education as a proportion of GNI may be a more appropriate measure.

Significance

There is some evidence that Ireland spends less than other European countries on public service provision (Timonen, 2003; National Economic and Social Council, 2005; Combat Poverty Agency, 2006), although direct comparisons can be difficult to make because of methodological and policy differences across countries. In Ireland, for example, disaggregation of total public expenditure on children has not, to date, been possible and only data on public expenditure on education are presented in this indicator.

Public spending, however, plays a fundamental role in improving well-being and the amount of public expenditure for public services is frequently used to assess a country's effort to foster well-being (Sen, 1981). While public spending in itself does not guarantee desirable outcomes (Timonen, 2003; Quiggan, 2001), strong and dependable public services are vital to extend opportunity, tackle social exclusion and improve people's quality of life (Combat Poverty Agency, 2006). The OECD has suggested that lower expenditure does not necessarily lead to lower achievement and notes, for example, that expenditures for Korea and the Netherlands are below the OECD average for primary and secondary education, yet both countries are among the best performers in the educational achievement (PISA) survey in 2003 (OECD, 2006). There is not a consensus on this. Quiggan (2001), for example, reported that in Australia, the quality of education services available to children from low-income families deteriorated as a result of cuts in public expenditure and this was reflected in declining rates of school completion and university enrolments.

Measure

**Public expenditure on education,
expressed as a percentage of Gross Domestic Product (GDP).**

Key findings

- In 2003, Irish expenditure on education as a percentage of GNI was similar to the EU average of 5.2% of GDP, although Irish expenditure as a percentage of GDP was lower than the EU average *(see Figure 43)*.
- Public expenditure on education in Ireland decreased from 5.9% of GDP in 1993 to 4.4% of GDP in 2003. In terms of GNI, this represented a decrease from a level of 6.4% in 1993 to 5.2% in 2003.[1]
- Ireland's expenditure on education, expressed as a percentage of GDP, was the 5th lowest among the EU25 in 2003 *(see Table 81)*. Denmark had the highest rate of expenditure, at 8.3% of GDP.

Figure 43: Public expenditure on education in Ireland and EU25 (1993-2003)

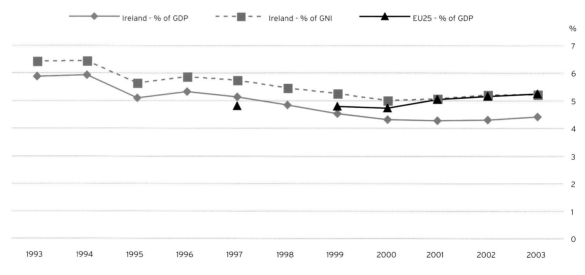

Source: Based on data provided to Eurostat and including expenditure by all Government Departments for education and training.

---

[1] Gross public expenditure on education (DES Voted Expenditure only) decreased from 5.3% of GDP in 1993 to 4.5% (provisional estimates) of GDP in 2005. In terms of GNI, this represented a decrease from a level of 5.8% in 1993 to 5.2% in 2005. These figures are based on Department of Education and Science Gross Voted Expenditure and differ from expenditure used by Eurostat which includes other Department votes. It should be noted that the proportion of GNI spent on education increased from 4.9 to 5.2% between 2003 and 2005 (DES Voted Expenditure).

Table 81: Public expenditure on education as % of GDP in EU25 (2001-2003)			
Country	2001	2002	% of GDP 2003
Denmark	8.4	8.4	8.3
Sweden	7.2	7.6	7.5
Cyprus	6.1	6.6	7.4
Finland	6.2	6.3	6.5
Belgium	6.0	6.1	6.1
Slovenia	6.1	6.0	6.0
France	5.8	5.8	5.9
Hungary	5.1	5.5	5.9
Estonia	5.5	5.7	5.7
Poland	5.4	5.4	5.6
Portugal	5.6	5.5	5.6
Austria	5.7	5.7	5.5
United Kingdom	4.7	5.2	5.4
Latvia	5.6	5.7	5.3
Ireland (% of GNI)	5.1	5.2	5.2
EU25	5.0	5.1	5.2
Lithuania	5.9	5.9	5.2
Netherlands	4.8	4.9	5.1
Malta	4.5	4.5	4.8
Germany	4.5	4.7	4.7
Italy	4.9	4.6	4.7
Czech Republic	4.2	4.4	4.6
Ireland (% of GDP)	4.3	4.3	4.4
Slovakia	4.0	4.4	4.4
Spain	4.2	4.3	4.3
Greece	3.9	3.9	4.2
Luxembourg	3.8	4.0	4.1

Source: Eurostat

■ Real non-capital public expenditure per student in Ireland increased by 112% for first level and by 91% for second level over the period 1996-2005, when measured in constant 2005 prices *(see Table 82)*. However, the corresponding increase in expenditure on third-level education over the same period was a more modest 28% in constant prices.

Table 82: Real non-capital public expenditure on education, by educational level (1996-2005)				
	Expenditure per pupil at constant (2005) prices (€) Educational level			€m (current prices)
Year	First	Second[1]	Third[2]	Total non-capital expenditure
1996	2,502	3,842	7,500	2,618
1997	2,706	4,182	8,715	2,971
1998	2,919	4,361	7,867	3,077
1999	3,094	4,540	8,249	3,333
2000	3,339	4,782	8,028	3,684
2001	3,553	5,380	8,544	4,166
2002	4,071	5,990	8,936	4,765
2003	4,567	6,605	9,001	5,399
2004	5,120	6,951	9,127	5,931
2005	5,300	7,347	9,563	6,365

[1] Includes Further Education sector (i.e. Post-Leaving Certificate courses).

[2] Based on full-time equivalents.

Source: Department of Education and Science

Technical notes

Non-capital public expenditure on education includes direct public expenditure on educational institutions, public subsidies to other private entities for education matters and public subsidies to households, such as scholarships and loans to students for tuition fees and student living costs.

The expenditure has been deflated to real prices by using the Consumer Price Index (CPI). The all items CPI at base December 2001 is shown below:

December 2001 = 100	
Year	All items CPI
1996	84.4
1997	86.2
1998	87.6
1999	90.6
2000	95.9
2001	100.0
2002	102.7
2003	106.3
2004	108.7
2005	111.3

Public expenditure on education as used for the international comparison includes both current and capital expenditure.

In the mid-1990s, undergraduate tuition fees were abolished in Ireland. In 1995/96, third-level students paid half-fees and from 1996/97 undergraduate fees were abolished.

Educational institutions are defined as entities that provide instructional services to individuals or education-related services to individuals and other educational institutions.

International data are collected through the joint UNESCO-OECD-Eurostat data collection questionnaires on educational finance. Countries provide data coming usually from administrative sources on the basis of commonly agreed definitions.

Data on total public expenditure on education are expressed as a percentage of GDP. National public expenditure as a percentage of GDP is calculated using figures in national currency both for public expenditure and for GDP. European averages are weighted and therefore take into account the relative proportion of the student population or the education expenditure of the considered countries. They are calculated taking into account all relevant countries for which data are available. They are considered of sufficient quality if countries with available data exceed 70% of the population or of the GDP of the European aggregate.

References

Combat Poverty Agency (2006) *Submission to the NESF on improving the delivery of quality public services.* Dublin: Combat Poverty Agency.

CSO (2006) *Measuring Ireland's Progress 2005.* Dublin: Central Statistics Office.

Department of Finance (2005) *Ireland − Stability Programme Update.* Dublin: The Stationery Office.

Department of Finance (2006) *Budgetary and Economic Statistics.* Dublin: The Stationery Office.

Department of Social and Family Affairs (2003) *National Action Plan against Poverty and Social Exclusion 2003-2005.* Dublin: The Stationery Office.

Department of the Taoiseach (2006) *Towards 2016: Ten-Year Framework Social Partnership Agreement 2006-2015.* Dublin: The Stationery Office.

Lawlor, J. and McCarthy, C. (2003) 'Browsing Onwards: Irish Public Spending in Perspective', *Irish Banking Review,* Autumn 2003.

National Economic and Social Council (2005) *The Developmental Welfare State.* Dublin: The Stationery Office.

OECD (2006) *Education at a glance: OECD Indicators.* Paris: Organisation for Economic Cooperation and Development.

Quiggan, J. (2001) *Social Capital and Public Expenditure in Australia.* Available at: www.uq.edu.au/economics/johnquiggin/JournalArticles02/SocialCapital02.pdf (accessed 3 September 2006).

Sen, A. (1981) 'Public Action and the Quality of Life in Developing Countries', *Oxford Bulletin of Economics and Statistics,* Vol. 43, No. 4, pp. 287-319.

Timonen, V. (2003) *Irish Social Expenditure in a Comparative International Context: Epilogue.* Dublin: Combat Poverty Agency.

PART 4: FORMAL AND INFORMAL SUPPORTS

Further information

■ OECD Education Statistics and Indicators Database (www.oecd.org/document/6/0,2340,en_ 2649_34515_37344774_1_1_1_1,00.html)

■ Eurostat Education Statistics Database (www.epp.eurostat.ec.europa.eu/portal/page?_ pageid=1996,45323734&_dad=portal&_schema =PORTAL&screen= welcomeref&open=/ &product=EU_MASTER_education_training&depth=2)

ECONOMIC SECURITY

Child poverty

Context

The United Nations Convention on the Rights of the Child highlights the right of children to an acceptable standard of living and to social development to reach their full potential. Ending child poverty has been identified as a national policy priority in Ireland (Department of the Taoiseach, 2002). The National Anti-Poverty Strategy (NAPS) sets out a commitment to reducing consistent poverty rates among children to 2% or less (Department of Social and Family Affairs, 1997). Within the NAPS, poverty is defined as follows: 'People are living in poverty if their income and resources (material, cultural and social) are so inadequate as to preclude them from having a standard of living which is regarded as acceptable by Irish society generally. As a result of inadequate income and resources people may be excluded and marginalised from participating in activities which are considered the norm for other people in society'.

The NAPS specifically notes that lack of an adequate income is only one aspect of child poverty (Department of Social and Family Affairs, 1997). The National Action Plan against Poverty and Social Exclusion 2003-2005 states as a key policy task 'to develop a more integrated policy and institutional structure to ensure adequate supports for children, their development and for those caring for them' (Department of Social and Family Affairs, 2003). The Social Partnership Agreement for 2003-2005, *Sustaining Progress,* contained a 'Special Initiative on ending Child Poverty' (Department of the Taoiseach, 2003) and the National Children's Strategy also provides a policy commitment to ending child poverty. These commitments are upheld in the most recent Social Partnership Agreement for 2006-2015, *Towards 2016* (Department of the Taoiseach, 2006).

Internationally, child poverty is also an issue (UNICEF, 2000 and 2005). The EU Social Inclusion Strategy sets out to make a decisive impact on poverty by 2010. Within this, there is a particular focus on actions to tackle child poverty by Member States.

Significance

According to Bradshaw (2002), the prevalence of poor children in a country is an important indicator of the well-being of children. There is substantial evidence, dating from the 1950s, that shows that children who are poor do less well educationally, are more likely to suffer ill health, become teenage parents, suffer child abuse and are vulnerable to homelessness and delinquent behaviour. In addition, such children are less likely to have opportunities in life (Nolan, 2000). The impact of child poverty lasts into adulthood and may lead to a life cycle of deprivation, which repeats itself from generation to generation (Department of Social and Family Affairs, 1997). Some families are more at risk of being poor than others and in Ireland, as elsewhere, research has found that child poverty rates are higher among single-income families (Layte *et al*, 2006). Households with four or more children also face a higher risk (Oxley *et al*, 2001).

Despite a large body of theoretical work, there is no universally accepted 'gold standard' measure for poverty. There are, however, two broad approaches to the measurement of socio-economic position: one based on the differential availability of resources (e.g. money) to people and the other on the conditions experienced by people (Salmond *et al*, 2006). In Ireland, 'consistent poverty', a measure developed by the ESRI for the Irish context, takes account of both aspects and for this reason is the official measure of poverty adopted by the Government. The measure identifies the proportion of people from those with an income of less than 60% of the median income who are also deprived of one or more goods or services considered essential by people in Ireland to meet a basic standard of living. This includes heating their home and being able to pay everyday household expenses without falling into debt. Consequently, the measure of consistent poverty can be understood as more comprehensive and multi-dimensional than a measure based on income alone (Maitre *et al*, 2006).

In Europe and elsewhere, the most common practice in recent years, particularly in comparative research, has been to rely on relative income poverty measures and this approach has been adopted in various influential studies for Eurostat, as well as those at a national level (Maître *et al*, 2006). The EU refers to this as the 'at risk of poverty' measure, which recognises that persons 'at risk of poverty' may not actually be in poverty as generally understood. The rationale for using the 'at risk of poverty' measure is that those falling below a certain income threshold in their society are less likely to be able to participate fully in the life of that society. Some limitations have been identified with this measure, including, for example, only moderate correlations with high deprivation scores and a failure to take into account differentials in standards of living between countries at different stages of economic development. In addition, the measure can be unstable in measuring poverty in countries at a time of high economic growth and this is considered to be a particular factor in the Irish context.

Consistent Poverty Measure

> **The number of children living in households with a household income below the national 60% median and experiencing basic deprivation, expressed as a proportion of all children.**

Key findings

- 9.7% of persons under 18 experienced consistent poverty in 2004 *(see Table 83)*.

Table 83: Percentage of persons at risk of poverty (2004)	
Persons under 18	9.7
All persons	6.8

Source: EU-SILC; CSO

- Households with children generally had higher poverty rates than those without children.
- In 2004, persons in households comprising a single adult with children had a consistent poverty rate of 31.1% *(see Figure 44).*

Figure 44: Percentage of children under 16 at risk of poverty in the EU (2004)

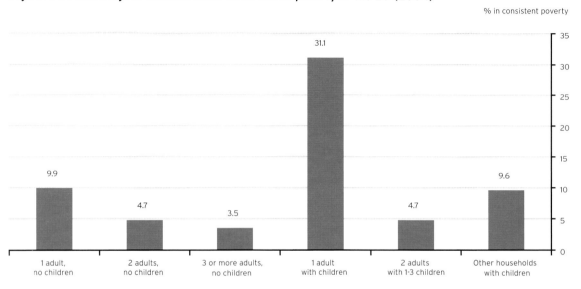

% in consistent poverty

Source: EU-SILC; CSO

Relative Income Poverty Measure

> **The number of children living in households with a household income below the national 60% median, equivalised using the national equivalence scale, expressed as a proportion of all children.**

Key findings

- In 2004, 22.7% of persons under 18 were considered to be at risk of poverty *(see Table 84).*
- Persons under 18 had a higher risk of being poor than the population as a whole (22.7% versus 19.4%).

Table 84: Percentage of persons at risk of poverty (2004)	
Persons under 18	22.7
All persons	19.4

Source: EU-SILC; CSO

■ In 2004, the number of persons under 16 living in households at risk of poverty in Ireland (22%) was higher that the EU average (20%) *(see Figure 45)*.

Figure 45: Percentage of children under 16 at risk of poverty in the EU (2004)

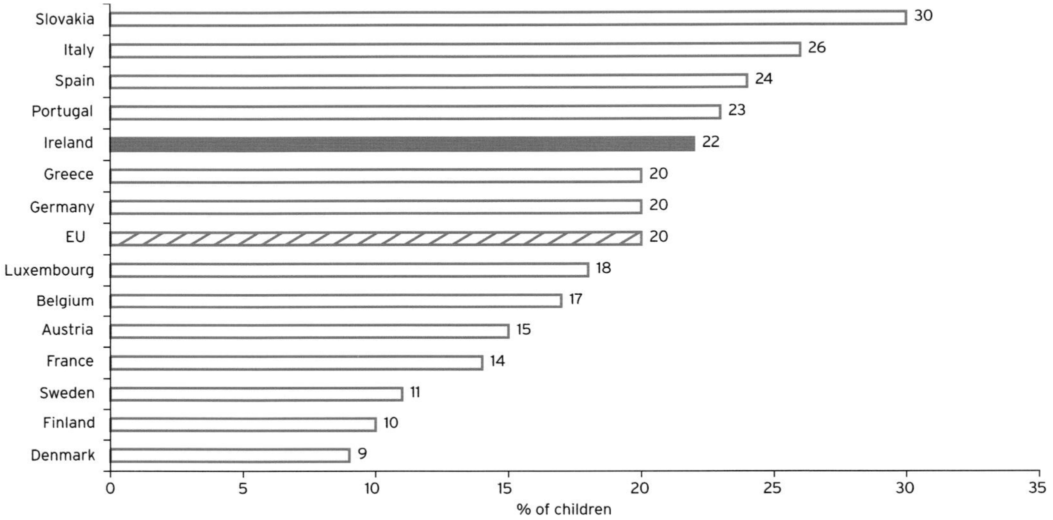

Source: Eurostat

Technical notes

The consistent poverty indicator is based on data collected in Ireland from the EU Survey on Income and Living Conditions (EU-SILC) for 2004. The survey provides information on poverty, deprivation and social exclusion. The sample size in 2004 was 5,477 households and 14,272 individuals. The concept of 'consistent poverty' used in this indicator refers to the share of persons at risk of poverty (with an equivalised income below 60% of the national median income) and experiencing deprivation on one or more of 8 basic deprivation indicators *(see below)*.

The national equivalised scale used for the consistent poverty indicator to obtain the equivalised household size attributes a weight of 1 to the first adult in a household, 0.66 to each subsequent adult (aged 14+ living in the household) and 0.33 to each child less than 14. The 8 deprivation indicators are:
■ no substantial meal for at least one day in the past two weeks due to lack of money;
■ without heating at some stage in the past year due to lack of money;
■ experienced debt problems arising from ordinary living expenses;
■ unable to afford two pairs of strong shoes;
■ unable to afford a roast once a week;
■ unable to afford a meal with meat, chicken or fish (or vegetarian equivalent) every second day;
■ unable to afford new (not second-hand) clothes;
■ unable to afford a warm water-proof coat.

The 'at risk of poverty' indicator is also based on data collected in Ireland from the EU Survey on Income and Living Conditions (EU-SILC) for 2004. The concept of 'at risk of poverty' used in this indicator refers to the share of persons with an equivalised income below 60% of the national median income. The figures in this indicator refer to income after social transfers are included.

224

The EU definition of income and at risk of poverty rate is slightly different from the national definition. The key difference between the national and EU definition of income is that the national definition includes income from private pensions, while the EU definition does not. For EU at risk of poverty rates, the equivalised disposable income for each person is calculated as the total net income figure divided by the equivalised household size according to the modified OECD scale (which gives a weight of 1.0 to the first adult, 0.5 to other persons aged 14 or over who are living in the household and 0.3 to each child aged less than 14).

The national equivalised scale used to obtain the equivalised household size attributes a weight of 1 to the first adult in a household, 0.66 to each subsequent adult (aged 14+ living in the household) and 0.33 to each child less than 14. The purpose of an equivalence scale is to account for the size and composition of different income units (households) and thus allows for a more accurate comparison between households.

References

Bradshaw, J. (2002) 'Comparisons of Child Poverty and Deprivation Internationally', in *The Well-Being of Children in the UK,* J. Bradshaw (ed.). York: Save the Children, pp. 17-26.

CSO (2005) *EU Survey on Income and Living Conditions: First Results 2003.* Dublin: Central Statistics Office.

Combat Poverty Agency (2005) *Ending Child Poverty.* Dublin: Combat Poverty Agency.

Department of Health and Children (2000) *The National Children's Strategy: Our Children – Their Lives.* Dublin: The Stationery Office.

Department of Social and Family Affairs (1997) *Sharing in Progress: National Anti-Poverty Strategy.* Dublin: The Stationery Office.

Department of Social and Family Affairs (2003) *National Action Plan against Poverty and Social Exclusion 2003-2005.* Dublin: The Stationery Office.

Department of the Taoiseach (2002) *An Agreed Programme for Government between Fianna Fáil and the Progressive Democrats.* Dublin: The Stationery Office.

Department of the Taoiseach (2003) *Sustaining Progress: Social Partnership Agreement 2003-2005.* Dublin: The Stationery Office.

Department of the Taoiseach (2006) *Towards 2016: Ten-Year Framework Social Partnership Agreement 2006-2015.* Dublin: The Stationery Office.

Layte, R., Maître, B., Nolan, B. and Whelan, C.T. (2006) *Day In, Day Out – Understanding the dynamics of child poverty.* Dublin: Combat Poverty Agency.

Maître, B., Nolan, B. and Whelan, C. (2006) *Reconfiguring the Measurement of Deprivation and Consistent Poverty in Ireland,* ESRI Policy Research Series Paper 58. Dublin: Economic and Social Research Institute.

Nolan, B. (2000) *Child Poverty in Ireland.* Dublin: Oak Tree Press.

Oxley, H., Thai-Thanh, D., Forster, M.F. and Pellizzari, M. (2001) 'Income inequalities and poverty among children and households in selected OECD countries', in *Child Well-Being, Child Poverty and Child Policy in Modern Nations,* K. Vleminckx and T.M. Smeeding (eds.). Bristol: The Policy Press.

Salmond, C., Crampton, P., King, P. and Waldegrave, C. (2006) 'NZiDep: A New Zealand index of socio-economic deprivation for individuals', *Social Science & Medicine*, No. 62, pp. 1474-85.

UN (1989) *Convention on the Rights of the Child.* Geneva: United Nations Office of the High Commissioner for Human Rights. Available at www.ohchr.org

UNICEF (2000) *A League Table of Child Poverty in Rich Nations,* Innocenti Report Card No. 1. Florence: United Nations Children's Fund.

UNICEF (2005) *Child Poverty in Rich Countries 2005,* Innocenti Report Card No. 6. Florence: United Nations Children's Fund.

Further information
- Office for Social Inclusion (www.socialinclusion.ie)
- Combat Poverty Agency (www.cpa.ie)

AVAILABILITY OF HOUSING FOR FAMILIES WITH CHILDREN

Housing waiting lists

Context

The Planning and Development Act 2000, as amended in 2002, aims to 'encourage and facilitate a level of housing supply to meet the housing needs of all sectors of the population' (Government of Ireland, 2000 and 2002). In 2005, a new housing policy framework was issued by Government, *Building Sustainable Communities* (Department of the Environment, Heritage and Local Government, 2005a). A key objective of this policy is 'to promote the conditions whereby the maximum number of people can access affordable accommodation through private provision'. The policy also recognises that a range of supports are required 'to assist those who cannot access such accommodation from their own resources'. These include delivering high-quality social housing in mixed communities and the rolling out of a programme of regeneration for all run-down estates (Department of the Environment, Heritage and Local Government, 2005b).

This 2005 policy builds on a number of other policy initiatives (Government of Ireland, 1988; Department of the Environment, 1991 and 1995; Department of the Environment and Local Government, 2000a and 2000b; Department of the Environment, Heritage and Local Government, 2005b). Most recently, a commitment has been made to increase the number of new housing commencements/acquisitions by 27,000 by 2009.

The National Action Plan against Poverty and Social Exclusion 2003-2005 also set targets for combating social exclusion in relation to housing, including a specific target on services for homeless persons (Department of Social and Family Affairs, 2003). There is also a commitment under the new Social Partnership Agreement to eliminate homelessness by 2010 (Department of the Taoiseach, 2006). The overall objective is 'to enable households experiencing poverty and disadvantage to have available to them housing or accommodation which is affordable, accessible, of good quality, suitable to their needs, culturally acceptable, located in a sustainable community and, as far as possible, in a secure tenure of their choice' (Department of Social and Family Affairs, 2002, p. 13). Since 2004, all local authorities have been asked to prepare 5-year social and affordable housing action plans (SAHAPs); these provide details of the output of social and affordable housing in each local authority's area and set targets against which progress can be measured (Brooke, 2006).

Significance

While local authorities in Ireland have the primary responsibility to ensure that all people have access to appropriate accommodation, the role of the voluntary and cooperative housing sector has increased in recent times (NESC, 2004; CORI Justice Commission, 2005). A number of studies have shown that some children in Ireland are living in accommodation that is overcrowded, damp and in disrepair (Halpenny *et al*, 2002; Costello and Kerrins, 2003). Certain groups are more at risk than others, including children in one-parent families, those living in rented accommodation and children from the Traveller community (Brooke, 2004). Although there has been a reliance in the past on Bed and Breakfasts (B&Bs) for emergency accommodation (Halpenny *et al*, 2002), this may not represent the current position (O'Flynn and Chaloner, 2006). Such temporary accommodation is, however, according to Barnardos (2005), unsuitable of children's well-being. B&B accommodation can be below standard, overcrowded and lack basic facilities for children (for example, cooking, washing and play areas).

It has been suggested that regular moves from one temporary accommodation unit to another threatens children's familial, social and educational stability (Barnardos, 2005). An important relationship has been found in respect of children who are in temporary accommodation and poorer health outcomes than the general population. These include histories of incomplete vaccinations, poor nutrition, retarded weight and height growth, and emotional and mental distress (Halpenny *et al*, 2002). The Open Your Eyes to Child Poverty Initiative (2000) noted that poor access to secure and stable accommodation can result in poor school attendance and early school-leaving.

Measure

> **The number of children in families on a local authority housing waiting list, expressed as a proportion of all children.**

Key findings

- 22,335 households with children were identified as being in need of social housing in the 2005 assessment of housing needs *(see Table 85)*. This represents a 24.2% (7,149) decrease compared with the 2002 assessment, when 29,484 households were identified as being in need of social housing.
- In 2005, 61.4% of family households in need of social housing were households with one child; 24.1% were households with 2 children; 8.9% were households with 3 children; and 5.7% of households included 4 or more children. This distribution had remained consistent over the period 1996-2005.

Table 85: Percentage of households with children in need of social housing (1996-2005)

No. of children	1996	1999	2002	2005 No.	2005 %
1	10,816	14,734	17,523	13,703	61.4
2	4,112	6,117	7,250	5,385	24.1
3	1,559	2,402	2,685	1,991	8.9
4	690	1,036	1,126	772	3.5
5 or more	596	896	900	484	2.2
Total	17,773	25,185	29,484	22,335	100.0

Source: Triennial Assessment of Housing Needs, Department of the Environment, Heritage and Local Government

■ In 2002, just over 60% of households with children in need of social housing had an income of €10,000 or less *(see Figure 46).* Less than 3% of these households had an income in excess of €25,000.

Figure 46: Households with children in need of social housing, by income band (2002)

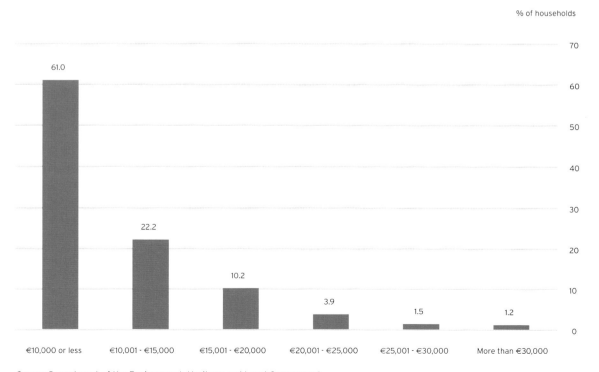

Source: Department of the Environment, Heritage and Local Government

PART 4: FORMAL AND INFORMAL SUPPORTS

229

Technical notes

The data for this indicator represent net need for social housing, meaning households who have been assessed as being in need of either local authority or voluntary housing. The terminology used to describe a local authority's housing needs varies. These figures are net of duplicate applications (i.e. applicants who have applied to more than one local authority). A local authority's waiting list may contain duplicate applications.

The guidelines for the Triennial Assessment of Housing Needs, conducted by the Department of the Environment, Heritage and Local Government, state that as far as possible particulars of the incomes of applicants should be verified by appropriate up-to-date evidence (e.g. a P60 or via PPSN).

One of the weaknesses of local authority assessments of housing needs (LAAHNs) is that they do not measure severity of housing need and all households on housing waiting lists are treated as though they have an equal level of housing need. This means that there may be some people registered on housing waiting lists who have a very low housing need. On the other hand, LAAHNs may underestimate other elements of housing need.

For example, local authorities are asked to exclude from the final figure certain households that are not assessed as suitable for local authority housing, namely:
- Households whose need for assistance could, in the opinion of the Authority, be more appropriately met by rent or mortgage supplementation under the Supplementary Welfare Allowance Scheme. Arguably, this highly unsatisfactory category was originally a euphemism for single people, who were not seen as appropriate for housing by local authorities.
- Households living in unfit local authority housing.
- Households living in overcrowded or materially unsuitable local authority housing.
- Households whose need could be more appropriately met by other social housing measures (this includes households with a particular need in addition to their housing need).

References

Barnardos (2005) *Seven steps to ending child poverty.* Dublin: Barnardos.

Brooke, S. (2004) *Housing Problems and Irish Children: The impact of housing on children's well-being.* Dublin: Children's Research Centre, University of Dublin, Trinity College.

Brooke, S. (2006) *Building for Inclusion: Housing Output and Part V of the Irish Planning and Development System.* Dublin: Focus Ireland.

CORI Justice Commission (2005) *Housing and Accommodation.* Dublin: CORI Justice Commission.

Costello, L. and Kerrins, L. (2003) *'A Place to call Our Own': Research on the housing and housing support needs of young lone parents in Tallaght.* Dublin: Centre for Social and Educational Research.

Department of Social and Family Affairs (2002) *Building an Inclusive Society.* Dublin: The Stationery Office.

Department of the Environment (1991) *A Plan for Social Housing.* Dublin: The Stationery Office.

Department of the Environment (1995) *Social Housing – The Way Ahead.* Dublin: The Stationery Office.

Department of the Environment and Local Government (2000a) *Action on Housing.* Dublin: The Stationery Office.

Department of the Environment and Local Government (2000b) *Circular HS/400 Guidelines for Planning Authorities. Part V of the Planning and Development Act 2000 Housing Supply.* Dublin: The Stationery Office.

Department of the Environment, Heritage and Local Government (2005a) *Housing Policy Framework: Building Sustainable Communities.* Dublin: The Stationery Office.

Department of the Environment, Heritage and Local Government (2005b) *Local Authority Assessments of Social Housing Needs.* Dublin: The Stationery Office.

Department of Social and Family Affairs (2003) *National Action Plan against Poverty and Social Exclusion 2003-2005.* Dublin: The Stationery Office.

Department of the Taoiseach (2006) *Towards 2016: Ten-Year Framework Social Partnership Agreement 2006-2015.* Dublin: The Stationery Office.

Government of Ireland (1988) *Housing Act.* Dublin: The Stationery Office.

Government of Ireland (2000) *Planning and Development Act.* Dublin: The Stationery Office.

Government of Ireland (2002) *Planning and Development (Amendment) Act.* Dublin: The Stationery Office.

Halpenny A.M., Keogh, A.F. and Gilligan, R. (2002) *A Place for Children? Children in families living in emergency accommodation: The perspectives of children, parents and professionals.* Dublin: Homeless Agency.

NESC (2004) *Housing in Ireland: Performance and Policy Background Analysis.* Dublin: National Economic and Social Council.

O'Flynn, J. and Chaloner, L. (2006) *Planning for Children: Improving Access to Services for Children in Private Emergency Accommodation in Dublin.* Dublin: The Homeless Agency.

Open Your Eyes to Child Poverty Initiative (2000) *Target an End to Child Poverty: Proposal to the Anti-Poverty Strategy.* Dublin: Open Your Eyes to Child Poverty Initiative.

Further information

■ Department of the Environment, Heritage and Local Government (www.environ.ie)

PART 4: FORMAL AND INFORMAL SUPPORTS

231

COMMUNITY CHARACTERISTICS

Perceived safety in the community

Context

There is a range of different ways of defining community. Most, however, include some reference to geography, culture and social stratification (Naidoo and Wills, 1994). There is some agreement that Ireland has a relatively good reputation in regard to community support and engagement, and this was evident in the countrywide involvement by people in the Special Olympic World Games held in 2003. The importance of individuals and organisations within communities working together is rooted within an understanding that values social capital. This has been defined by the OECD as 'networks together with shared norms, values and understandings that facilitate cooperation within or among groups' (OECD, 2001, p. 41).

This understanding is shared and supported by the Irish Government. In the recent publication by the Task Force on Active Citizenship (2006), it was noted that 'many significant problems can be solved when individuals and organisations work together and include all concerned in making and implementing decisions'.

The Department of Community, Rural and Gaeltacht Affairs funds, and in some cases administers, a range of support programmes for community development so that socially excluded groups and local communities can be active participants in identifying and meeting their own development needs, working alongside the statutory agencies and others involved in local development initiatives. ADM Ltd. is an intermediary company established by the Irish Government, in agreement with the European Commission, to promote social inclusion, reconciliation and equality, and to counter disadvantage through local social and economic development. ADM Ltd. administers a number of different programmes, including the Social Inclusion Programme, RAPID and PEACE II Programmes on behalf of the Department of Community, Rural and Gaeltacht Affairs.

An important measure of community is the extent to which children feel safe and secure in their local community. The single greatest threat to the survival of children once they have passed the infant stage comes from accidents. In Ireland, child road safety is specifically addressed through an extensive education programme that targets school children of both primary and post-primary age. The Road Safety Strategy sets out a range of engineering, education, enforcement and legislative targets with an impact on child safety (NDA, 2004). A number of initiatives have been implemented, including a 'Safer routes to school' Pilot Programme by the Dublin Transportation Office in 2002. In addition, the road safety officers of the National Safety Council make regular calls to schools, delivering lectures and showing videos highlighting road safety awareness. The National Play Policy, published by the National Children's Office, also draws attention to issues of safety in respect of children's play areas (NCO, 2004). Other issues relating to safety include freedom from crime and active engagement in local communities.

Significance

This indicator can help to provide an understanding of social capital of young people. It has grown out of a recognition that behaviours are shaped and constrained by a range of social and community contexts, and that the ways in which an individual relates to social networks and communities have important effects on their health and well-being (Morrow, 1999).

Data presented in this indicator take account of one aspect of social capital, that of local identity. This indicator was introduced and validated for the HBSC Survey in 1998 (Mullan *et al,* 2001; Ford, 2000). Social capital in the Irish context has been subject to review by Healy (forthcoming), who identifies the following three broad dimensions as important:
- informal social ties and norms of obligation and trust;
- community (including voluntary) involvement;
- social contact and communication with others.

There is some evidence that higher levels of social capital in local communities can lead to better health outcomes (Malmstrom *et al,* 1999; Yen and Kaplan, 1999; Kawachi *et al,* 1997). A number of prospective studies of professional men in the USA, for example, found that those with the lowest levels of social trust were significantly more likely to die from cardiovascular disease, accidents and suicides, although these findings were questioned by other researchers (Mullan *et al,* 2001). Other studies suggest that living in an unsafe local area is associated with high stress levels (Steptoe and Feldman, 2001) and increased social isolation, including restriction on activities (Saelens *et al,* 2003). However, it is unclear to what extent low social economic status acts as a mediator in these associations (Ross and Mirowsky, 2001). Runyan *et al* (1998), looking at social capital more broadly, found that the presence of social capital acted as a buffer against the negative effects of unfavourable (e.g. abusive and/or neglectful) environments.

Measure

> **The proportion of children aged 10-17 who report feeling safe in area where they live.**

Key findings

- In 2002, 87.4% of children aged 10-17 reported feeling safe in the area where they lived *(see Table 86).*

Differences by age, social class and gender
- The percentage of children who reported feeling safe in the area where they lived was relatively stable across age and gender.
- A higher percentage of children from social class 1-2 (91.1%) reported this compared with children from social class 5-6 (86.0%).

Table 86: Percentage of children who report feeling safe in area where they live, by age, social class and gender (2002)

	Boys	Girls	Total
Total	86.7	87.8	87.4
Years of age			
10-11	86.1	88.4	87.4
12-14	86.5	88.4	87.6
15-17	87.4	86.9	87.1
Social class			
SC 1-2	90.6	91.5	91.1
SC 3-4	87.7	87.7	87.7
SC 5-6	84.1	87.6	86.0

Source: HBSC Survey

Differences by geographical area

■ Children living in the former North-Western Health Board area were most likely (92.2%) to report feeling safe where they live, while children in the former Eastern Regional Health Authority were least likely (83.7%) to report this *(see Figure 47)*.

Figure 47: Percentage of children who report feeling safe in the area where they live, by former health board area

% of children

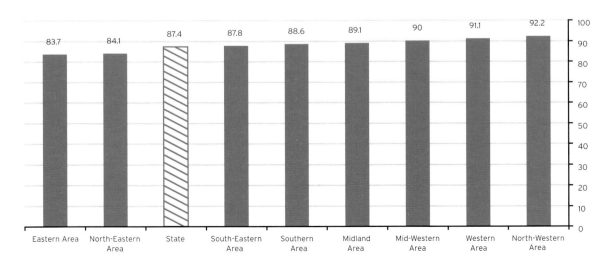

Source: HBSC Survey

International comparisons

■ From the 2002 HBSC Survey, using the ages of 11, 13 and 15 only to draw international comparisons, 86.5% of Irish children reported feeling safe in the area where they live *(see Figure 48)*. This compared with the HBSC average of 89.6%.

■ Among all 16 countries that used this HBSC item, the lowest percentage for this indicator was found among Latvian children (65.7%) and the highest among children from Norway (97.8%).

■ Among 13 countries that used this item among 11-year-old students, Irish 11-year-old children were ranked 10th. Among 16 countries that used this item among older children, Irish 13-year-old children were ranked 12th and Irish 15-year-old children were ranked 14th.

Figure 48: Percentage of children who report feeling safe in the area where they live, by country, (2002)

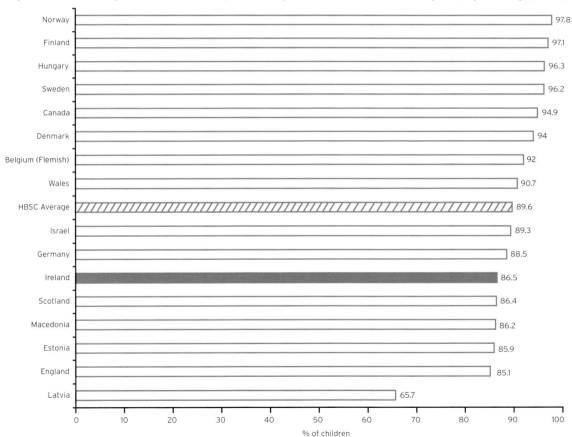

Source: HBSC Survey

PART 4: FORMAL AND INFORMAL SUPPORTS

235

Technical notes

The indicator presented here is part of a more comprehensive social capital index and as such does not capture the whole phenomenon. In addition, the HBSC uses a self-completion questionnaire, which leaves the definition of 'good places in your area' to the interpretation of the respondent.

Percentage differences are presented for descriptive purposes only and may not reflect a statistically significant finding.

References

Ford, K. (2000) *A Report of the HEA's Social Action Research Project Network meeting.* London: Health Education Authority.

Healy, T. (forthcoming) *The Level and Distribution of Social Capital in Ireland*, Dublin: *Statistical and Social Society of Ireland.*

Kawachi, I., Kennedy, B.P., Lochner, K. and Prothrow-Stith, D. (1997) 'Social Capital, Income and Inequality', *American Journal of Public Health,* Vol. 87, No. 9, pp. 1491-98.

Malmstrom, M., Sundquist, J. and Lohansson, S.E. (1999). 'Neighbourhood Environment and Self-reported Health Status: A Multilevel Analysis', *American Journal of Public Health,* Vol. 89, No. 8, pp. 1181-86.

Morrow, V. (1999) 'Conceptualising social capital in relation to the well-being of children and young people: A Critical Review', *The Sociological Review,* No. 44, pp. 744-65.

Mullan, E., Currie, C., Boyce, W., Klanins, I. and Holstein, B. (2001) 'Focus Area Rationale: Social Inequalities', in *Health Behaviour in School-aged Children: A World Health Organization Cross-national Study: Research Protocol for the 2001/02 Survey,* C. Currie, O. Samdal, W. Boyce and R. Smith (eds.). Edinburgh: Child and Adolescent Health Research Unit, University of Edinburgh.

Naidoo, J. and Wills, J. (1994) *Health Promotion: Foundations for Practice.* London, Bailliere Tindall.

NCO (2004) *Ready, Steady Play! A National Play Policy,* National Children's Office. Dublin: The Stationery Office.

NDA (2004) *Road Safety Strategy.* Dublin: National Roads Authority.

OECD (2001) *The Well-being of Nations: The Role of Human and Social Capital.* Paris: Organisation for Economic Cooperation and Development.

Ross, C.E. and Mirowsky, A. (2001) 'Neighbourhood disadvantages, disorder and health', *Journal of Health and Social Behaviour,* Vol. 42, No. 3, pp. 256-76.

Runyan, D., Hunter, W., Socolar, R. Amaya-Jackson, L., English, D., Landsverk, J., Dubowitz, H., Browne, H., Bangdiwala, S.I. and Mathew, R.M. (1998) 'Children who prosper in unfavourable environments: The relationship to social capital', *Paediatrics*, No. 101, pp. 12-18.

Saelens, B.E.P., Sallis, J.F.P., Black, J.B.B.A. and Chen, D.B.A. (2003) 'Neighbourhood-based differences in physical activity: An Environment Scale Evaluation', *American Journal of Public Health,* Vol. 94, No. 3, pp. 774-802.

Steptoe, A. and Feldman, P.J. (2001) 'Neighbourhood problems as source of chronic stress: Development of a measure of neighbourhood problems, and associations with socio-economic and health', *Annals of Behavioural Medicine*, Vol. 23, No. 3, pp. 177-85.

Task Force on Active Citizenship (2006) *'Together we're better'. Task Force on Active Citizenship: Consultation Document.* Dublin: Task Force on Active Citizenship.

Yen, I.H. and Kaplan, G.A. (1999) 'Neighbourhood social environment and risk of death: Multilevel evidence from the Alameda County Study', *American Journal of Epidemiology*, Vol. 149, No. 10, pp. 898-907.

PART 4: FORMAL AND INFORMAL SUPPORTS

237

ENVIRONMENT AND PLACES

Context

The National Children's Strategy (Department of Health and Children, 2000) highlights the importance of the built and natural environment in children's lives. A range of initiatives are identified within the Strategy:

- the publication of play and recreation policies;
- enhancing the design of open space provision and improving safe access to it for children;
- consideration given to children's safety while walking or cycling;
- ensuring children can play their part in protecting and enhancing the environment.

The *Ready, Steady, Play! A National Play Policy*, published in 2004, is designed to help address the needs of younger children in this area (NCO, 2004). A National Recreation Policy will follow in 2007 and this will focus on aspects to support older children and adolescents; the public consultation on this policy has recently been completed (OMC, 2006a). In addition to these developments, the Department of the Environment, Heritage and Local Government provides funds to support environmental awareness projects. It also provides a public information service on the environment, called ENFO, to encourage children to be environmentally responsible. An Taisce have a lead role in organising the Green Schools Programme, which awards schools that attain a level of excellence in environmental management. This, along with other school and neighbourhood-based programmes, encourages environmentally responsible behaviour by children and young people (OMC, 2005).

Significance

Children's environments are important to them and a well-designed environment is important for ensuring the physical and emotional well-being of the whole community, including children (Nic Gabhainn and Sixsmith, 2005). In a national study of young people, De Roiste and Dineen (2005) examined young people's views about opportunities, barriers and supports to recreation and leisure. The research provides information about what young people do in their free time and also highlights the barriers and supports they experience.

The findings suggest that the vast majority of young people enjoy their free time and almost 88% are involved in a wide range of activities, including participation in community clubs or groups, involvement in sports and engaging in hobbies. The findings also show that over 90% of young people aged 12-18 enjoy 'hanging out' with their friends. A number of environmental issues, however, impact on their recreational opportunities. These include a strong perception of inadequate recreation provision, issues around safety and difficulties in accessing leisure activities because of lack of public transport.

A recent consultation with children on the implementation of the United Nations Convention on the Rights of the Child (UNCRC), conducted by the Office of the Minister for Children, also found evidence of these views (OMC, 2006b).

Measure

> **The proportion of children aged 10-17 who report there are good places in their area to spend their free time.**

Key findings

- In 2002, 43.9% of children aged 10-17 reported that there were good places in their area to spend their free time *(see Table 87)*.

Differences by age, social class and gender

- The percentage of children who reported that there were good places in their area to spend their free time was higher among boys and younger children, with little variation found across the social classes:
  - 47.8% of boys reported this, compared with 41.0% of girls;
  - 59.6% of 10-11 year-olds reported this, compared with 32.6% of 15-17 year-olds.

Table 87: Percentage of children who report that there are good places in their area to spend their free time, by age, social class and gender (2002)			
	Boys	Girls	Total
Total	47.8	41.0	43.9
Years of age			
10-11	60.0	59.4	59.6
12-14	52.4	43.7	47.5
15-17	34.9	31.0	32.6
Social class			
SC 1-2	50.1	38.4	43.0
SC 3-4	47.4	42.2	44.4
SC 5-6	46.6	42.0	44.1

Source: HBSC Survey

Differences by geographical area

■ Children in the former Eastern Regional Health Authority were most likely (51.3%) to report that there were good places in their area to spend their free time, while children in the former North-Eastern Health Board area were least likely (36.9%) to report this *(see Figure 49)*. There was little difference between the other health board areas.

Figure 49: Percentage of children aged 10-17 who report that there are good places in their area to spend their free time, by former health board area

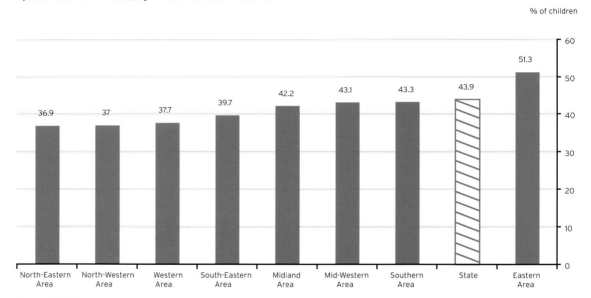

% of children

Source: HBSC Survey

International comparisons

■ From the 2002 HBSC Survey, using the ages of 11, 13 and 15 only to draw international comparisons, 45.3% of Irish children reported that there were good places in their area to spend their free time *(see Figure 50)*. This compared with the HBSC average of 57.3%.

■ Among all 15 countries that used this HBSC item, the lowest percentage for this indicator was found among children from Finland (40.2%) and the highest among German children (73.9%).

■ Overall, Irish children ranked 14th among all 15 countries participating in the survey. Among 12 countries that used this item among 11-year-old students, Irish 11-year-old children were ranked 12th. Among 15 countries that used this item among older children, Irish 13- and 15-year-old children were ranked 13th.

240

Figure 50: Percentage of children who report that there are good places in their area to spend their free time, by country (2002)

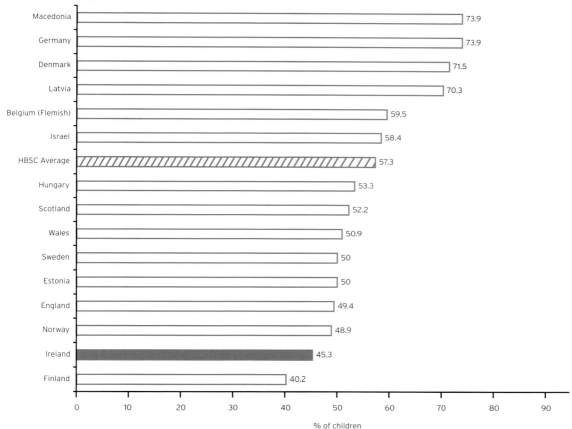

Source: HBSC Survey

Technical notes

The indicator presented here is part of a more comprehensive social capital index and as such does not capture the whole phenomenon. In addition, the HBSC uses a self-completion questionnaire, which leaves the definition of 'good places in your area' to the interpretation of the respondent.

Percentage differences are presented for descriptive purposes only and may not reflect a statistically significant finding.

References

Department of Health and Children (2000) *The National Children's Strategy: Our Children – Their Lives.* Dublin: The Stationery Office.

De Roiste, A. and Dineen, J. (2005) *Young People's Views about Opportunities, Barriers and Supports to Recreation and Leisure,* National Children's Office. Dublin: The Stationery Office.

NCO (2004) *Ready, Steady Play! A National Play Policy,* National Children's Office. Dublin: The Stationery Office.

Nic Gabhainn, S. and Sixsmith, J. (2005). *Children's Understandings of Well-Being,* National Children's Office. Dublin: The Stationery Office.

OMC (2005) *2004 Progress Report on the Implementation of the National Children's Strategy.* Dublin: Office of the Minister for Children (accessed from http://www.nco.ie/publications/56/ on 18 September 2006).

OMC (2006a) *Report of the Public Consultation for the Development of the National Recreation Policy for Young People,* Office of the Minister for Children. Dublin: The Stationery Office.

OMC (2006b) *How We See It. Children and Young People's Views on the Implementation of the UNCRC in Ireland,* Office of the Minister for Children. Dublin: The Stationery Office.

REFERRALS TO GARDA JUVENILE DIVERSION PROGRAMME

Context

The Children Act (Government of Ireland, 2001) provides the primary legal framework for dealing with children who are in difficulty and sets out a structure within which the youth justice system can operate. The Act gives a statutory basis to the Garda Juvenile Diversion Programme, which aims to divert young offenders away from crime and the criminal justice system through the use of cautions, supervision and restorative justice. In order to be admitted to the Garda Juvenile Diversion Programme, a child must be over the age of criminal responsibility and under 18, accept responsibility for the offence(s) and consent to being cautioned and supervised. Where a child is not admitted to the Diversion Programme, the case may be taken forward for prosecution.

Garda Youth Diversion Projects commenced in 1991 with the aim of diverting young people from becoming involved in criminal or anti-social behaviour. They provide suitable activities to facilitate personal development and encourage civic responsibility, and work towards the long-term employability of the participants. By 2001, the number of these projects had increased to 64 (Department of Justice, Equality and Law Reform, 2002) and will be increased to 100 by the end of 2007.

The *Report on the Youth Justice Review* was published in 2006 (Department of Justice, Equality and Law Reform, 2006). On the basis of its recommendations, a new Irish Youth Justice Service (IYJS) has been established, under the Department of Justice, Equality and Law Reform and co-located and operating within the strategic environment of the Office of the Minister for Children. The IYJS will bring together all services for young offenders under one governance and management structure, with the following objectives:

■ development of a specific youth justice policy from a single unified perspective;
■ responsibility for services for young offenders, including detention, community sanctions, restorative justice conferencing and diversion projects;
■ improved delivery of services through the development of national and local mechanisms to drive change.

Significance

Each child whose criminal behaviour comes to the attention of the Gardaí is referred to the Juvenile Diversion Programme. Referrals are therefore an accurate representation of the total number of children who offend. The Diversion Programme has proven to be highly successful in diverting young people away from crime by offering guidance and support to juveniles and their families. In the more serious cases, juveniles are placed under the supervision of Garda Juvenile Liaison Officers, who are specially trained members of the Garda Síochána responsible for administering the programme at local level. The Criminal Justice Act (Government of Ireland, 2006) introduced the concepts of restorative justice, specifically restorative cautioning and restorative conferencing, to the Juvenile Diversion Programme.

PART 4: FORMAL AND INFORMAL SUPPORTS

243

An evaluation of the effectiveness of Garda Youth Diversion Projects found that they do have an impact on offending and anti-social behaviour (Centre for Social and Educational Research, 2001). Young people involved in the projects were positive about them and a number of positive learning outcomes were identified (Bowden and Higgins, 2000). In addition, the young people involved noted that the projects facilitated the creation of positive, trusting and supportive relationships with adults and also provided them with alternative leisure, creative and developmental opportunities.

Recent changes in the youth justice system and further anticipated changes — including the full implementation of the Children Act (Government of Ireland, 2001), as amended by the Criminal Justice Act (Government of Ireland, 2006) — are intended to have a positive impact on the level of offences committed by children. This indicator would reflect any decrease in youth offending rates or any changes to the type or severity of offences committed.

Measure

> **The number of children referred to the Garda Juvenile Diversion Programme, expressed as a proportion of all children.**

Key findings

■ A total of 17,517 children aged 7-17 were referred to the Garda Juvenile Diversion Programme in 2005 *(see Table 88)*. This total excludes the 50 children from outside the jurisdiction. In the State as a whole, about 21% of children referred to the Diversion Programme were female. This proportion was reflected is most Garda regions, with the South-Eastern region having the highest proportion of females referred to the programme, at just over 24%.

Table 88: Number of children within the jurisdiction referred to Garda Juvenile Diversion Programme, by Garda Division and gender (2005)

Garda Division	Boys	Girls	Total
Dublin Metropolitan Region	4,974	1,254	6,228
Southern Region	2,970	779	3,749
Eastern Region	1,999	518	2,517
South Eastern Region	1,599	511	2,110
Western Region	1,348	365	1,713
Northern Region	995	205	1,200
Total	13,885	3,632	17,517
Total referrals	17,232	4,265	21,497
Children referred as % of 7-17 age group	4.4	1.2	2.8

Source: An Garda Síochána

■ The number of referrals does not correspond to the number of children since some children were referred more than once. There were 21,497 referrals to the Diversion Programme in 2005, a rate of 1.2 referrals per child referred.

■ The rate of referral for children aged 7-17 to the Garda Juvenile Diversion Programme in 2005 was 349 referrals per 10,000 children in that age group. The highest referral rate was in the 15-17 age group, with 15,430 referrals *(see Figure 51)*. This amounted to 884 referrals per 10,000 persons aged 15-17. This age group represented just over 70% of all referrals to the programme in 2005.

Figure 51: Referrals to the Garda Juvenile Diversion Programme, by age group (2005)

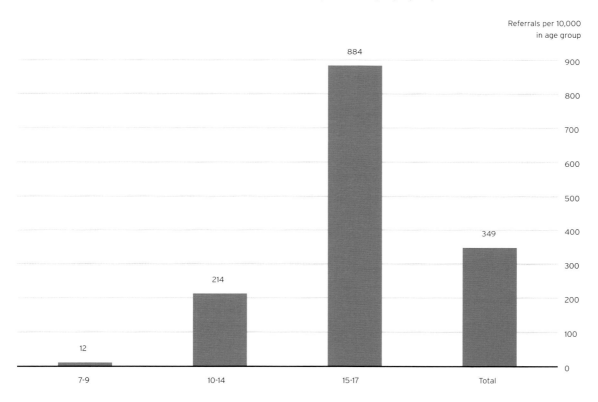

Source: An Garda Síochána

■ Alcohol-related offences were the single highest cause of referrals to the Garda Juvenile Diversion Programme in 2005, representing just under 20% of all referrals *(see Figure 52)*. Theft and criminal damage accounted for a further 18% and 10% of referrals respectively. Just over 6% of referrals were for possession of drugs.

PART 4: FORMAL AND INFORMAL SUPPORTS

245

Figure 52: Referrals to the Garda Juvenile Diversion Programme, by offence (2005)

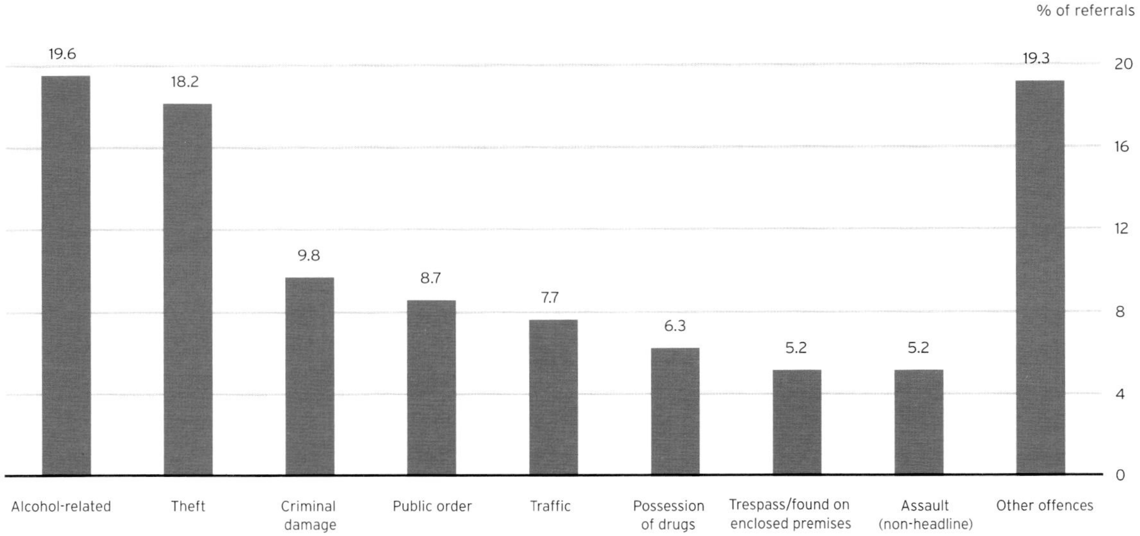

Source: An Garda Síochána

Technical notes

Table 88 shows the number of children referred to the Garda Juvenile Diversion Programme in the reference year. Figures 51 and 52 show the number of referrals to the programme. A child may have more than one referral in the reference year, therefore the number of referrals exceeds the number of children referred. In 2005, 17,517 children were referred to the Diversion Programme, while the total number of referrals was 21,497.

References

Bowden, M. and Higgins, L. (2000) *The Impact and Effectiveness of the Garda Special Projects: Final Report to the Department of Justice, Equality and Law Reform.* Dublin: Children's Research Centre, University of Dublin, Trinity College.

Centre for Social and Educational Research (2001) *Study of Participants in Garda Special Projects,* Department of Justice, Equality and Law Reform. Dublin: The Stationery Office.

Department of Justice, Equality and Law Reform (2002) *Garda Youth Diversion Project Guidelines.* Dublin: The Stationery Office.

Department of Justice, Equality and Law Reform (2006) *Report on the Youth Justice Review.* Dublin: The Stationery Office.

Government of Ireland (2001) *Children Act.* Dublin: The Stationery Office.

Government of Ireland (2006) *Criminal Justice Act.* Dublin: The Stationery Office.

ANTENATAL CARE

Context

In Ireland, the Maternity and Infant Care Scheme provides an agreed programme of care, free at the point of delivery, to all expectant mothers who are ordinarily resident in Ireland. The service, described as combined care, is provided jointly by a general practitioner, hospital obstetricians and midwives. Each expectant mother is entitled to seven examinations during the pregnancy, which may be alternated with visits to the maternity unit/hospital.

Mothers' rights to take paid time-off from employment to attend antenatal appointments (including some antenatal classes) are protected in Irish law through the Maternity Protection Act (Government of Ireland, 1994), the Maternity Protection (Amendment) Act (Government of Ireland, 2004), the Maternity Protection (Time off for Antenatal and Post-natal Care) Regulations (Government of Ireland, 1995a) and the Maternity Protection (Disputes and Appeals) Regulations (Government of Ireland, 1995b).

Significance

In high-income and middle-income countries today, the use of antenatal care services by pregnant women is almost universal. The World Health Organization notes that, ideally, the first visit should occur in the first trimester, around, or preferably before, week 12 of pregnancy (WHO, 2002). Maximum benefit, however, requires an early initiation of antenatal care in order that the following issues can be appropriately addressed (WHO, 2006):

- complications of pregnancy itself;
- diseases that may affect a pregnant woman and those that may be aggravated by pregnancy;
- negative effects of unhealthy lifestyles on the outcome of pregnancies.

There is a consensus that failure to receive appropriate antenatal care during pregnancy can lead to undesirable outcomes for both mother and infant, including maternal morbidity, low birth weight or even maternal and perinatal mortality (WHO, 2006). McCaw-Binns *et al* (1995) found that late attenders for antenatal care were more likely to be teenagers and unmarried, while Gissler and Hemminki (1995), using data from 57,108 women in Finland, showed that women who began antenatal care after the 16th week of gestation had the poorest outcomes, including higher incidence of low birth weight (whether due to pre-term birth or impaired intrauterine growth), Caesarean section and instrumental delivery.

The timing of the first antenatal contact between the pregnant woman and the health services can, therefore, be an important predictor of pregnancy outcome. In Ireland, some difficulties arise in respect of the reporting of timing of first antenatal check-up due to an absence of data of first contact with general practitioner services.

Measure

The distribution of timing of first antenatal visit by trimester for all women delivering live or stillborn babies.

Key findings

■ In 2003, 64.8% of women presented for antenatal care in the first trimester, 22.2% in the second trimester and 7.9% in the third trimester *(see Table 89)*.

■ In 2003, women aged 35-39 were least likely to attend for their first antenatal care in the third trimester (4.6%).

■ There has been an inconsistent upward trend in the percentage of women attending for their first antenatal visit in the third trimester.

■ First antenatal visits in the first trimester are lowest among the lower socio-economic groups, such as the unemployed *(see Figure 53)*. Women who are primarily engaged in home duties also have one of the lowest proportions of first antenatal visit in the first trimester.

■ The highest proportion of women attending for antenatal care in the first trimester are those whose occupations are categorised as 'unskilled manual workers' and 'salaried employees'.

Figure 53: Percentage of mothers attending for antenatal care in the first trimester of pregnancy, by occupation of mother (2003)

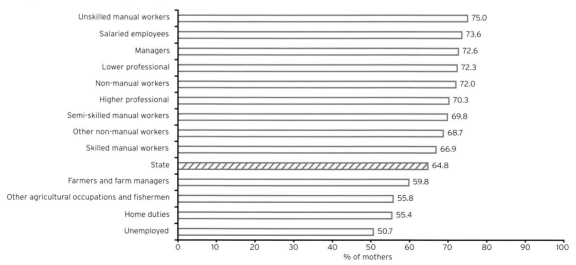

Source: National Perinatal Reporting System, Economic and Social Research Institute

Table 89: Percentage distribution of timing of first antenatal visit, by trimester and mother's age (1999-2003)																				
	1999				2000				2001				2002				2003			
Years of age	1st	2nd	3rd	n/s*	1st	2nd	3rd	n/s	1st	2nd	3rd	n/s	1st	2nd	3rd	n/s	1st	2nd	3rd	n/s
Under 15	41.7	0.0	25.0	33.3	25.0	41.7	25.0	8.3	50.0	33.3	16.7	0.0	30.0	50.0	10.0	10.0	26.7	46.7	20.0	6.7
15-19	56.9	31.6	8.1	3.4	57.5	30.7	9.4	2.4	52.4	34.4	10.9	2.7	52.5	35.0	11.0	1.5	53.9	33.1	11.5	1.6
20-24	59.0	29.6	7.9	3.5	59.6	27.6	10.1	2.6	55.7	28.8	12.4	3.1	55.7	29.5	12.7	2.2	58.0	28.9	11.4	1.7
25-29	66.8	22.8	5.3	5.1	67.3	21.4	7.2	4.2	61.4	22.5	10.3	5.8	60.6	22.7	11.9	4.8	62.6	22.3	10.7	4.4
30-34	69.0	20.0	4.4	6.7	69.4	19.4	5.3	5.9	66.3	19.3	6.4	8.1	65.7	19.8	6.7	7.8	68.2	19.7	6.1	6.0
35-39	66.2	21.6	5.0	7.2	68.9	19.9	4.9	6.4	66.4	19.3	5.6	8.7	66.0	21.0	5.2	7.9	68.7	20.0	4.6	6.7
40-44	63.1	22.6	6.2	8.1	65.6	22.4	5.9	6.1	62.9	22.9	5.9	8.3	65.3	22.5	5.8	6.5	66.5	21.0	5.2	7.3
45 and over	55.0	30.0	6.3	8.8	67.7	25.0	4.4	2.9	52.5	28.8	8.8	10.0	55.9	23.5	11.8	8.8	65.3	20.8	8.3	5.6
Not stated	46.7	11.7	3.3	38.3	54.2	29.2	8.3	8.3	13.6	22.7	18.2	45.5	25.5	27.5	13.7	33.3	39.3	18.0	11.5	31.2
Total	65.5	23.2	5.5	5.8	66.5	21.9	6.7	4.9	62.7	22.4	8.3	6.6	62.4	23.0	8.7	5.9	64.8	22.2	7.9	5.1

* n/s = not stated

Source: National Perinatal Reporting System, Economic and Social Research Institute

■ Almost 90% of mothers in Donegal attend for antenatal care in the first trimester compared with 29.7% in Mayo *(see Figure 54)*. This may be due, in part at least, to some differences in recording first contact with general practitioner services.

Figure 54: Percentage of mothers attending for antenatal care in the first trimester of pregnancy, by county of residence of mother (2003)

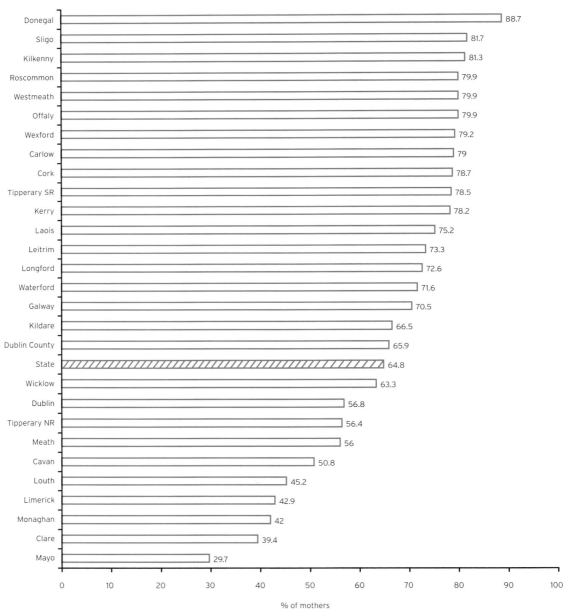

County	%
Donegal	88.7
Sligo	81.7
Kilkenny	81.3
Roscommon	79.9
Westmeath	79.9
Offaly	79.9
Wexford	79.2
Carlow	79
Cork	78.7
Tipperary SR	78.5
Kerry	78.2
Laois	75.2
Leitrim	73.3
Longford	72.6
Waterford	71.6
Galway	70.5
Kildare	66.5
Dublin County	65.9
State	64.8
Wicklow	63.3
Dublin	56.8
Tipperary NR	56.4
Meath	56
Cavan	50.8
Louth	45.2
Limerick	42.9
Monaghan	42
Clare	39.4
Mayo	29.7

% of mothers

Source: National Perinatal Reporting System, Economic and Social Research Institute

250

Technical notes

The National Perinatal Reporting System (NPRS) dataset provides details of national statistics on perinatal events (live births, late foetal deaths or stillbirths). Information on every birth that occurs either in hospital or at home is returned to the NPRS. The information collected includes data on pregnancy outcomes, with particular reference to perinatal mortality and important aspects of perinatal care. The period to which the information applies is from 22 week's gestation to the first week of life. In addition, descriptive social and biological characteristics of mothers giving birth and their babies are recorded.

All births are registered and notified on a standard four-part form, which is completed where the birth takes place, either at the hospital or by the attending independent midwife. The first part of the form is sent to the Registrar of Births and subsequently to the Central Statistics Office. The second part of the form goes to the community care area where the mother resides. The NPRS dataset is compiled from the third part of the form. The fourth part is retained by the hospital. The Economic and Social Research Institute (ESRI) is contracted by the Department of Health and Children to manage the NPRS system.

The collection of data on timing of first antenatal contact variable attempts to capture important information on Irish women's first contact with the healthcare services during pregnancy. This variable acts as an indicator of the length of antenatal care each mother has received and can be examined with birth, stillbirth and mortality rates. The completion of this indicator at present, however, may not provide an accurate estimation of this information. If the data are examined more closely, it is seen that in 2003, for example, 75% of all babies born had antenatal care recorded as 'combined care'. Of these, over 40% of patient records have recorded 'date of first visit to the hospital' only. If hospitals are not recording the mother's first antenatal visit to their GP or any other healthcare provider, the NPRS is effectively only reporting on time of first visit to the hospital. As a result, the percentage of mothers attending antenatal care during the first trimester is an underestimate and is very low at 65% of all births. This is much lower than other European countries, where the percentages of mothers attending antenatal care during the first trimester are in the region of 90%.

References

Gissler, M. and Hemminki, E. (1995) 'Amount of Antenatal Care and Infant Outcome', *Obstetrical & Gynaecological Survey,* Vol. 50, No. 5, pp. 338-40.

Government of Ireland (1994) *Maternity Protection Act.* Dublin: The Stationery Office.

Government of Ireland (1995a) *Maternity Protection (Time off for Antenatal Care and Post-natal Care) Regulations.* Dublin: The Stationery Office.

Government of Ireland (1995b) *Maternity Protection (Disputes and Appeals) Regulations.* Dublin: The Stationery Office.

Government of Ireland (2004) *Maternity Protection (Amendment) Act.* Dublin: The Stationery Office.

McCaw-Binns, A., La Grenade, J. and Ashley, D. (1995) 'Under-users of Antenatal Care: A comparison of non-attenders and late attenders for antenatal care, with early attenders', *Social Science and Medicine,* Vol. 40, No. 7, pp. 1003-12.

WHO (2002) *WHO Antenatal Care Randomized Trial: Manual for the Implementation of the New Model.* Copenhagen: World Health Organization.

WHO (2006) *The World Health Report 2006 – Working Together for Health.* Copenhagen: World Health Organization.

CHILDHOOD IMMUNISATION

Context

There is a national policy of promoting childhood immunisation as a simple, safe and effective way of protecting children against certain diseases. Vaccinations are provided free of charge, either by a general practitioner or through the school health service. The current Irish childhood immunisation schedule recommends that infants should receive three doses of vaccines against diphtheria, tetanus, pertussis (whooping cough), poliomyelitis and Meningococcal meningitis type C. They should receive their first dose of each vaccine at 2 months of age and subsequent doses at 4 and 6 months of age. Children should receive the first dose of the MMR (measles, mumps and rubella) vaccine between 12 and 15 months of age (Department of Health and Children, 2002).

Significance

Immunisation programmes are regarded as an important public health measure in preventing the spread of infectious diseases and are regarded as the most effective of all health-promoting interventions after clean water, shelter and food. Large-scale immunisation programmes have significantly impacted on the prevention of vaccine-preventable diseases. Worldwide, smallpox has been eradicated and in Ireland, as in the rest of Europe, polio transmission has been successfully eliminated (WHO, 2005).

A recent study by Deady and Thornton (2005) on Irish parents' knowledge of, and attitude towards, the primary childhood immunisations in one area of Dublin noted that parents who were in single-parent families and those with lower educational attainment levels were significantly less aware of the severity of diseases for which immunisation was available. In addition, older parents were more likely to question immunisation safety compared with younger ones.

Measure

> **The percentage uptake of D3/P3/T3/Hib3/Polio3 and Meningococcal C3 vaccinations at (a) 12 months and (b) 24 months of age; and the percentage uptake of MMR1 vaccinations at 24 months of age.**

Key findings

- Overall, the level of uptake of immunisation has increased among children aged up to 12 months, from about 76.5% in 2000 to about 83% in 2004 *(see Table 90)*.
- The percentage uptake of immunisation in 2001 was about 69%. This was the lowest over the 5-year period under examination.

Table 90: Immunisation uptake rates at 12 months (2000-2004)					
Vaccine	2000	2001	2002	2003	2004
DTaP3/DT3	76.6	69.5	-	-	-
D3T3	-	-	75.1	80.7	83.1
P3	-	-	74.3	80.2	82.9
HIB3	76.5	69.3	75.1	80.5	83.0
Polio3	76.5	68.8	74.8	80.6	83.1
MenC3	-	-	73.8	80.2	82.6

Source: Immunisation Uptake Statistics, Health Protection Surveillance Centre

- The level of uptake of immunisation among children aged up to 24 months also increased over this period, from about 84% in 2000 to about 89% in 2004 *(see Table 91)*.
- The increase was more marked for the Meningococcal meningitis type C vaccine: in 2002 the percentage uptake was 74.7% for children aged 24 months, while in 2004 this percentage had increased to 87.9%.

Table 91: Immunisation uptake rates at 24 months (2000-2004)					
Vaccine	2000	2001	2002	2003	2004
DTaP3/DT3	85.9	84.3	-	-	-
D3T3	-	-	83.2	86.4	89.4
P3	-	-	81.5	85.3	88.9
HIB3	85.4	83.8	82.7	86.0	89.1
Polio3	85.7	84.1	82.5	86.1	89.3
MenC3	-	-	74.7	83.6	87.9

Source: Immunisation Uptake Statistics, Health Protection Surveillance Centre

Differences by geographical area
- In 2004, immunisation rates for the 12-month-old cohort were at about 83% for the State as a whole *(see Table 92)*. Uptake rates were lowest in the former Eastern Regional Health Authority, at about 79%, and highest in the former Midland Health Board area, at just under 90%.

Table 92: Immunisation uptake rates at 12 months, by former health board area (2004)

	D3T3	P3	HIB3	Polio3	MenC3
Eastern Regional Health Authority	79.0	78.9	79.0	79.1	78.5
Midland Health Board	89.9	89.6	89.9	89.9	89.8
Mid-Western Health Board	86.2	85.9	86.1	86.2	86.0
North-Eastern Health Board	86.3	86.0	86.2	86.3	85.8
North-Western Health Board	89.2	88.9	88.7	89.3	88.5
South-Eastern Health Board	86.4	85.9	86.2	86.4	85.8
Southern Health Board	83.3	83.0	83.2	82.9	82.9
Western Health Board	81.0	80.7	80.9	81.0	79.4
Mean average - State	**83.1**	**82.9**	**83.0**	**83.1**	**82.6**

Source: Immunisation Uptake Statistics, Health Protection Surveillance Centre

■ Similar regional patterns were apparent for the 24-month-old cohort. In 2004, the national immunisation uptake rates for this cohort were at about 88%-89% *(see Table 93)*. The lowest rates (84%-86%) were in the former Eastern Regional Health Authority, while the highest rates (89%-91%) were in the former Midland and North-Western Health Boards areas.

Table 93: Immunisation uptake rates at 24 months, by former health board area (2004)

	D3T3	P3	HIB3	Polio3	MenC3
Eastern Regional Health Authority	86.1	85.8	85.9	86.0	84.5
Midland Health Board	94.0	92.7	94.0	94.0	93.9
Mid-Western Health Board	89.2	88.2	88.8	89.1	88.2
North-Eastern Health Board	93.3	93.0	92.7	93.1	92.1
North-Western Health Board	95.1	94.9	94.1	94.8	93.4
South-Eastern Health Board	91.5	90.8	91.3	91.5	90.3
Southern Health Board	89.3	88.9	89.1	89.2	88.4
Western Health Board	89.8	89.4	89.7	89.7	86.5
Mean average - State	**89.4**	**88.9**	**89.1**	**89.3**	**87.9**

Source: Immunisation Uptake Statistics, Health Protection Surveillance Centre

■ In 2004, the rate of completed vaccination for diphtheria, tetanus, pertussis and polio in Ireland was amongst the lowest in the EU, at 89% *(see Figures 55 and 56)*. 16 EU countries had completed vaccination rates of 95% or higher in the same year.

Childhood immunisation

Figure 55: Percentage of relevant age group receiving 3rd dose of diphtheria, tetanus and pertussis vaccines, by country (2004)

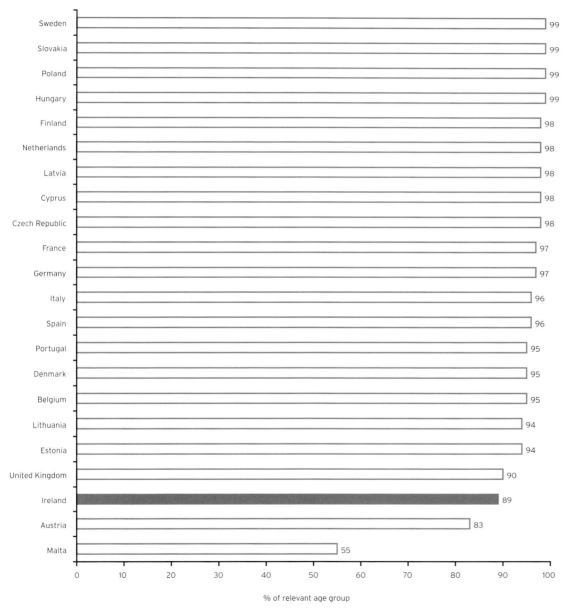

% of relevant age group

Source: Immunisation Uptake Statistics, Health Protection Surveillance Centre

PART 4: FORMAL AND INFORMAL SUPPORTS

255

Figure 56: Percentage of relevant age group receiving 3rd dose of polio vaccine, by country (2004)

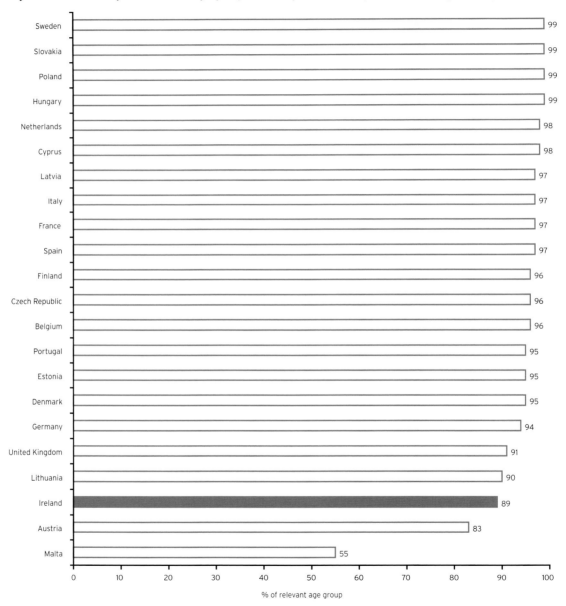

% of relevant age group

Source: Immunisation Uptake Statistics, Health Protection Surveillance Centre

■ In 2000, 78.9% of children aged up to 24 months had received their first dose of the MMR vaccine *(see Figure 57 and Table 94)*. This proportion dropped to 73.2% in 2001, but has increased since, rising to 81.1% in 2004.

Figure 57: MMR1 vaccine uptake rate (2000-2004)

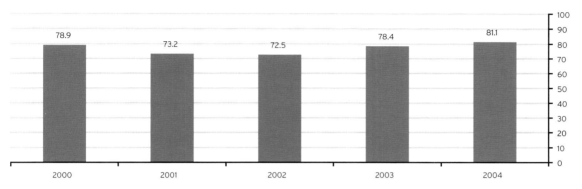

Source: Immunisation Uptake Statistics, Health Protection Surveillance Centre

Table 94: MMR1 vaccine uptake rate, by former health board area (2000-2004)	2000	2001	2002	2003	2004
Midland Health Board	75.0	72.2	71.9	88.0	91.0
North-Western Health Board	73.6	77.6	79.6	83.4	87.0
South-Eastern Health Board	89.7	86.8	81.6	83.2	86.6
Mid-Western Health Board	76.9	73.9	80.1	80.1	83.7
Southern Health Board	76.8	76.1	76.1	79.7	83.5
North-Eastern Health Board	80.1	78.5	79.5	80.9	82.6
Western Health Board	83.1	76.0	73.8	74.3	77.5
Eastern Regional Health Authority	77.3	65.5	64.0	74.2	76.1
Mean average – State	78.9	73.2	72.5	78.4	81.1

Source: Immunisation Uptake Statistics, Health Protection Surveillance Centre

■ Uptake rates of the MMR1 vaccine increased in 5 of the 8 former health board areas between 2000 and 2004 *(see Figure 58)*.
■ The former Midland Health Board showed the largest increase − of 16 percentage points over the period.
■ The uptake rates for the MMR1 vaccine decreased over the same period in the former Eastern, South-Eastern and Western health boards.

Figure 58: MMR1 vaccine uptake rate, by former health board area (2000 and 2004)

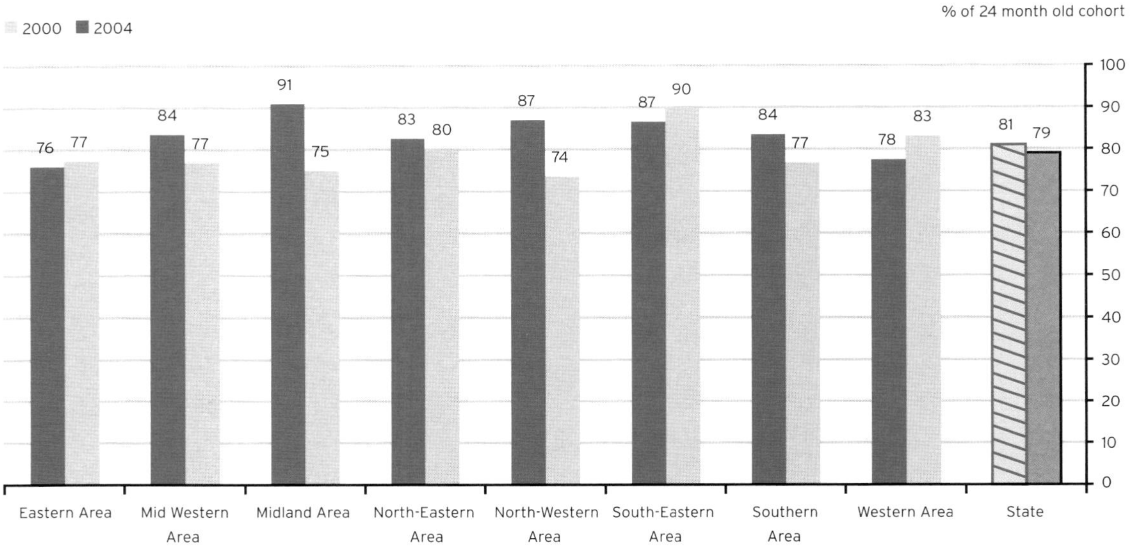

2000 2004

% of 24 month old cohort

Eastern Area: 76, 77
Mid Western Area: 84, 77
Midland Area: 91, 75
North-Eastern Area: 83, 80
North-Western Area: 87, 74
South-Eastern Area: 87, 90
Southern Area: 84, 77
Western Area: 78, 83
State: 81, 79

Source: Immunisation Uptake Statistics, Health Protection Surveillance Centre

- In 2004, Ireland had the second lowest uptake of measles-containing vaccine in the EU, at 81% *(see Figure 59)*.

Figure 59: Percentage of relevant age group receiving measles-containing vaccine, by country (2004)

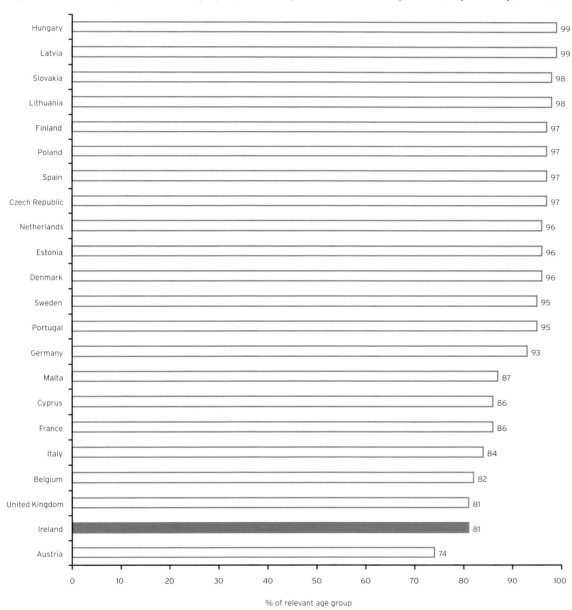

% of relevant age group

Source: Immunisation Uptake Statistics, Health Protection Surveillance Centre

PART 4: FORMAL AND INFORMAL SUPPORTS

259

Technical notes

Irish statistics on immunisation are compiled by the Health Protection Surveillance Centre (HPSC) using data from the former health board areas. There is no national database on immunisation.

International data on immunisation coverage is collected by the World Health Organization to monitor and assess the impact of strategies and activities for reducing morbidity and mortality of vaccine-preventable diseases. In most countries, the data collected refer to the number of doses administered to the target population divided by the total estimated number of people in the target population. The target population groups vary from country to country and are dependent on the national immunisation schedule in place.

In Ireland, each former health board area is responsible for maintaining an immunisation register. A listing of all birth notifications in the area is received from the General Register's Office (GRO). Public health nurses follow up on all new births, visit the mother and register the child's details and details of the GP nominated by the mother to perform the required immunisations. This information is returned to the local immunisation office and recorded on the childhood immunisation register used by that area. The office monitors the child's immunisation record and issues reminders when immunisations fall due. Following each vaccination, the GP makes a return to the local immunisation office, indicating details of the vaccine and date of administration. This information is maintained on the local immunisation register and is provided to the HPSC for the compilation of immunisation uptake statistics.

Immunisation against Meningococcal meningitis type C was introduced in October 2000. Rates of uptake of this vaccine are available from 2002 onwards.

In the tables for this indicator, the reference year refers to the year in which the recipients of the vaccine reached either 12 or 24 months of age, depending on the cohort being considered. Therefore, for example, the rate of 76.6% for the DTaP3/DT3 vaccines in Table 90, which refers to the 12-month-old cohort, indicates that 76.6% of children born between 1 January 1999 and 31 December 1999 received this vaccine.

The following are the definitions of the vaccines referred to in these indicators:

DTaP3/DT3   These terms refer respectively to 3 doses of a combined diphtheria, tetanus and pertussis vaccine (DTaP3) or 3 doses of a combined diphtheria and tetanus vaccine (DT3). The figures shown in Tables 90 and 91 represent the proportion of children in the relevant age group who had received one or other of these vaccines. Completed vaccination (three doses) among children in subsequent years was registered by disease-specific vaccines (D3, P3 and T3).

D3T3   Refers to a combined diphtheria and tetanus vaccine, administered in 3 doses at 2, 4 and 6 months of age.

P3   Refers to a pertussis vaccine, administered in 3 doses at 2, 4 and 6 months of age.

HIB3   Refers to the vaccine for Haemophilus Influenzae type B, administered in 3 doses at 2, 4 and 6 months of age.

POLIO3   Refers to the vaccine for poliomyelitis, administered in 3 doses at 2, 4 and 6 months of age.

MenC3   Refers to the vaccine for Meningococcal meningitis type C, administered in 3 doses at 2, 4 and 6 months of age. This vaccine was introduced in October 2000. Data on uptake of the vaccine is available from 2002 onwards.

MMR1   Refers to the first dose of the combined vaccine for measles, mumps and rubella, administered between the ages of 12 and 15 months.

References

Deady, J. and Thornton, L. (2005) 'Parents' knowledge of, and attitude towards, the primary childhood immunisations', *Irish Medical Journal,* Vol. 98, No. 1, pp. 7-8.
Department of Health and Children (2002) *Immunisation Guidelines for Ireland.* Dublin: The Stationery Office.
WHO (2005) *The World Health Report 2005 – Make Every Mother and Child Count.* Copenhagen: World Health Organization.

Further information
- Health Protection Surveillance Centre (www.ndsc.ie/hpsc/)
- Health Service Executive, immunisation information (www.immunisation.ie)

SCREENING FOR GROWTH AND DEVELOPMENT

Context

The provision of a primary and secondary preventive child health service has its roots in Section 2(1) of the Notification of Births (Extension) Act (Government of Ireland, 1915) and the Public Health (Medical Treatment of Children) Act (Government of Ireland, 1919), which provided for a public health home-visiting service for families with children. The service is delivered through the public health nursing, area medical officer and general practitioner service, and is universally free at the point of delivery.

A review of this service and a strategic plan for its development were published in 1999 under the title *Best Health for Children* (Denyer *et al*, 1999). Two main goals were identified:
■ that all children would have the opportunity to realise their full potential in terms of good health, well-being and development;
■ that remediable disorders would be identified and acted upon as early as possible.

In line with an evidence-based approach, a second review was carried out in 2005 and made recommendations for a revised national core programme for child health contacts between the child health services and the family (National Core Child Health Programme Review Group, 2005). These contacts are now scheduled to take place at the following times: at birth, as soon as possible after mother and infant are discharged from maternity services, at 6-8 weeks, 3 months, 7-9 months, 18-24 months, 3.25-3.5 years of age, primary school entry and primary school-leaving. With the exception of the birth examination (carried out by midwives, other obstetric or paediatric staff, usually in hospital), the 6-week contact (GP and practice nurse) and the 7-9 month contact (which may be undertaken by either public health nurses or area medical officers), all remaining contacts are undertaken through the public health nursing service. This service provides physical and developmental examinations, including growth monitoring and advice and support on issues of parenting (e.g. feeding, safety, parent-infant interactions, sibling management and age-appropriate play).

Significance

Rationales underpinning the Irish public health nursing service to families with infants have been restated by Denyer *et al* (1999, p. 3), including:
■ the acceptability of this service to the public;
■ the importance of the identification of children's needs (including social, medical, emotional and educational needs);
■ the provision of an opportunity for families who may not usually come in contact with health professionals to access services;

- the advocacy role played by these services in facilitating access to appropriate services by families with identified needs;
- the unique opportunity to access the population at a critical age in life, which facilitates assessment of population health status and enables the collation of epidemiological information;
- the facilitation of health promotion;
- the development of a high level of expertise, by professionals involved in the service, in a wide range of areas of child health.

Although there has not been a longitudinal evaluation of the Irish child health service to families, there is a substantial literature from elsewhere that demonstrates significant benefits for families when a similar service is provided in the early years. Short-term benefits identified include reassurance for mothers (Earle and Burman, 1998); increased parental knowledge (Kerr *et al*, 1997); improved parental problem-solving strategies (Astill *et al*, 1998); and higher levels of reported positive infant mood (Olds *et al*, 1986). Long-term follow-up of one home nursing service showed positive outcomes for children, with lower levels of juvenile delinquency at aged 21 years in those children who had been home-visited (Olds *et al*, 1998).

The data presented next refer only to the percentage of families visited by the Public Health Nurse (PHN) within 48 hours of discharge from hospital; data do not include families who are visited outside this time.

PART 4: FORMAL AND INFORMAL SUPPORTS

263

Public Health Nurse visit

Measure

> **The percentage of mothers of newborn children visited by a Public Health Nurse (PHN) within 48 hours of discharge from hospital.**

Key findings

- In 2004, the percentage of mothers of newborn babies visited by a Public Health Nurse (PHN) within 48 hours of discharge from hospital ranged from 59% to 95.5% *(see Table 95)*.
- Although the data provided in respect of this indicator are not fully comprehensive, they show considerable variation both within and between former health board areas. Within the former North-Eastern Health Board area, for example, 92% of mothers with newborn infants in Cavan/Monaghan were contacted by a PHN within 48 hours of discharge from hospital, compared with 54.5% in Meath.

Table 95: Percentage of mothers of newborn infants visited by a Public Health Nurse within 48 hours of discharge from hospital, by former health board area (2003-2004)		
	2003	2004
Eastern Regional Health Authority	59	59[1]
Southern Health Board	90	94[2]
South-Eastern Health Board	75	78.5
Mid-Western Health Board	76	76
Western Health Board	94	95.5
Midland Health Board	93	89
North-Western Health Board	88	89
North-Eastern Health Board		
Cavan/Monaghan	90	92
Louth	73	73.5
Meath	41.5	54.5

[1] Only includes data from a small number of community care areas.

[2] Refers to the number seen within 24 hours of notification.

Source: National Health Services Performance Indicators, Department of Health and Children

264

Technical notes

Analysis of commentary presented with the data suggests that there are a number of issues arising in respect of this indicator, namely:

■ Different definitions were in use at the time of data collection. Although the majority of former health board areas appeared to use the definition of 'the percentage visited within 48 hours of discharge from hospital', at least one health board area used 'the percentage seen within 24 hours of notification'.

■ The majority of former health board areas indicated that they are reporting only on the percentage of 'face-to-face contact', while a small number report on 'telephone contact' as well as 'face-to-face contact'.

■ The notification of the discharge of a mother with a new infant appears to operate differently in different places. A number of former health board areas make reference to the manual transfer of information to PHNs and also to difficulties in ensuring the notification gets to the right PHN because of maternal change of addresses. In some areas, the notification operates in a consistent and timely way. In others, however, difficulties arise, such as:
  - delays in the PHNs receiving the birth or discharge notification;
  - incorrect addresses or other misinformation;
  - the birth notification is received, but the infant is still in hospital.

■ In most former health board areas, there is no service at weekends or on bank holidays unless the infant needs to have a Guthrie test to screen for inborn errors of metabolism.

Developmental screening

Measure

The percentage uptake of developmental screening at 7 to 9 months.

Key findings

- The data from 2003 show considerable variation within and between former health board areas for this indicator *(see Table 96)*.
- Developmental screening at 7-9 months by area medical officers does not appear to be available in some geographical areas. The highest percentage coverage (68%) is in the former Western Health Board area.

Table 96: Percentage uptake of Child Health Core Screening Programme at 7 to 9 months as outlined in 'Best Health for Children' 1999 guidelines, by former health board area (2003)	
Eastern Regional Health Authority	49
Southern Health Board	0
South-Eastern Health Board	11.3
Mid-Western Health Board	57
Western Health Board	68
Midland Health Board	55
North-Western Health Board	35
North-Eastern Health Board	
Cavan/Monaghan	0
Louth	36.3
Meath	0

Source: National Health Services Performance Indicators, Department of Health and Children

Technical notes

There was less information available for analysis with this indicator than with the indicator on PHN contact within 48 hours of discharge from hospital *(see p. 264)*. However, commentary suggests that the contact between families with 7-9 month infants and the area medical officers was not consistent. In the former Southern Health Board, for example, it was noted that no service was being provided by the area medical officer (AMO) service. There were clinics at this time, however, provided by PHNs. In 2003, the definition applied to this indicator included service delivery involving the AMO service. Areas providing a PHN-led service therefore recorded lower than actual uptake rates, but had the option to correct this in the commentary section.

References

Astill, W., Halliwell, K. and Gareze, C. (1998) 'Outcome measures: The value of health visiting interventions', *Community Practitioner,* Vol. 71, No. 5, pp. 181-82.

Denyer, S., Thornton, L. and Pelly, H. (1999) *Best Health for Children. Developing a Partnership with Families. Report to the Chief Executive Officers of the Health Boards of Ireland on behalf of the Directors of Public Health.* Dublin: Best Health for Children. Available at: www.pacirl.ie

Earle, L.P. and Burman, M.E. (1998) 'Benefits and barriers to well-child care: Perceptions of mothers in a rural state', *Public Health Nursing,* Vol. 15, No. 3, pp. 180-87.

Government of Ireland (1915) *Notification of Births (Extension) Act.* Dublin: The Stationery Office.

Government of Ireland (1919) *Public Health (Medical Treatment of Children) Act.* Dublin: The Stationery Office.

Kerr, S., Jowett, S. and Smith, L. (1997) 'Education to help prevent sleep problems in infants', *Health Visitor,* Vol. 70, No. 6, pp. 224-25.

National Core Child Health Programme Review Group (2005) *Report from the National Core Child Health Programme Review Group to the Health Service Executive: Best Health for Children Revisited.* Dublin: Programme of Action for Children. Available at: www.pacirl.ie

Olds, D.L., Henderson, C.R., Tatelbaum, R. and Chamberlin, R. (1986) 'Preventing child abuse and neglect: A randomised trial of nurse home visitation', *Paediatrics,* No. 78, pp. 65-78.

Olds, D., Henderson, C.R., Cole, R., Eckenrode, J., Kitzman, H., Luckey, D., Pettitt, L., Sidora, K., Morris, P. and Powers, J. (1998) 'Long-term effects of nurse home visitation on children's criminal and anti-social behaviour: Fifteen-year follow-up of a randomized controlled trial', *Journal of the American Medical Association,* No. 280, pp. 1238–44.

Further information
- Health Service Executive (www.hse.ie)

ACCESSIBILITY OF BASIC HEALTH SERVICES FOR CHILDREN AND YOUNG PEOPLE

Context

Article 24 of the United Nations Convention on the Rights of the Children asserts 'the right of the child to the enjoyment of the highest attainable standard of health possible and to facilities for the treatment of illness and rehabilitation of health' (UN, 1989). This Article also recognises children's 'right of access to such health services' and calls upon governments to ensure that 'no child is deprived' of this right. The Convention also obligates State Parties 'to ensure to the maximum extent possible the survival and development of the child' (Article 6) and to respect all rights set forth in the Convention 'without discrimination of any kind' (Article 2).

In 1993, the Department of Health introduced the Waiting List Initiative (WLI) to deal with a persistent waiting list problem in the acute hospitals. WLI funding was provided in addition to normal hospital funding and was intended to:

■ incentivise hospitals and former health boards to perform extra elective procedures;
■ be targeted specifically at patients waiting longer than target times in the selected specialities;
■ be ring-fenced, i.e. kept separate from other funding of elective procedures.

In addition, Action 81 of the National Health Strategy, *Quality and Fairness: A Health System for You* (Department of Health and Children, 2001), stated that 'a comprehensive set of actions will be taken to reduce waiting times for public patients'. In accordance with this, the National Treatment Purchase Fund (NTPF) was established in April 2002 as one mechanism for reducing long-term waiting lists. The NTPF was set up initially to deal with adults who were waiting a year or longer for an operation and for children who were waiting 6 months or more for an operation. The NTPF sources treatment for qualifying patients in hospitals in Ireland, Northern Ireland and England.

Significance

The Institute of Public Health in Ireland (2001) stated in its report *Equity of Access to Health Services:* 'Health is influenced by many factors, including genetic endowment, early life experiences, material conditions such as income and housing, education, psycho-social factors such as social support networks, health-related behaviour and biological risk factors, and medical care.' While recognising this, it is also important to recognise that health services can play an important role in combating health inequalities and enhancing population health (WHO, 1998; Combat Poverty Agency, 2005).

268

In general, the size of waiting lists has traditionally been viewed as an important measure of the quality of healthcare services (Thornorethardottir *et al*, 2002). It has been noted that excessive waiting time for treatment can lead to a deterioration in health, prolongation of suffering (Hurst and Siciliani, 2003) and growing public dissatisfaction with healthcare services provided (Watson and Williams, 2001). This is particularly the case for children, where, for example, a failure to provide early intervention in areas such as speech therapy, hearing loss and emotional difficulties can have lifelong implications. The Children's Rights Alliance (2001) have suggested that the elimination of waiting lists is the first step to ensuring all children can achieve the 'highest attainable standard of health possible' (according to Article 24 of the UN Convention on the Rights of the Child) through the same quality of access to health services irrespective of income levels, class standing, race, ethnicity, gender or geographical location.

Measure

The number of children on hospital waiting lists.

Key findings

- In April 2006, 1,761 children were known to be on a hospital waiting list awaiting treatment *(see Table 97)*.
- The hospitals in the Dublin area account for approximately three-quarters of the total number of children waiting for treatment (1,322).

Table 97: Number of children on hospital waiting lists, by hospital and waiting time (2006)				
	3-6 months	6-12 months	Over 12 months	Total
Beaumont Hospital	11	8	6	25
The Children's University Hospital	145	147	96	388
Our Lady's Hospital for Sick Children, Crumlin	317	274	246	837
Royal Victoria Eye and Ear Hospital	22	24	8	54
Tallaght Hospital	11	5	2	18
Cork University Hospital	48	42	56	146
Mercy University Hospital, Cork	14	17	13	44
South Infirmary Hospital Cork	38	8	0	46
Kerry General Hospital	7	2	0	9
Mid-Western Regional Hospital	24	36	15	75
St. John's Hospital, Limerick	1	1	0	2
University College Hospital, Galway	65	38	14	117
Total	703	602	456	1,761

Source: Patient Treatment Register, National Treatment Purchase Fund

Differences by waiting time

■ 40% (703) of the 1,761 children awaiting treatment were on the hospital waiting list for 3-6 months, 34% (602) for 6-12 months and 26% (456) for one year or more *(see Figure 60).*

Figure 60: Number of children, by hospital waiting time (2006)

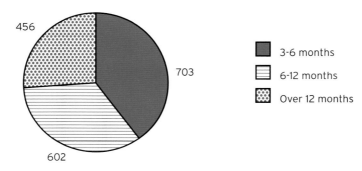

Source: Patient Treatment Register, National Treatment Purchase Fund

Differences by speciality

■ Approximately, two-thirds of the 1,761 children awaiting treatment were on the hospital waiting list for a surgical procedure and approximately one-third for a medical procedure *(see Figure 61).*

Figure 61: Number of children on waiting list, by type of procedure (2006)

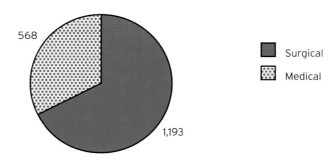

Source: Patient Treatment Register, National Treatment Purchase Fund

■ For the 10 most common child surgical procedures, 87% are waiting less than 6 months *(see Table 98).* Overall, for 8 of the 10 most common child procedures, patients are waiting 2-5 months.

Table 98: Paediatric patient waiting times for 10 most common surgical procedures

	Cumulative median waiting time	Beaumont Hospital	Children's University Hospital	Our Lady's Hospital for Sick Children	Royal Victoria Eye and Ear Hospital	Tallaght Hospital	Cork University Hospital	Kerry General Hospital	Mercy University Hospital, Cork	South Infirmary Victoria Hospital, Cork	Mid-Western Regional Hospital, Limerick	St. John's Hospital, Limerick	University College Hospital, Galway
	Mths	Mths	Mths	Mths	Mths	Mths	Mths	Mths	Mths	Mths	Mths	Mths	Mths
Otoplasty (set back prominent ears)	9	0	11	5	-	-	20	-	-	-	-	-	2
Circumcision	6	0	7	5	-	7	-	2	6	9	4	-	4
Surgical removal of tooth	5	0	-	6	-	-	-	-	-	-	2	-	-
Excision	5	2	6	5	0	0	14	-	0	4	3	0	3
Tonsillectomy	4	0	5	5	2	4	-	1	-	2	1	0	1
Coronary angiogram	4	-	-	4	-	0	-	-	-	-	-	-	-
Orchidopexy (testes surgery)	4	-	3	0	-	-	4	-	-	-	-	-	-
Correction of squint	4	-	2	4	4	-	2	-	0	-	9	-	6
Adenidectomy	2	2	8	2	8	2	-	-	-	2	0	-	2
Myringotomy (removal of fluid from middle ear)	1	0	-	1	-	-	-	-	-	0	-	-	-

Source: Patient Treatment Register, National Treatment Purchase Fund

Technical notes

The Patient Treatment Register (PTR) is the first online verified database of public in-patient and day-case waiting lists in Ireland. It was developed with cooperation from the Department of Health and Children, the Health Service Executive and the public hospitals. Phase One, which included 7 hospitals, has been up and running since September 2005. A further 12 hospitals have now been added and the PTR is being rolled out nationally, with the remaining target hospitals to be delivered by the end of 2006.

The National Treatment Purchase Fund (NTPF) has statutory responsibility for the collation, management and publication of waiting list data from hospitals. Currently, 19 hospitals are participating, which means that 74% of the patient population, as measured under the old waiting list system, is covered by the PTR. The participating hospitals are:

Dublin North Regional Area	**Dublin Mid-Leinster Regional Area**
■ Beaumont Hospital ■ Cappagh Orthopaedic Hospital ■ Connolly Hospital, Blanchardstown ■ The Children's University Hospital, Temple Street ■ The Mater Hospital	■ Tallaght Hospital ■ St. Vincent's Hospital, Elm Park ■ St. James's Hospital ■ Royal Victoria Eye and Ear Hospital ■ Our Lady's Hospital for Sick Children, Crumlin
Western Regional Area	**Southern Regional Area**
■ St. John's Hospital, Limerick ■ Merlin Park Hospital, Galway ■ Mid-Western Regional Hospital, Limerick ■ Mid-Western Regional Orthopaedic Hospital, Croom ■ University College Hospital, Galway	■ Cork University Hospital ■ Kerry General Hospital ■ Mercy University Hospital, Cork ■ South Infirmary – Victoria Hospital, Cork

References

Children's Rights Alliance (2001) *National Health Strategy 2001. Submission by the Children's Rights Alliance.* Dublin: Children's Rights Alliance.

Combat Poverty Agency (2005) *Health Services and the National Anti-Poverty Strategy.* Dublin: Combat Poverty Agency.

Department of Health (1993) *Waiting List Initiative.* Dublin: The Stationery Office.

Department of Health and Children (2001) *Quality and Fairness: A Health System for You.* Dublin: The Stationery Office.

Hurst, J. and Siciliani, L. (2003) *Tackling excessive waiting times for elective surgery: A Comparison of policies in twelve OECD countries.* Paris: Organisation for Economic Cooperation and Development.

Institute of Public Health in Ireland (2001) *Equity of Access to Health Services.* Dublin: Institute of Public Health in Ireland.

Thornorethardottir, S., Halldorsson, M. and Guethmundsson. S. (2002) 'Gender and age differences in waiting time on hospital waiting list', *Laeknabladid,* Vol. 88, No. 9, pp. 635-39.

UN (1989) *Convention on the Rights of the Child.* Geneva: United Nations Office of the High Commissioner for Human Rights. Available at www.ohchr.org

Watson, D. and Williams, J. (2001) *Perceptions of the Quality of Health Care in the Public and Private Sectors in Ireland: Report to the Centre for Insurance Studies, Graduate Business School, UCD.* Dublin: Economic and Social Research Institute.

WHO (1998) *Health 21 – The Health for All Policy for the WHO European Region.* Copenhagen: World Health Organization.

CHILDREN AND YOUNG PEOPLE IN CARE

Context

The United Nations Convention on the Rights of the Child recognises in its preamble that 'the child, for the full and harmonious development of his or her personality, should grow up in a family environment, in an atmosphere of happiness, love and understanding'.

Under the Child Care Act (Government of Ireland, 1991), the Health Service Executive (HSE) is empowered to provide family support services so that children can grow up in their own families, even in adverse circumstances. Where this is not possible, however, the HSE is legislated to provide for children in care and the Child Care Act, 1991 provides the basis for this. Children may be admitted into care either voluntary (with the consent of the child's parents) or under a Court order. Children who are in foster care (under 18 years) remain legally part of their family of origin, although guardianship responsibilities are taken on by the local health service. Foster care is legislated for under the Child Care Act, 1991 and with the associated Child Care (Placement of Children in Foster Care) Regulations (Government of Ireland, 1995a) and Child Care (Placement of Children with Relatives) Regulations (Government of Ireland, 1995b).

Although the majority of children in the care of the HSE are in foster care, almost 450 children are in residential care. These care centres are provided either by the HSE or by non-statutory agencies and are inspected either by the Social Services Inspectorate (SSI) or the registration and inspection units of the HSE. Inspection reports are published by the SSI and are available on its website (www.issi.ie). Registration and inspection unit reports are available on request under the terms of the Freedom of Information Act (Government of Ireland, 1999). National standards have also been developed for children's residential centres, special care units and foster care services (Department of Health and Children, 2001a and 2001b, 2003).

Significance

Children in care are a particularly vulnerable group and while it has been found that some children do better in certain respects if left in care than if returned home (Sinclair and Gibbs, 2002), the effect of being placed in care can also be damaging for the child. Children in care, for example, are more likely than other children to experience high levels of behavioural and emotional problems. In particular, research suggests that children in care fare less well in education than other children, insofar as they are more likely to be suspended or expelled from school, more likely to exhibit low levels of school engagement (Daly and Gilligan, 2005) and more likely to leave school without an academic qualification (Kelleher *et al,* 2000). Children in care are also more likely to be bullied at school (Daly and Gilligan, 2005).

Other research suggests that children in care are also more likely to have received mental health services, to have a limiting physical, learning or mental health condition, or to be in poor or fair health (Sinclair and Gibbs, 2002). Being placed in foster care with relatives, being placed with a sibling and/ or being placed in long-term care, however, has been shown to mediate some of these difficulties (O'Brien, 2001; Daly and Gilligan, 2005). In Ireland, children and young people tend to remain in care and more than three-quarters are in care for one year or longer (Daly and Gilligan, 2005).

Measure

> **The number of children who are in the care of the Health Service Executive (HSE), expressed as a proportion of all children. This can be subdivided by type of care arrangement: (a) foster care - general; (b) foster care - special; (c) foster care - relatives; (d) pre-adoptive placement; (e) residential - general; (f) residential - special; (g) at home under care order; and (h) other.**

Key findings

- Over the period 2000-2004, the number of children in the care of the former health board areas rose from 4,424 children to 5,060 children *(see Table 99)*. This translates to a rate of 43 per 10,000 children to 50 per 10,000 children under 18 years of age.
- The former Eastern Regional Health Authority consistently recorded the highest number of children in care, while the former North-Western Health Board consistently recorded the lowest number.
- In 2004, 57% of children in care were voluntarily accommodated because they or their parents had asked for this. The remaining 43% were in care because the Courts had ordered it.

Table 99: Number of children in the care of the former health board areas (2000-2004)	2000	2001	2002	2003	2004
Eastern Regional Health Authority	1,732	2,830	2,116	2,163	2,080
Southern Health Board	560	589	653	621	704
South-Eastern Health Board	538	540	574	558	575
Mid-Western Health Board	405	391	417	407	438
North-Eastern Health Board	447	434	421	423	437
Western Health Board	285	268	270	309	322
Midland Health Board	240	244	258	293	300
North-Western Health Board	217	221	212	210	204
State	4,424	5,517	4,921	4,984	5,060
Rate per 10,000	43	54	49	49	50

Source: Childcare Interim Dataset, Department of Health and Children

Differences by gender

■ In general, there are no significant gender differences among children in the care of the HSE *(see Figure 62).* In 2004, 52% (2,609) of the children in care were male and 48% (2,451) were female.

Figure 62: Percentage of children in care, by gender (2004)

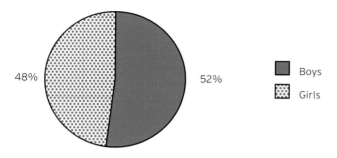

Source: Childcare Interim Dataset, Department of Health and Children

Differences by length of stay

■ In 2004, 37% (1,807) of children were in care for 5 years or more; 45% (2,307) were in care for between 1-5 years; and 18% (946) were in care for less than one year *(see Figure 63).*

Figure 63: Percentage of children in care, by length of stay (2004)

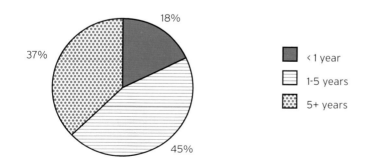

Source: Childcare Interim Dataset, Department of Health and Children

Differences by type of placement

■ Over the period 2000 to 2004, the percentage of children in 'kinship care' (i.e. foster care with relatives) has increased significantly, from 18.0% to 26.7%, while the percentage of children in residential care settings has fallen over the same period *(see Table 100)*.

■ In 2004, almost 85% of all children in the care of the former health boards lived in foster family homes. 57.2% were in foster family homes with non-relatives, while 26.7% lived in foster family homes with relatives.

Table 100: Number of children in the care of the former health boards, by type of care arrangement (2000-2004)										
	2000		2001		2002		2003		2004	
	No.	% of total	No.	% of total	No.	% of total	No.	% of total	No.	% of total
Foster Care - General	2,494	56.4	2,641	47.9	2,648	53.8	2,718	54.5	2,869	56.7
Foster Care - Special	93	2.1	42	0.8	23	0.5	31	0.6	25	0.5
Foster Care - Relative	797	18.0	973	17.6	1,184	24.1	1,237	24.8	1,349	26.7
Pre-adoptive placement	47	1.1	35	0.6	33	0.7	30	0.6	38	0.8
Residential - General	539	12.2	467	8.5	484	9.8	441	8.8	365	7.2
Residential - Special	97	2.2	102	1.8	34	0.7	29	0.6	27	0.5
Residential - High Support	-	-	-	-	42	0.9	57	1.1	50	1.0
At home under supervision	139	3.1	56	1.0	34	0.7	39	0.8	32	0.6
Other	218	4.9	1,201	21.8	439	8.9	402	8.1	305	6.0
Total	4,424	100.0	5,517	100.0	4,921	100.0	4,984	100.0	5,060	100.0

Source: Childcare Interim Dataset, Department of Health and Children

Technical notes

Data for the Childcare Interim Dataset is collected by the former health board areas and collated by the Department of Health and Children.

References

Daly, A. and Gilligan, R. (2005) *The educational and social support experiences of young people aged 13-14 years in long-term foster care.* Dublin: Children's Research Centre, University of Dublin, Trinity College.

Department of Health and Children (2001a) *National Standards for Children's Residential Centres.* Dublin: The Stationery Office.

Department of Health and Children (2001b) *National Standards for Special Care Units.* Dublin: The Stationery Office.

Department of Health and Children (2003) *National Standards for Foster Care.* Dublin: The Stationery Office.

Government of Ireland (1991) *Child Care Act.* Dublin: The Stationery Office.

Government of Ireland (1995a) *Childcare (Placement of Children in Foster Care) Regulations.* Dublin: The Stationery Office.

Government of Ireland (1995b) *Child Care (Placement of Children with Relatives) Regulations.* Dublin: The Stationery Office.

Government of Ireland (1999) *Freedom of Information Act.* Dublin: The Stationery Office.

Kelleher, P., Kelleher, C. and Corbett, M. (2000) *Left out on their own: Young people leaving care in Ireland.* Dublin: Focus Ireland.

O'Brien, V. (2001) 'Family Fostering: Children's experiences of care by relatives', in U*nderstanding Children. Volume 2: Changing Experiences and Family Forms,* A. Cleary, M. Nic Ghiolla Phádraig and S. Quin (eds.). Cork: Oak Tree Press.

Sinclair, I. and Gibbs, I. (2002) 'Looked after children', in *The Well-Being of Children in the UK,* J. Bradshaw (ed.). York: Save the Children, pp. 122-35.

UN (1989) *Convention on the Rights of the Child.* Geneva: United Nations Office of the High Commissioner for Human Rights. Available at www.ohchr.org

Further information

■ Social Services Inspectorate (www.issi.ie)

PART 4: FORMAL AND INFORMAL SUPPORTS

277

MENTAL HEALTH REFERRALS

Context

The Mental Health Act (Government of Ireland, 2001) provides the legislative framework for mental health services in Ireland and by November 2006, all provisions of this Act will have been enacted. A detailed reference guide to the Mental Health Act 2001 as it relates to children is available (Mental Health Commission, 2005a). The Act sets out the overarching statutory functions of the Mental Health Commission, which are to promote, encourage and foster the establishment and maintenance of high standards and good practices in the delivery of mental health services and to take all reasonable steps to protect the rights of persons detained in approved centres. Recently, the Mental Health Commission has given consideration to the issues that will influence and underpin future development of mental health in Ireland. It has focused on two areas of particular interest – a move towards a recovery-based mental health service (Mental Health Commission, 2005b) and multidisciplinary team working (Mental Health Commission, 2006).

At present, child and adolescent psychiatric services are provided almost exclusively in out-patient settings (Working Group on Child and Adolescent Psychiatric Services, 2003). A new database, COMCAR, is currently being piloted by the Health Research Board and will record activity at community care level, including out-patient clinics, day centres and day hospitals. Information from this database will provide a better picture of the prevalence of mental health problems for children in Ireland in the future. At present, however, the data presented below represents only the number of in-patient admissions to psychiatric hospitals.

Significance

In Ireland, as in other Western countries, mental health problems among children and teenagers are common. Lynch *et al* (2004) conducted a prevalence study on 720 Irish 12-15 year-old adolescents at risk of psychiatric disorders and suicide ideation in the Dublin area. They found that almost 20% of adolescents in this age group were at risk of having a mental health disorder. Of the 720 participants, 12% expressed possible suicide intent and 45.7% expressed suicide ideation.

A more rural-based study by Martin *et al* (2005) screened 3,374 children aged 1.5-18 years. An overall prevalence rate of 17.5% was found for mental health problems. Differences were identified according to age: problems were identified in 17% of children aged less than 5 years, 10% of national school children and 26% of secondary school children. This study also found some 10% of all 12-18 year-olds had experienced suicide ideation in the previous 6 months and 7% had deliberately harmed themselves.

Measure

The number of admissions to psychiatric hospitals among children.

Key findings

- In 2005, there were 333 admissions to hospital for psychiatric care among children *(see Figure 64)*.
- Over the period 2002-2005, the number of admissions to hospital for psychiatric care has fallen significantly – from 452 to 333.

Figure 64: Number of children admitted to hospital for psychiatric in-patient care (2001-2005)

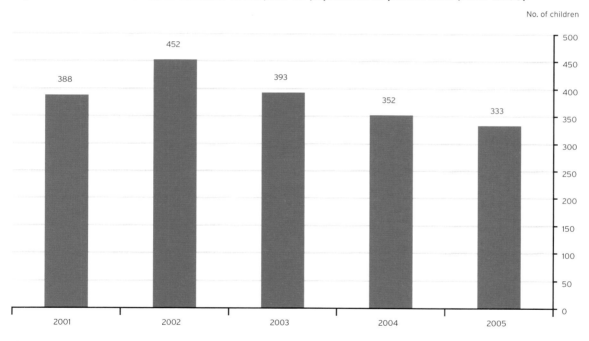

Source: National Psychiatric In-Patient Reporting System (NPIRS), Health Research Board

Differences by age

■ Children aged 15-17 accounted for 85.9% (286) of these admissions *(see Table 101)*.

Table 101: Number of admissions aged under 18 to psychiatric hospitals, by age group (2001-2005)						
Years of age	2001	2002	2003	2004	2005	
	No.	No.	No.	No.	No.	%
0-4	0	0	0	0	0	0.0
5-9	5	3	4	5	1	0.3
10-14	46	47	43	38	46	13.8
15-17	337	402	346	309	286	85.9
Total	388	452	393	352	333	100.0

Source: National Psychiatric In-Patient Reporting System (NPIRS), Health Research Board

Differences by gender

■ Over the period 2001-2003, the number of admissions to hospital for psychiatric care was consistently higher for girls than for boys *(see Table 102)*. Since 2004, the trend has reversed, with more boys than girls being admitted to hospital for psychiatric care.

■ Again, in 2005, there were more boys (54.4%) admitted to hospital for psychiatric care than girls (45.6%).

Table 102: Number of admissions aged under 18 to psychiatric hospitals, by gender (2001-2005)						
	2001	2002	2003	2004	2005	
	No.	No.	No.	No.	No.	%
Boys	177	208	163	185	181	54.4
Girls	211	244	230	167	152	45.6
Total	388	452	393	352	333	100.0

Source: National Psychiatric In-Patient Reporting System (NPIRS), Health Research Board

Differences by conditions

■ In 2005, the most common reason for children being admitted to hospital for psychiatric care was for depressive disorders (26.4%) *(see Table 103)*. Other common reasons included schizophrenia (9.0%), neuroses (18.9%), personality disorders (10.8%) and drug dependence (9.9%).

Table 103: Number of admissions aged under 18 to psychiatric hospitals, by cause (2001-2005)						
Diagnosis	2001	2002	2003	2004	2005	
	No.	No.	No.	No.	No.	%
Depressive disorders	107	120	111	79	88	26.4
Neuroses	53	74	71	75	63	18.9
Personality disorders	52	81	44	40	36	10.8
Drug dependence	36	29	31	32	33	9.9
Schizophrenia	42	48	32	27	30	9.0
Other psychoses	17	13	20	13	14	4.2
Alcoholic disorders	29	9	24	17	13	3.9
Mania	27	33	13	22	11	3.3
Mental handicap	‹5	5	‹5	5	6	1.8
Organic psychoses	14	14	‹5	7	‹5	‹1.5
Unspecified	7	26	40	35	34	10.2
Total	388	452	393	352	333	100.0

Source: National Psychiatric In-Patient Reporting System (NPIRS), Health Research Board

Differences by geographical area

- In 2005, 27.0% of children admitted to hospital for psychiatric in-patient care were from Dublin, 10.2% from Cork and 9.9% from Galway *(see Table 104).*

Table 104: Number of admissions aged under 18 to psychiatric hospitals, by county (2001-2005)						
County	2001	2002	2003	2004	2005	
	No.	No.	No.	No.	No.	%
Carlow	<5	7	<5	<5	<5	<1.0
Cavan	<5	<5	<5	<5	<5	<1.0
Clare	<5	14	15	5	<5	<1.0
Cork city	39	32	31	34	34	10.2
Donegal	6	12	<5	9	<5	<1.0
Dublin	97	119	84	99	90	27.0
Galway city	31	37	44	44	33	9.9
Kerry	12	25	13	13	13	3.9
Kildare	22	38	18	19	21	6.3
Kilkenny	<5	<5	7	<5	<5	<1.0
Laois	<5	5	8	9	<5	<1.0
Leitrim	<5	<5	<5	<5	<5	<1.0
Limerick city	20	22	25	12	8	2.4
Longford	8	18	8	<5	6	1.8
Louth	12	16	16	<5	<5	<1.0
Mayo	8	15	10	5	<5	<1.5
Meath	12	6	8	12	16	4.8
Monaghan	<5	<5	<5	<5	<5	<1.0
Offaly	5	7	<5	16	5	1.5
Roscommon	7	<5	7	6	6	1.8
Sligo	12	<5	7	<5	<5	<1.0
Tipperary	29	36	26	16	<5	<1.0
Waterford city	9	8	15	9	9	2.7
Westmeath	16	6	9	6	8	2.4
Wexford	14	8	16	7	16	4.8
Wicklow	14	6	7	10	10	3.0
England and NI	<5	<5	<5	<5	<5	<1.0
Unspecified	<5	<5	6	<5	36	10.8
Total	388	452	393	352	333	100.0

Source: National Psychiatric In-Patient Reporting System (NPIRS), Health Research Board

Technical notes

The National Psychiatric In-Patient Reporting System (NPIRS) database is the only national psychiatric in-patient database in Ireland. It was established in 1963, arising from the recommendations of the *Commission of Enquiry on Mental Illness* (Department of Health, 1966). It has been maintained by the Medico-Social Research Board (MSRB) and subsequently by the Health Research Board (HRB) since 1971. The database records data on all admissions to, and discharges from, psychiatric in-patient facilities in Ireland each year. The publication of annual reports (Activities of Irish Psychiatric Services) on the NPIRS data since 1965 plays a central role in service delivery and planning. Regional newsletters, presenting data from the former health boards, have been produced since 2000. The NPIRS database structure is also used as the basis for carrying out decennial censuses of the in-patient population, the most recent of which was carried out in 2001. The results of this census are available in the report *Irish Psychiatric Hospitals and Units Census 2001* (Daly and Walsh, 2002). The NPIRS database is also used as the basis for epidemiological research on mental illness.

The data collected for the NPIRS include demographic data relating to each patient (such as gender, date of birth, marital status, address from which admitted and socio-economic group), together with clinical and diagnostic information (such as date of admission/discharge, legal category, order of admission, diagnosis on admission and discharge in accordance with the WHO International Classification of Diseases categories (ICD 10), and reason for discharge).

In response to changing patterns of patient care, the HRB has developed a new database, COMCAR, designed to record activity at community care level, including out-patient clinics, day centres and day hospitals.

Percentage differences are presented for descriptive purposes only and may not reflect a statistically significant finding.

References

Daly, A. and Walsh, D. (2002) *Irish Psychiatric Hospitals and Units Census 2001.* Dublin: Health Research Board.

Department of Health (1966) *Commission of Enquiry on Mental Illness.* Dublin: The Stationery Office.

Government of Ireland (2001) *Mental Health Act.* Dublin: The Stationery Office.

Lynch, F., Mills, C., Daly, I. and Fitzpatrick, C. (2004) 'Challenging times: A study to detect Irish adolescents at risk of psychiatric disorders and suicidal ideation', *Journal of Adolescence*, Vol. 27, No. 4, pp. 441-51.

Martin, M., Carr, A., Carroll, L. and Byrne, S. (2005) *The Clonmel Project. Mental health service needs of children and adolescents in the south-east of Ireland: A preliminary screening study.* Clonmel: Health Service Executive.

Mental Health Commission (2005a) *Reference Guide Mental Health Act 2001: Part 2 Children.* Dublin: Mental Health Commission.

Mental Health Commission (2005b) *A Vision for a Recovery Model in Irish Mental Health Services. Discussion Paper.* Dublin: Mental Health Commission.

Mental Health Commission (2006) *Multidisciplinary Team Working: From Theory to Practice Discussion Paper.* Dublin: Mental Health Commission.

Working Group on Child and Adolescent Psychiatric Services (2003) *Second Report,* Department of Health and Children. Dublin: The Stationery Office.

Further information
- Health Research Board (www.hrb.ie)
- Mental Health Commission (www.mhcirl.ie)

MAIN DATA SOURCES

Title: **Census of the Population**
Source: Central Statistics Office (www.cso.ie)
Description: Population statistics, including housing, employment, education and family structure
Frequency: Every 5 years

Title: **Childcare Interim Data Set**
Source: Department of Health and Children (www.doh.ie)
Description: Statistics on children in care or at risk
Frequency: Annual

Title: **Education Welfare Board Database**
Source: National Education Welfare Board (www.newb.ie)
Description: Statistics on children absent from school for 20 or more days
Frequency: Annual

Title: **European Schools Project on Alcohol and Drugs (ESPAD) Survey**
Source: St. Patrick's College, Drumcondra (www.spd.dcu.ie)
Description: European survey of the behaviours, knowledge and beliefs concerning cigarettes, alcohol, solvents and illegal drugs among 15-year-old children
Frequency: Every 3 years

Title: **European Union Survey on Income and Living Conditions (EU-SILC)**
Source: Central Statistics Office (www.cso.ie)
Description: European survey on income, living conditions and basic deprivation
Frequency: Annual

Title: **Garda Annual Report**
Source: An Garda Síochána (www.garda.ie)
Description: Crime statistics, including arrests and diversions to the Garda Juvenile Diversion Programme
Frequency: Annual

Title: **Health Behaviour of School-aged Children (HBSC) Survey**
Source: National University of Ireland, Galway (www.nuig.ie)
Description: International survey of the health behaviours of children aged 10-17, covering areas such as general health, food and nutrition, exercise, alcohol consumption and children's perceptions of happiness
Frequency: Every 4 years

Title: **Health Services National Performance Indicators**
Source: Department of Health and Children (www.doh.ie)
Description: Statistics on health and healthcare services, including mental health, child and adolescent health, and child care
Frequency: Annual

Title: **Hospital In-Patient Enquiry (HIPE)**
Source: Economic and Social Research Institute (www.esri.ie)
Description: Statistics on hospital stays, including date of birth, gender, marital status, medical card status, diagnosis, procedure and length of stay
Frequency: Annual

Title: **Immunisation Uptake Statistics**
Source: Health Protection Surveillance Centre (www.ndsc.ie/hpsc)
Description: Statistics on infectious diseases and vaccinations
Frequency: Quarterly

Title: **KIDSCREEN**
Source: Programme of Action for Children (www.hse.ie)
Description: European survey of the health-related quality of life of 8-11year-old and 12-17 year-old children
Frequency: Currently being piloted

Title: **National Intellectual Disability Database (NIDD)**
Source: Health Research Board (www.hrb.ie)
Description: Statistics on those with an intellectual disability (mild, moderate, severe and profound) in receipt of, or on a waiting list for, specialist services
Frequency: Annual
Title: **National Perinatal Reporting System (NPRS)**

Source: Economic and Social Research Institute (www.esri.ie)
Description: Demographic statistics (including stillbirths, perinatal and maternal deaths, mother and father's date of birth, nationality, occupation and marital status) and basic clinical information (including birth weight, period of gestation, type of feeding and congenital anomalies for every birth)
Frequency: Annual

Title: **National Physical and Sensory Disability Database (NPSDD)**
Source: Health Research Board (www.hrb.ie)
Description: Statistics on those with a physical and/or sensory disability in receipt of, or on a waiting list for, specialist services
Frequency: Annual

Title: **National Psychiatric In-Patient Reporting System (NPIRS)**
Source: Health Research Board (www.hrb.ie)
Description: Statistics on all admissions to, and discharges from, psychiatric in-patient facilities in Ireland. The data collected for the NPIRS include demographic data relating to each patient (such as gender, date of birth, marital status, address from which admitted and socio-economic group), together with clinical and diagnostic information
Frequency: Annual

Title: **Patient Treatment Register (PTR)**
Source: National Treatment Purchase Fund (www.ntpf.ie)
Description: Statistics on public in-patient and day-case waiting lists in Ireland
Frequency: Annual

Title: **Post-Primary Pupil Database**
Source: Department of Education and Science (www.education.ie)
Description: Statistics on pupil participation and retention rates
Frequency: Annual

Title: **Programme for International Student Assessment (PISA) Survey**
Source: Education Research Centre, Drumcondra (www.erc.ie)
Description: International survey of reading, mathematics and science achievement of 15-year-old children
Frequency: Every 4 years

Title: **Quarterly National Household Survey (QNHS)**
Source: Central Statistics Office (www.cso.ie)
Description: Statistics on births, marriages and deaths
Frequency: Quarterly

Title: **Triennial Assessment of Housing Needs, published in the** *Quarterly Bulletin on Housing Statistics*
Source: Department of the Environment, Heritage and Local Government (www.environ.ie)
Description: Statistics on families on housing lists and homelessness
Frequency: Every 3 years

Title: **Tuarascáil Staitistiúil**
Source: Department of Education and Science (www.education.ie)
Description: Statistics on schools and examinations
Frequency: Annual

Title: **Vital Statistics**
Source: Central Statistics Office (www.cso.ie)
Description: Large-scale, nationwide survey of households in Ireland
Frequency: Quarterly

INDEX

A

abuse and neglect
    assessments, 132–33
        legislation and policy on, 130–31
        substantiated notifications, 134–36
ADM Ltd., 232
alcohol consumption. *See* drinking
antenatal care, 247–51
asylum, separated children seeking, 32–34

B

binge drinking. *See* drinking
birth rate, 9, 12
birth weight, 98–103
breakfast, eating of. *See* eating habits
breastfeeding, 105–9
bullying, 67–71

C

Cardiovascular Health Strategy, 190
care
    children in, 273–76
    legislation on, 273
    State care, a history of, 207
    See also homelessness
Child Care Act (1991), 32, 130, 206, 273
Child Protection Notification System. *See* abuse
    and neglect
child welfare and protection concerns. *See* abuse
    and neglect
childcare arrangements, 76–78
Childcare Interim Dataset, 276
Children Act (2001), 8, 243, 244
Children First: National Guidelines for the Protection
    and Welfare of Children, 130
Children's Rights Alliance, 269
COMCAR database, 278, 283
Comhairle Leabharlanna, An, 146
communities
    children feeling safe in, 232–36
    'good places in area to spend free time', 238–41
    social capital, 232–33
    support programmes, 232
Constitution of Ireland, 23, 86
Consumer Price Index, 218
Criminal Justice Act (2006), 244
Crisis Pregnancy Agency, 173

D

data sources, 3, 5, 285–88
death rate. *See* mortality
DEIS Programme. *See* education
disability
    databases on, 128
    intellectual disability, 121–24, 128
    legislation and policy on, 119
    physical and/or sensory disability, 125–28
domestic violence, 131
drinking
    children's habits, 160–64
    homeless people, 207
    legislation and policy on, 160–61
drug use
    children's habits, 166–72
    homeless people, 207
    legislation and policy on, 166

E

eating habits, 200–204
economic security. *See* poverty
education
    DEIS Programme, 80, 86
    early childhood, 76–78
    early school-leaving, 81, 86, 94
    in Constitution of Ireland, 86
    legislation and policy on, 27, 35, 62, 80, 86, 119, 178
    lifelong learning, 27
    literacy/numeracy, 86–94
    parental education level, 27–31
    physical education in schools, 190, 191
    public expenditure on, 214–19
    school attendance, 80–83
    sex education in schools, 174
    special needs, 86, 119
    SPHE Programme, 62, 166, 178
    transfer to second-level, 84–85
environmental awareness, 238
EU comparisons. *See* individual indicators
EU Social Inclusion Strategy, 221
European Charter on Alcohol, 160
exercise. *See* physical activity

F

family
    importance for children of, 44
    in Constitution of Ireland, 23
    legislation and policy on, 23, 44
    lone-parent families, 23-26
    structure of, 23-26
Family Support Agency, 23
family support services, 23, 131, 273
father and child relationship, 49-51
Food and Nutrition Guidelines for Primary Schools, 200
foster care, 273, 274, 276
friendships between children, 62-66

G

Gaf Café, Galway, 62
Garda Juvenile Diversion Programme. *See* Juvenile Diversion Programme
Green Schools Programme, 238

H

health
    access to health services, 268-72
    antenatal care, 247-51
    birth weight, 98-103
    breastfeeding, 105-9
    child health service, 110, 262-66
    disability, 119-28
    drinking, 160-64
    drug use, 166-72
    homeless people, 207
    hospital waiting lists, 269-71
    hospitalisation of children, 110-17
    immunisation for children, 252-60
    legislation on, 110
    mental health, 178-88
    nutrition and eating habits, 200-201
    physical activity, 190-98
    screening for growth and development, 262, 266
    sexual health and behaviour, 173-76
    smoking, 150-58
    SPHE Programme, 62, 166, 178
    WHO definition of, 183
Health Protection Surveillance Centre, 260
Health Research Board, 128, 278, 283
Health Service Executive (HSE)
    responsibilities of, 32, 110, 130, 206, 273

homelessness
    children and young people, 206-10
    definitions of, 206
    legislation and policy on, 206
    See also care
Hospital In-Patient Enquiry (HIPE) System, 117
hospitalisation of children, 110-17
    main causes of, 111-16
hospitals
    children on waiting lists, 269-71
    psychiatric care admissions, 278-83
    Waiting List Initiative, 268
household, definition of, 31
housing, social
    children in families on waiting lists, 228-30
    legislation and policies on, 227
    local authority assessments, 230
    Triennial Assessment of Housing Needs, 230

I

immigration
    intercultural policies, 9-10
    legislation and policy on, 9-10, 32
    levels of, 9
immunisation for children, 252-60
Institute of Public Health in Ireland, 268
intercultural policies, 9-10
international comparisons. *See* individual indicators
Irish Sports Council, 161, 190
Irish Youth Justice Service, 243

J

Juvenile Diversion Programme, Garda, 243-46

L

leisure activity, 146-47, 238-41
    See also physical activity
library services and facilities, 146
literacy
    difficulties with, 87
    mathematics, 90-91, 94
    reading, 88-89, 146-49
    science, 92-93
local authority housing. *See* housing, social
local identity, 233
    See also social capital

M

maltreatment. *See* abuse and neglect
maternity, legislation on, 247
Medico-Social Research Board, 283
mental health
    children in care, 274
    COMCAR database, 278, 283
    disorders among youth, 131, 278, 280
    homeless people, 207
    legislation and policy on, 278
    Mental Health Commission, 278
    psychiatric hospital admissions, 278-83
    self-esteem and self-perception, 178-81
    self-reported happiness, 183-85
    suicide, 187-88
    WHO reports on, 183
minority communities, legislation for, 35
mortality
    among children, 9, 15-18
    among infants, 15, 17, 36, 98
    causes of death, 16
mother and child relationship, 46-48

N

National Action Plan against Poverty and Social
    Exclusion (2003-2005), 86, 98, 173, 214, 221, 227
National Action Plan against Racism (2004), 10
National Alcohol Policy for Ireland (1996), 160
National Anti-Poverty Strategy (1997), 221
National Anti-Poverty Strategy (2002-2007), 10
National Childcare Investment Programme (2006-2010),
    8, 76
National Children's Strategy (2000)
    ending child poverty, 221
    implementation of, 8
    importance of environment, 238
    views and participation of children, 140
    vision of, 8
    whole child perspective of, 2
National Consultative Committee on Racism and
    Interculturalism, 10
National Disability Strategy (2004), 119
National Drugs Strategy (2001-2008), 166
National Education Welfare Board, 80
National Health Promotion Strategy (2000-2005),
    150, 160, 166, 173, 178, 190, 200

National Health Strategy (2001), 110, 268
National Longitudinal Study of Children in Ireland, 5
National Nutritional Policy (2006), 200
National Perinatal Reporting System, 103, 251
National Play Policy (2004), 110, 190, 232, 238
National Psychiatric In-Patient Reporting System, 283
National Recreation Policy, 62, 146, 190, 238
National Strategy for Action on Suicide Prevention
    (2005-2014), 187
National Treatment Purchase Fund, 268, 272
numeracy. *See* literacy
nutrition. *See* eating habits

O

obesity. *See* eating habits
offenders, young. *See* Juvenile Diversion Programme
Office of the Minister for Children
    participation of children, 140
    role of, 8

P

parents
    children's relationships with, 43-59
    educational level of, 27-31
    lone-parent families, 23-26
participation of children, 140-44
Patient Treatment Register, 272
peers, children's relationships with, 61-71
physical activity
    PE in schools, 191
    policies on, 190
    sports played, 191
    time spent in, 192-98
play policies, 110, 190, 232, 238
population of children
    non-Irish nationals, 19-21
    separated children seeking asylum, 32-34
    total in Ireland, 11-14, 174
    Traveller community, 35-37
poverty
    children affected by, 221-25
    consistent poverty, 5, 24, 222-23
    ending child poverty commitments, 221
    EU definition of, 225
    EU policy on, 221
    Irish definition of, 222, 224

policies on, 221
relative income poverty, 223-24
teenage mothers, 173
public expenditure on education, 214-19
public health nursing service, 262-65
public services
access to, 119
expenditure on, 215

R

racism, tackling, 9
reading as leisure activity, 146-49
reading literacy. *See* literacy
recreation policies, 62, 146, 190, 238
residential care, 273, 276
road safety
programmes for, 232
traffic accidents involving children, 113-15

S

safety
children feeling safe in local community, 232-36
play areas, 232
road safety programmes, 232
schools
attendance at, 80-83
early school-leaving, 81, 94
PE education, 191
School Meals Programme, 80, 200
sex education, 174
Social, Personal and Health Education (SPHE)
Programme, 62, 166, 178
student councils, 140-44
screening for growth and development, 262, 266
self-esteem, self-perception and 'happiness'.
See mental health
self-harm, 187, 278
separated child, definition of, 32
sexual health and behaviour
age of consent, 173
teenage pregnancy, 173-76
Síolta, 76
smoking
children's habits, 150-58
legislation on, 150

social capital, 232-33
social inclusion, 9
Social Partnership Agreement (2003-2005), 221
Social Partnership Agreement (2006-2015), 8, 86,
206, 214, 221, 227
Social Services Inspectorate, 273
Social, Personal and Health Education (SPHE)
Programme, 62, 166, 178
socio-demographics of children in Ireland, 7-38
SPHE. *See* Social, Personal and Health Education
(SPHE) Programme
sports. *See* physical activity
Springboard Programme, 131
Stay Safe Programme, 131
stillborn babies, 18, 103, 176
student councils in schools, 140-44
Substance Abuse Prevention (Education) Programme,
166
Sudden Infant Death Syndrome. *See* mortality, causes
of death
suicide among youth, 187-88
suicide ideation, 131, 278

T

teenage pregnancy, 173-76
tobacco use. *See* smoking
Traveller community
infant mortality, 36
legislation for, 35
population of children in, 35-37
Traveller Health Strategy, 35
truancy. *See* education, early school-leaving

U

unaccompanied minor, definition of, 32
United Nations Convention on the Rights of the Child
(1989)
guiding principles of, 8
Ireland's implementation of, 183
views of the child, 140
United Nations Geneva Convention on Status of
Refugees, 32

V

vaccination. *See* immunisation for children

W

waiting lists. *See* hospitals; housing
well-being, children's
    indicators of, 2-4, 87, 167, 221
    WHO definition of, 183
World Health Organization Declaration on Young
    People and Alcohol (2001), 160

Y

Young People's Facilities and Services Fund, 166
Youth Homelessness Strategy (2001), 206
youth justice system, 243-44